The Second Palestinian Intifada

T0341746

The Second Palestinian Intifada

A Chronicle of a People's Struggle

RAMZY BAROUD

Foreword by Kathleen and Bill Christison
Introduction by Jennifer Loewenstein
Photographs by Mahfouz Abu Turk
and Matthew Cassel

PLUTO PRESS

First published 2006 by Pluto Press
345 Archway Road, London N6 5AA
and 839 Greene Street, Ann Arbor, MI 48106

www.plutobooks.com

British Library Cataloguing in Publication Data
A catalogue record for this book is available from the British Library

ISBN   0 7453 2548 3 hardback
ISBN   978 0 7453 2548 4 hardback

ISBN   0 7453 2547 5 paperback
ISBN   978 0 7453 2547 7 paperback

ISBN 1 84964 321 0 PDF
ISBN 978 1 8496 4321 4 PDF

Library of Congress Cataloging in Publication Data applied for

10   9   8   7   6   5   4   3   2   1

Designed and produced for Pluto Press by
Chase Publishing Services Ltd, Fortescue, Sidmouth, EX10 9QG, England
Typeset from disk by Stanford DTP Services, Northampton, England
Printed and bound by CPI Group (UK) Ltd, Croydon, CR0 4YY

*To Zarefah, Iman, and Sammy,
my life's inspiration*

Contents

Foreword

Kathleen and Bill Christison

In a poignant piece included in this book, Ramzy Baroud tells the story of his grandfather, a refugee from the Palestinian village of Beit Daras who spent nearly 40 years until his death at a very old age in a Gaza refugee camp constantly listening to a transistor radio, hoping that someday it would bring the news that Palestinian refugees would be allowed to return to their homes, lost in 1948 when Israel was created and 750,000 Palestinians were forced from their homes.[1] Ramzy's grandfather, like the Palestinian people themselves, lived in what might be called a state of suspended animation, wrapped in memory, holding before him a vision of Palestine that would never be recreated. His long but ultimately, for him, fruitless vigil symbolizes at once the tragedy of the Palestinian people and their great strength.

A predominant, and perhaps the most salient, feature of the history of Zionism and the establishment of Israel as a Jewish state has been the Zionist effort to ignore—and therefore ultimately to erase from the political landscape—the Palestinian people who were native to the land that became Israel. Throughout the nearly 60 years since Israel's creation and the Palestinians' dispossession, and for the several decades before this when Zionism was gaining strength, Zionists and their supporters in the United States and Europe have made a concerted effort to dehumanize the Palestinians, render them invisible, and delegitimize them as true claimants to a national life in Palestine. From the Balfour Declaration pledging British support for a "Jewish national home" in Palestine, at a time when Palestinians made up 90 percent of the population; through the United Nations decision 30 years later to partition Palestine and give the Zionists over half the territory for a Jewish state, when Jews constituted no more than one-third of the population and owned only 7 percent of the land; through the Palestinians' decades of statelessness and displacement following 1948; to the Second Palestinian Uprising, the most recent of the Palestinians' struggles to assert their right to independence and self-governance in their own homeland, Zionism has persuaded much of the world that the Palestinians' presence in and claim to the land of Palestine are of no consequence.

The effort to ignore Palestinians continues unabated, even into the twenty-first century. As the years have passed, it has become ever easier for people the world over, as well as for politicians and policymakers, to forget the Palestinians because they do not constitute a state (or an effective political lobby), and, in a cruel vicious circle, the longer Palestinian national aspirations are ignored, the less their claim to any kind of national sovereignty is seen as legitimate. A body of assumptions and misconceptions has grown up, centering on the notions that Israel is the victim, that Palestinians have no rational basis for their hostility to Israel, and that the only real issue is Palestinian hatred of Jews and refusal to accept Israel's existence. These very fundamental misperceptions have never been adequately challenged and, with the passage of time, have become more widespread and firmly entrenched. As misperception has built on misperception, it has become easier for Israel to justify pushing the Palestinians aside, ever more openly oppressing the whole Palestinian population, and for the world to look away. Each Palestinian uprising, each attempt to assert a national right, seems to strengthen an ever-growing belief that Palestinians have no inherent rights in Palestine and are driven only by hatred of Jews to contest what is widely thought to be the Jews' inherent right to patrimony there. Few remember, because it is now inconvenient to remember, that Ramzy Baroud's grandfather and 750,000 other innocent civilians were displaced nearly 60 years ago and that their descendants still live under oppression and in exile. The body of misperceptions surrounding the Palestinians has not simply grown haphazardly, but has been carefully shaped and nurtured by a skillful pro-Israeli propaganda machine that operates around the world but primarily in the United States. As a result, the U.S.—from the public to the media to politicians and policymakers— has completely bought into the images of Israelis as innocent victims and Palestinians as unworthy of more than secondary consideration. This set of images, and the political mindset that accompanies them, has grown cumulatively with time, gradually blotting out the historical record, blurring memory, and creating what passes for political reality, until the prevailing mindset has become so dominant that few challenge it.

What was once a tacit U.S. acceptance of Israel's occupation of the West Bank, Gaza, and East Jerusalem and its undemocratic dominance over the territories' three million Palestinians has become under President George W. Bush an eager endorsement of Israel's policies. The growing U.S. inability to view the conflict from any but

Israel's perspective, and the Bush administration's outright animus toward the Palestinians, have opened the door to unrestrained Israeli oppression of the Palestinians. If it was not clear before, it is now indisputable that Israel's actions are designed, with U.S. concurrence, to erase the Palestinians as a people and a national entity. Israeli settlements encircle Palestinian towns and cities. Israeli roads cut through Palestinian agricultural land, separating one town from another and preventing any Palestinian growth. The separation wall winds through the West Bank, destroying or confiscating prime Palestinian agricultural land and fresh water wells, razing thousands of Palestinian olive trees, destroying Palestinian markets and halting commerce, demolishing homes, separating children from schools and adults from workplaces, totally severing East Jerusalem from the West Bank, leaving Jerusalem Palestinians with no hinterland and West Bankers with no capital and no religious or civic center. Israeli tanks occupy Palestinian cities; Israeli bulldozers demolish Palestinian homes; Israeli authorities confiscate Palestinian residency permits; most maps published in Israel depict the West Bank and Gaza as part of Israel. Gaza is caged and in ruins, worse than Dresden of 1945. The Israeli occupation army has demolished every Palestinian government and security headquarters building throughout the West Bank and Gaza, ransacked every Palestinian civilian ministry, even destroyed Palestinian census records and land registry records. What is the Israeli purpose here other than to erase all trace of Palestinian existence?

The Palestinian–Israeli conflict has gone beyond being a mere political problem, beyond the stuff of cool political debate. It is a human disaster that can no longer be treated with dispassion, no longer addressed by an equal weighing of rights and wrongs on both sides. The Israeli appropriation of the Palestinians' land, livelihood, and very existence is terrorist violence, as surely as any suicide bombing is terrorism. The massive difference between the terrorism of the two sides, however, is that one employs a few youth to express an entire people's rage through individual acts of murder, while the other employs the vast military power of a strong nation to smother another people. There is another critical difference: in international media coverage of the two sides, only Israel's story is told, so that Palestinian violence has no context and no reason, whereas Israeli violence is portrayed as "reasonable" and "unavoidable." Studies of newspaper and television coverage in both the U.S. and Britain have shown that Israel is consistently portrayed as the besieged victim despite its military power, that Palestinian casualties are consistently minimized despite their far higher numbers, that Israeli grievances and justifications for Israeli actions are consistently reported, without similar reporting of Palestinian grievances and justifications.[2] The result is that even the media-savvy publics in the U.S. and Europe know next to nothing about the Palestinians, about the Israeli occupation, about the killing of Palestinians, about the root causes of Palestinian "terrorism."

How should the Palestinians respond to the ethnocide being committed against them? In these circumstances, with no one listening, no one hearing their grievances, and no feasible way to stop the Israeli machine, many desperate Palestinians have felt they had no other course than to lash out with murderous acts against individual Israelis. Attacks on innocent civilians can never be justified, but few critics even seem to notice when the Palestinians use a non-violent strategy. Neither Israel nor the U.S. nor the American and international media have noted that Palestinian protest activities against the separation wall for the last two years have been totally non-violent. Nor have they noted that in general non-violence has become a unilateral Palestinian enterprise—that when Palestinians use non-violence, Israel continues gratuitous violence against Palestinians through assassinations and assaults on Palestinian towns. In reality, the obstacle to peace has always been Israel's occupation, not Yasser Arafat or Mahmoud Abbas or Hamas; the source of violence is not Palestinian "terrorism," but Israel's occupation and the land theft, oppression, and ethnic cleansing that go with it. It is Israel that is not a partner for peace, Israel's violence that impedes peace.

The Palestinians' tragedy, as symbolized by Ramzy Baroud's grandfather and his obsession with listening for news of his salvation, is that they and their leadership have always been too ready to let others do for them—to let the Arab states fight for them or the United States bring them peace, always hoping, as if in a dream, that the radio will soon bring good news. They have never known how, and therefore have never tried adequately, to prevail in the public-relations contest with Israel—never known how to frame their story in a way that would win the sympathy of a public enraptured by the story of Jewish suffering in the Holocaust. There may never in fact have been anything they could do, given the Israel-centered frame of reference that has shaped public discourse, and ultimately policy, for over half a century. But the Palestinians have never made a serious attempt to break the almost total media blackout in the United States that has left their narrative unknown. The leadership has also never been able to make the transition from revolutionary movement to state-building institution. With no coherent territory to govern over and no true governing authority anywhere, the leadership has never known how to balance resistance to the Israeli occupation with preparation for governing a state. Where once Yasser Arafat and Fatah and the P.L.O. were rallying points and unifiers for the Palestinians, in the half-light of the Oslo so-called "peace process," where they were able neither to control the pace of negotiations nor freely to advance the interests of their own people, the leaders and the organizations all soon descended into mundane political hackery and corruption. In this volume, Baroud discusses the level of betrayal felt by ordinary Palestinians because of this failure of leadership, as well as the crippling corruption that has become pervasive within Palestinian institutions. But the long vigil of Baroud's grandfather also demonstrates the Palestinians' great strength: their resilience and remarkable endurance. Even in the face of being ignored, exiled, repeatedly dispossessed, oppressed by successive conquerors, occasionally massacred, the Palestinians carry on vigorously. Baroud's grandfather obviously had a clear sense that the injustice done to him and to all around him was so very great that redress simply had to come sometime soon. And so he waited in that state of suspended animation. And, it must be asked, what better way is there after all to carry on in the face of massive power and gross injustice?

This puts one in mind of the great Palestinian novel, *The Secret Life of Saeed, the Pessoptimist*, by Emile Habiby, about the difficult life of the small remnant of the Palestinian people who remained in Israel in 1948. In one episode, the Palestinian hero, the Pessoptimist, watches as an Israeli military governor drives a Palestinian woman and her child away at gunpoint from a field where she is working. "At this point," says the hero,

I observed the first example of that amazing phenomenon that was to occur again and again.... For the further the woman and child went from where we were, the governor standing and I in the jeep, the taller they grew. By the time they merged with their own shadows in the sinking sun, they had become bigger than the plain of Acre itself. The governor still stood there awaiting their final disappearance, while I remained huddled in the jeep. Finally he asked in amazement, "Will they never disappear?"

The answer to that Israeli question is no, the Palestinians will endure. Palestinians like Ramzy Baroud and his grandfather will make it so.

Preface

The Second Palestinian Uprising will be etched in history as an era in which a major shift in the rules of the game occurred. From the shock of witnessing scores of young people voluntarily blowing themselves up, to the shame of the construction of one of the largest walls in history to create an eternal divide between two peoples, it has been a time in which both sides, oppressor and oppressed, have become intimately and painfully affected by the scourge of the Israeli occupation and the subsequent Palestinian resistance.

I was a teenage boy in high school when the First Palestinian Uprising erupted in December 1987. As the world's media wrangled in an attempt to construe or misrepresent the actual causes of violence throughout the Occupied Territories, the impoverished and persistently grief stricken residents of my Gaza refugee camp were consumed with other more worldly matters: would they eat today, would they find clean water, would they seize their long-awaited freedom? Family members, friends and neighbors lost their lives in that evocative fight in which the Palestinian people once again reclaimed their rightful role in the struggle. It was an awesome awakening which forced all parties that had traditionally laid claim to the Palestinian struggle to relinquish their stake. Ordinary Palestinians took to the streets, defying the Israeli army and articulating a collective stance that echoed a seemingly eternal commitment across the generations: "Our souls and our blood are forfeited to free you Palestine." I grew up hearing the echoes of that chant and soon joined in.

My house was positioned at the forefront of what the refugees referred to as Red Square. There, many of my peers fell to a cruel fate, the trails of their blood leaving stains that would last forever. Directly beside Red Square was the ever-expanding graveyard, wherein many graves were adorned by the colors of the Palestinian flag, marking the resting places of the many martyrs. It was in those dismal yet stirring surroundings that I began to write. In my earliest attempts, I wrote poetry. Many of my verses would soon evolve into chants that would resound throughout the camp, in times of celebration and in times of grief. My first works were published all along the walls of Gaza's refugee camps. Sadly, that is where they would stay, along with the other countless screams inscribed on those pockmarked walls. The

Israeli occupation was impenetrable, and our hopes as well as our legitimate grievances would remain cloistered within the camps, perhaps never to reach the outside world. Palestinians were intensely aware of the relationship between the virtual indifference toward their plight and the role of the media in misrepresenting their struggle and national aspirations. That awareness bred untold frustration among Palestinians, for their hands were tied as the narrative of their life and death was determined almost exclusively by the Israeli military and government.

I was studying in the United States when the Second Palestinian Uprising erupted in September 2000. The world's media once again wrangled to construe or misrepresent the causes of the violence. Palestinians were duly blamed and condemned. Venomous hate speech was spat out everywhere and by every media, reducing the Palestinians to the role designated to them by the official Israeli account—they were the wrongdoers, innately violent, politically conniving and manipulative, twisted and essentially terrorist. It was an arduous task to counter these fraudulent yet prevailing interpretations. For most Americans, as for the world at large, the Palestinians had been criminalized through decades of relentless propaganda devised so carefully that challenging it seemed utterly futile. But the same force that ignited courage in the hearts of millions of Palestinians throughout the Occupied Territories to confront an increasingly violent occupation empowered those who dared to challenge the ingrained and one-sided narrative that saw Israel as a "besieged" nation fighting for its survival amidst hordes of barbaric Philistines.

This book is my contribution to what I believe is the largely neglected Palestinian narrative of the Second Uprising and the Palestinian struggle as a whole. One of the largest controversies throughout the past five years—highlighted time and again within activist groups, intellectual circles and the media—concerned the growing rate of violent resistance employed by Palestinians against Israeli military forces and civilians. Because this topic was of great consequence, and the violence had in many arenas compromised the credibility of the Uprising, I felt that it was critical to contextualize this phenomenon, not to justify it, but to present the Palestinian response as a tragic yet predictable human reaction to decades of subjugation—as well expressed in the foreword to this book by Kathleen and Bill Christison. While I find it difficult to reconcile myself to the point of view embraced by those many supporters of

Palestinian rights around the world who find any sort of violent resistance reprehensible, I have a profound respect for their life-long activism, and this book is by no means an attempt to discredit their principles.

Equally central is the issue of the fragmentation of Palestinian nationhood, as eloquently addressed by Jennifer Loewenstein, one of the most prominent Jewish-American activists at the forefront of the struggle for Palestinian rights. In the Introduction that follows, Loewenstein examines the relationship between the decades-long Israeli military occupation, Israel's policy of isolating and breaking up Palestinian communities, whether at home or in Diaspora, and the palpable disintegration of the long-aspired-to notion of Palestinian nationhood. Her contribution is most pertinent.

This volume is divided into five chapters, each representing one of the five years of the Uprising. The first chapter, entitled "The Intifada Takes Off," covers the end of 2000 and the year 2001, and focuses on the circumstances which led to the onset of the Uprising. Chapter 2, entitled "Intifada International," deals with the events of 2002, and addresses the ever-growing international solidarity which Palestinians garnered from people and organizations around the world. The third chapter, "Calls for Reform," addresses the growing problem of corruption within the Palestinian Authority (P.A.), their subsequent loss of credibility in the eyes of ordinary Palestinians, and how such corruption was manipulated by Israel and the U.S. to exert pressure on the P.A. Chapter 4, "Profound Changes, Insurmountable Challenges," commemorates the many events that occurred in the year 2004, from Israel's snubbing of the International Court of Justice's ruling on the illegality of the Israeli Separation Wall, to the death of Palestinian leader Yasser Arafat. Finally, Chapter 5, "End of the Intifada?" addresses the many issues of 2005 that led to the inevitable demise of the Intifada altogether. While the chapters of this book refer mostly to the Second Uprising of 2000, it derives many of its references from the First Uprising of 1987.

This book is by no means intended as a platform to vent, censure or settle scores, nor is it an attempt to chronicle an encyclopedia of events, so that by the end the reader may conclude who is at fault and who is not. However, an exhaustive timeline is provided in an Appendix, outlining noteworthy events within each particular year. Unfortunately, it was impossible to mention every significant event that took place throughout the past five years; such a timeline would have required its own published volume. The book is intended as a means to articulate an independent Palestinian view that holds no allegiance to any political party, individual, or official entity of any sort. In this it is simply an attempt to cling to the same principles espoused by countless refugees in small and over-crowded refugee camps where freedom is proudly cherished over life.

Acknowledgements

I wish to thank all of those who have supported me in my effort to bring attention to the Palestinian struggle: to newspaper editors around the world for publishing my essays and commentaries; to every student group and university department that invited me to speak about the Palestinian struggle, about peace and justice; to every person who dared to stand for what is right no matter how detested the word of truth may be. A special thank you to Roger van Zwanenberg of Pluto Press for his support, patience, and highly appreciated input and important suggestions that helped shape this volume. To Sejal Chad at Pluto, thank you so much for your valuable feedback and suggestions during the editing process. I also want to extend my deepest gratitude to the staff at the Palestinian Initiative for the Promotion of Global Dialogue & Democracy (MIFTAH), for their kind assistance in gathering valuable data regarding Palestinian and Israeli losses during the Second Palestinian Uprising. Thank you to the many inspiring individuals that contributed to this book: Kathleen and Bill Christison, Jennifer Loewenstein, Professor Noam Chomsky, Dr. Hanan Ashrawi, Norman Solomon, Professor Norman Finkelstein, Professor Robert Jensen, and Professor Ilan Pappe. Thanks also to Matthew Cassel and Mahfouz Abu Turk for their contribution of fantastic photos to this work. To all of these dedicated individuals and to many more I am deeply indebted. My deepest gratitude to my wife Suzanne, my editor for the last twelve years. What I owe her cannot be relayed in a few words. Finally, for those who have been a great support during this process, thank you to Scott Davis, June Rugh, Paul Cowan, Aijaz Sayed, Michelle Gasparek, Elizabeth Gimmestad, Hani Yarid, Mohammed Lamin, Lamis Andoni, and Nabil Hijazi, Jennifer Johnson, and Andrew Borland. Your support was invaluable.

I extend my gratitude to the editors of the following publications for kindly hosting many articles on the basis of which much of this volume was composed:

Al-Ahram Weekly (Egypt); *Japan Times* (Japan); *Seattle Post Intelligencer* (U.S.); *Washington Post* (U.S.); *International Herald Tribune* (U.S.); *Christian Science Monitor* (U.S.); *Arab News* (Saudi Arabia); *Middle East Times* (Egypt); *Asia Times* (Hong Kong); *Jordan Times* (Jordan); *Khaleej*

Times (U.A.E.); *The Peninsula* (Qatar); *Gulf Times* (Qatar); *Frontier Post* (Pakistan); *Gulf News* (U.A.E.); *Palestine Times* (U.K.); *African Perspective* (South Africa); *Daily Mail* (Pakistan); *Daily Star* (Lebanon); *Milli Gazette* (India); *Jordan Star* (Jordan); *Gulf Daily News* (Bahrain); *The Miami Herald* (U.S.); *Austin-American Statesman* (U.S.); *Seattle Times* (U.S.); *Sacramento Bee Daily* (U.S.); *Z Magazine* (U.S.); *Sunday Times* (South Africa); *Monday Times* (Moldavia); *Global Outlook* (Canada); *Yemen Observer* (Yemen); *The New Nation* (Bangladesh); *Pakistan Observer* (Pakistan); *Daily Times* (Pakistan); *Zaman Daily* (Turkey); *Iran Daily* (Iran); *Trust Weekly* (Nigeria); *Muslim Weekly* (U.K.); *Social Press* (Italy); *Taiwan News* (Taiwan); *Yemen Times* (Yemen); *Greater Kashmir Daily* (India); *India Monitor* (India); *Middle East Affairs Journal* (U.S.).

Introduction
Setting the Stage

Jennifer Loewenstein

Except for the Israeli soldiers on duty, the al-Ram checkpoint was deserted at 11:30 on Monday night, May 28, 2001. I and my three traveling companions had spent a longer-than-planned day in Ramallah and needed to get back to our hotel in East Jerusalem. We had been advised to arrive at the checkpoint earlier, but owing to a lively evening at a local restaurant with friends, our return journey began later than scheduled. Just finding a taxi to take us to Qalandia had required some effort—even the cash-strapped drivers were not enthusiastic about taking four Americans to the crossings so late. Indeed, we walked a good half-hour through town just to find someone who would drive us to our first stop.

People familiar with the internal checkpoint system in place in the occupied West Bank at that time (this was before the advent of the wall) will understand that we could not take one taxi from Ramallah to East Jerusalem, but would require three—each at a different location—and that at each checkpoint we would go through the same routine of having our IDs checked, our belongings scrutinized, and our motivations questioned. This was the "good" treatment, the treatment for foreigners, who usually got through each checkpoint with ease.

We arrived at al-Ram, the last stop, tired and hoping to get through quickly so we could be on our way. As we approached the booth for internationals, we took out our passports to have them ready for inspection. A soldier, a boy about 19, came up to us, gun slung over his shoulder, and began asking what we had been doing in Ramallah and why we were coming back so late. We described our day—visiting friends, shopping, eating out—briefly and with no unnecessary detail. A second soldier came up behind the first to see who we were. He separated us into two groups: I and my companion Margaret from our two male companions, Ali and Jeremy.

Ali was an Iranian-American. His passport listed his place of birth as Iran. The first soldier examined it and said sarcastically, "ALI—*that's* a very American name," but Ali ignored him, saying he was with us

1

as part of a U.S. delegation. Meanwhile, the second soldier began questioning Margaret and me. "Why were you so late in Ramallah?" he asked. "Don't you know they don't like Americans?" he said haughtily. Margaret, tired and annoyed by his attitude, snapped back, "well they liked us!" This was not the appropriate tone to take with people who control your movement and it contributed to an already uncomfortable feeling about us. Should they have wished to make our lives difficult, these soldiers could have detained us all night so it was best to cooperate. At that point, the soldier questioning Ali beckoned me to come over. Jeremy, who'd been mostly silent up to now, tried to humor the soldier by talking about his Bar Mitzvah. Jeremy was a Jewish student from New York who'd arranged to go on this delegation to see for himself what was happening in the Occupied Territories. His efforts at defusing the situation there at the checkpoint proved fruitless, however, as the soldier emptied the contents of Ali's backpack onto a large cement block in front of us. He picked up a bottle of cologne Ali had purchased in Ramallah, opened it, and sprayed it in my face. "Do you like that?" he said snidely. "Does it make you love Ahhh-Liiiii?"—he exaggerated Ali's name, apparently bothered by the fact that it was so obviously Muslim, and then continued to fish around the items spilled out in front of us for something more interesting. The second soldier strode up behind Ali, "you can have your things back." He barked out these words, distracting all of us from the antics of his comrade. "Thank you," said Ali, again refusing to be rattled by their having singled him out for harassment. The soldier glanced at his companion with a quick smile and began stuffing Ali's things back into his backpack. "I think we've seen enough," he said, suddenly sounding disinterested. "You can go on." He accompanied us to the gate of the crossing where we were allowed to pass to the other side and hail our last taxi for the night.

It was now after 1:00am and we were all eager to get out of there. But halfway back to the hotel, Ali let out a groan. "Oh my God," he said, "I can't believe this. Tell me it's not true." He began searching furiously through his backpack in the back seat of the taxi. All of us looked concerned. Ali's passport was missing—the one he'd just shown to the soldiers at the booth. We didn't know what to do—it was so late and we'd already had trouble at the checkpoint. Should we return in the morning? Margaret, who spoke Arabic, asked our driver for his advice. "Go back and get it now," he urged, "or you will never see it again." Conferring for a minute, we agreed to return to the checkpoint. Without his passport, Ali would have enormous difficulties. With his dark, Middle Eastern features and accent, it would not be easy convincing people he was an American citizen. His travel plans could be seriously delayed until he received a new passport or clearance from the U.S. Embassy, and for the remainder of our trip he would not be able to travel with us because without his passport he would never be allowed to cross in and out of the West Bank and the Gaza Strip each day (something still relatively easy for Americans during the first year of the Al-Aqsa Intifada). We had to go back. I agreed to accompany Ali while Margaret and Jeremy stayed in the cab. I was plainly American and it was still assumed that soldiers would not harass 'nice, white' U.S. citizens, especially Jewish U.S. citizens, traveling about Occupied Palestine.

Walking back to the checkpoint, we saw the two soldiers noting our arrival. They whispered something to each other. The one who had sprayed the cologne in my face then sauntered towards us. "I'm SO sorry," he drawled, a faked apologetic smile on his lips. "I forgot to give you back your passport." We hadn't said a thing; he just reached into his back pocket and then shoved the passport into Ali's hands. "Have a good night." He turned and laughed, lifting up his machine gun and firing it into the night air. We got back into the cab and by 2:00am were finally in our rooms at the Jerusalem Hotel near the Damascus Gate. Thus continued my initiation into the world of Israel's occupation—one that had begun twenty years earlier on a tour bus in the Gaza Strip when I'd come to Israel on a study abroad semester. I hadn't expected back then to encounter things that would make me question Israel's policies, but the shock (among other things) of seeing a refugee camp in Gaza began a journey that would take me far away from the easy belief that Israel was a 'light unto nations' whose creation and existence were noble causes to be honored and defended at all costs.

For me, Ali's experience at the checkpoint highlighted the fault lines of a society whose existence is premised on the willed non- or sub-standard existence of another people; whose celebration as an enlightened, democratic outpost in the Middle East worthy of unlimited and unconditional U.S. assistance has to be maintained by a meticulously cultivated image of a nation constantly fighting for its life, besieged by intractable Muslim and Arab hatred. The lengths to which Israel has gone to diminish the human standing of the non-Jewish population over which it retains control are awe-inspiring, especially considering the success with which they have been met in influential circles across the United States. The accepted narrative is non-negotiable. This is what makes the personal and documentary challenges to that narrative so important: as the full picture of what has happened to the people of Palestine emerges, that narrative loses its power. Indeed, it begins to read like the obscenity it actually is.

Ali's experience was trivial. After all, he was American and only so much harassment was acceptable in front of three other American witnesses. What Palestinians have had to face—and continue to face with each passing day—makes his trial at the checkpoint a shadow of the current reality. This is what makes the situation both in the Occupied Territories and for Palestinians living in Israel so shameful. As I write, the dismemberment of Palestinian culture and society is taking place, in full view of the rest of the world, notably its principal sponsor, the United States. Each "step toward peace," spun and managed by Israel's political protectors and a largely complicit media, brings the total disintegration of Palestine even closer. A cursory look at the various levels upon which Israel is attempting to assure this disintegration should give readers a sense of its seriousness— and of the need for a closer look at the significance of the Second Palestinian Uprising.

PHYSICAL DISMEMBERMENT

I remember when the full physical reality of the occupation hit me: I was traveling around with Samer, an employee of the Alternative Tourism Group based in Beit Sahour. He had taken a small group of us to an Arab village located in a valley just outside Jerusalem. It looked dusty and forlorn. I did not see many people on the streets and it felt like a ghost town, though it was in fact overcrowded with people. This was in 2001, well before the appearance of the Wall that now cuts across the land like a jagged scar, reinforcing the system of land theft and dispossession. On the hilltops above and surrounding us we could see the shiny red rooftops of new Jewish settlements— neatly packed housing units side by side, cheerfully clean, with an assortment of modern businesses available to its residents. Some of the homes had swimming pools; all of them had small, green gardens. Landscapers had lined the streets with flowers, glossy green shrubs, and well-tended little trees. Across the entire West Bank this pattern is repeated: poor Arab villages huddled together in valleys overlooked by hilltop settlements or, worse, encircled by Israeli Defense Forces (I.D.F.) military outposts with their watchtowers, barbed wire fences, jeep patrols and Israeli flags, and flanked in all directions by scores of entrapping checkpoints. The big cities are cut off from the smaller towns which in turn are cut off from the villages which are cut off from farmland, water resources, businesses, schools, clinics, and access to the outside world. Jewish-only bypass roads link the settlements, the military infrastructure, and the state of Israel together, enabling easy access everywhere for Jews and Israelis while they choke off the separate Palestinian communities from each other and from any viable outlets.

Key to understanding this geography is seeing how the major Jewish settlements in and around Jerusalem (East and West) have severed the West Bank into two separate zones and isolated and encircled Palestinian East Jerusalem. These areas are, in turn, cut off from Gaza, a miserable strip of ruined land, desperately overcrowded and surrounded yet again by barbed wire fences, watchtowers, armed guards, motion censors, and concrete walls, except along the coast where the waters are patrolled by Israeli gunboats. The recent handover of the Philadelphi Corridor, the border between Gaza and Egypt, to joint Egyptian–P.A. control is farcical in that anything the Israelis object to will continue to be prohibited. Israel's success at fragmenting physical and geographical Palestine is matched by its success in having shattered the social, political, and economic strata as well. Most of the efforts to dismember Palestine have been systematic and ongoing since well before the Second Intifada. The latter, however, provided pretexts on the basis of which the process of destroying Palestine could be accelerated and intensified. Thus, for example, during "Operation Defensive Shield" in the spring of 2002, I.D.F. soldiers were responsible for destroying the records of civic institutions and N.G.O.s throughout the West Bank city of Ramallah, very often the central location for these offices.

SOCIAL DISMEMBERMENT

Ransacking soldiers left furniture and appliances wrecked beyond repair. Food, drink, mud, urine, faeces, and trash covered the floors, and graffiti was scrawled across the walls. After removing computer hard drives (which were transported to Israel) soldiers smashed up the computers and printers rendering them permanently unusable. They spilled out the contents of filing cabinets, burned or shredded documents and papers leaving them strewn across the floors or scattered in the streets. Soldiers also burned, shredded, and sometimes shot at personal photographs, posters, and pictures on the walls. In addition to the destruction of these offices, I.D.F. soldiers vandalized radio and TV stations, banks, schools, hospitals, medical clinics, and cultural centers. Many soldiers broke or shot bullets through office windows, destroyed office, medical, and school supplies, trashed the lavatories, and broke down the doors to the buildings. The I.D.F. justified this wanton destruction as a necessary part of the "war against terror," though such crimes were reminiscent of similar ones committed against Palestinian civil society such as in Beirut in 1982 when, under the command of then Defense Minister Ariel Sharon, the Israeli army confiscated the archives of the Palestine Research Center, destroying some of it and sending much of it back to Israel, in an unprecedented attempt at wiping out recorded Palestinian history.

What is amazing about these actions is that they have been largely forgotten, perhaps in the wake of more sensational and deadly crimes such as the imprisonment of Palestinian Authority President Yasser Arafat in his Muqata' compound, the killing, large-scale destruction, and invasion into Nablus, and the obliteration of the Jenin refugee camp in April 2002. In these cases, witnesses, among whom I count myself, saw what the occupying Israel army could do quite literally to the physical surroundings of Palestinians. The I.D.F. left nothing in Jenin but a desert of rubble on an unrecognizable area of land, dozens of dead (including many civilians), hundreds of wounded, and thousands of shell-shocked people—men, women, children, old and young, civilians and combatants, trying to make sense of the chaos that had descended upon them. More than 13,000 people lost their homes and thousands of others were detained and imprisoned leaving family members behind with no knowledge of their whereabouts and therefore no way to contact them. Disturbingly, Israel managed to prevent an international fact-finding mission on the destruction of Jenin from ever taking place—leaving that history, as well as the rest of what happened that horrible spring, to the vanquished, and therefore erased from the official narrative.

In the meantime, the curfews and closures continued, with families unable to visit relatives, students unable to get to school, workers unable to reach their jobs, the sick unable to get proper medical attention, and farmers unable to tend their land. These circumstances persist today as the whims of the occupier dictate which checkpoints to open and which curfews to impose when and for how long. Travel permits are issued arbitrarily and infrequently, and Israel maintains ultimate control over the Palestinian population registry—in which the names and addresses of the entire Palestinian population are kept, often with devastating consequences. (Persons born in Gaza, for example, who have nonetheless resided in the West Bank for decades, can, at the will of the Israeli authorities, be deported back to Gaza with no recourse to return to their families, friends, and places of employment on the grounds that they are "illegally residing" in the West Bank, i.e. because the Israeli occupation authorities refused to allow the change of address.) The social effects of these, and other, policies can be barely imagined. The veteran Israeli reporter Amira Hass has pointed to the resurrection of traditional tribal and familial authorities in the cities, towns, and villages at the expense of a national authority, since the latter is incapable of imposing an efficient or effective national government. Equally, much of Palestinian society has been thrown backwards in time, forced to resort to such things as travel by donkey cart over narrow, bumpy mountain roads, since the normal means of transportation have been all but cut off. The implications for the future of a single, national Palestine beyond its abstract conception are immense.

Rather than condemn these acts of collective punishment and internal dispersion and demand their immediate cessation, however, U.S. politicians, Middle East "experts," and media analysts (and their Israeli counterparts) choose to laud Israel's "easing of restrictions"— when routine daily life becomes slightly less impossible—as if these should be the preconditions for the Palestinian Authority to sign away the remainder of its ravaged lands.

ECONOMIC DISMEMBERMENT

One way to try to guarantee the destruction of a people is to take away its land—either by expulsion or by expropriation or both. Another is to sever the civic and social bonds of the national community (indeed, this is partly accomplished by the first). A third is to destroy the economies of those who remain behind. As we have seen, Israel has demonstrated great success with the first two. It appears to be excelling at the third as well.

Economically, Israel floods the territories with produce and goods manufactured within Israel, largely preventing the importation of competitive products from other countries, and then charges artificially high prices for them. Residents have little choice than to purchase these products if (among other things) they want to eat, despite rising levels of poverty, unemployment, and malnutrition throughout Palestinian lands and especially in the Gaza Strip. This integration of Israel's economy with those of its Occupied Territories undermines local Palestinian economies and is accelerating the economic separation of the northern and southern West Banks, East Jerusalem, and Gaza—a corollary to the geographic and socio-political separation of these regions. Israel's recent threat to breach the quasi-customs union it has with Gaza (linking it with the West Bank), unless it is allowed to maintain "real time" camera surveillance over the people entering Gaza through the Rafah Crossing as well as full control over the passage of goods and people in and out of Gaza at the new Kerem Shalom border terminal, illustrates (among other things) its desire to break the remaining economic bonds between the primary Palestinian cantons. Israel continues to close the Erez, Karni, and Sufa crossings between Gaza and Israel at will and to conduct widespread military operations into Gaza in "retaliation" for terror attacks in Israel—even when such attacks originated in the West Bank and were themselves a response to I.D.F. killings. All of these actions point to the key fact that the Gaza Strip is still occupied, despite all the media hype behind the redeployment of I.D.F. forces and the evacuation of 8000 illegal Jewish settlers in the August 2005 Gaza "Disengagement."

Most of this hype is for Western, particularly U.S., consumption since those living in Gaza are under no illusions over who ultimately controls their lives. It is only a matter of time before the process of economic separation is completed, the quasi-customs union breached, and the donor nations left with the bill for Israel's occupation—compounded by the fact that those Gazans who still have permission to work inside Israel for sub-standard wages will soon lose this privilege, according to the Disengagement document itself, a document drawn up largely by U.S. Deputy National Security Advisor, Elliot Abrams and Israeli Prime Minister Ariel Sharon's Senior Advisor, Dov Weisglass. All of the focus on redeveloping Gaza now that Israel has left its interior suggests a breach with reality or a failure to comprehend even the most basic facts about Israel's long-term intentions for its occupied lands. A report published by the World Bank in December 2004 concludes, for example, that poverty and unemployment will both continue to rise in Gaza even under the best post-Disengagement scenario possible.

When Israel handed over nominal control of the Philadelphi Corridor (the Gaza–Egypt border) to the Egyptians and the P.A. in September 2005, Palestinians in Gaza rushed the crossing and flooded out of the Strip in great numbers, in particular to the Egyptian city of Al-Arish in the Sinai desert. Friends wrote of what it was like in Gaza City to see almost no taxis in the streets (they'd all been hired for the ride to the Rafah crossing). People took off from work and school to get out of Gaza for the first time in years—to experience the psychological freedom of an open border, to go to the beaches in Rafah (a prohibited visit during the Intifada), and, significantly, to purchase cheap Egyptian goods in Al-Arish and take them home to their families. Subsequent attempts on the part of the crossing authorities to keep people back and to re-seal the border failed, as members of militant organizations and others broke down the barriers again and again until closure was forcefully restored days later. This scenario offers a glimpse into the Gaza pressure-cooker, the Gaza prison in which 1.4 million people have been locked without relief for more than five years. It also hints at the social and political implosion that will take place over the next few years as conditions in the Strip continue to worsen—an implosion the Israelis are doubtless expecting and, indeed, banking on for it will allow them to justify any and all military actions against Gaza in the name of national security and to claim the high ground of "no longer being occupying authorities"—at least in their books. According to the final version of the Disengagement document, once disengagement is complete, Israel is no longer legally obligated in any way to the inhabitants of the Gaza Strip as they were as the occupying authority—not that they ever honored those obligations.

POLITICAL DISMEMBERMENT

"Gaza is descending into chaos before my eyes," writes Said Abdelwahed, Professor of English at the Al Azhar University in Gaza City.

[L]ife in Gaza is becoming more complicated and gloomier than ever before. This ... is the logical result of such a lawless situation. Family feuds and street scuffles ... have become daily practices. The P.A. has no control on the street. Indeed, ordinary people do not respect [the] P.A. [because of] its history of corruption and its reputation for not caring about anyone but themselves. It has done nothing to try to regain some respect and authority on the streets of Gaza. I do not exaggerate when I say that the P.A. cannot even control the traffic.

The political meltdown of Gaza and the West Bank—primarily the struggle between the weakened and disintegrating Palestinian

Authority under Fatah and the growing strength of the Islamist movement Hamas—is the latest manifestation of what Baruch Kimmerling calls "Politicide," a deliberate policy on the part of the Sharon government to destroy the leadership and political infrastructure of Palestine. Five years of extrajudicial assassinations, deportations, imprisonments, and policies of divide and conquer have left political Palestine in a shambles. A direct result of this was the central role gained by the Islamic Resistance Movement (Hamas) following its decisive win in the Palestine Legislative Council elections of January 2006.

Ostensibly the opposite of what the Israeli government hopes for, the rise of Hamas is a predictable outcome of the breakdown of the P.A. This has been especially true since the signing of the Oslo Accords. With Arafat's death, Marwan Barghouti's imprisonment, and the ineffectual leadership of Mahmud Abbas and others marking the last five years of misery, it should be no surprise that many Palestinians are looking elsewhere for answers. Of course, Hamas is strongest in Gaza, and other groups such as the P.F.L.P., Mustafa Barghouti's Palestine National Initiative, and a new party headed by former P.A. Finance Minister Salim Fayyad are not without their followings. Still, the political disintegration of Palestine has potentially disastrous implications for its future. Israel has willfully exacerbated and exploited these political divisions within the West Bank and the Gaza Strip. Indeed some would argue it is largely responsible for them, though this should not absolve the P.A. of responsibility for its woefully poor management of public affairs and its refusal to put an end to rampant corruption. It is not surprising that the morale of those in the pay of the P.A., in particular the Palestinian police, is so low.

OPEN SEASON

It was a hot afternoon in Ramallah the day I rejoined my traveling companions. I'd been spending time with friends in the tiny village of Kufr Na'ima. I remember going to the village the day before, and getting into a white van watched carefully by I.D.F. personnel. Before we left, a heavily armed soldier slid open the door to ask for people's IDs. I handed him my American passport and, although he was unimpressed, there was a slight sense of relief inside the van as if having me there was somehow securing. This, of course, was before the deaths of Rachel Corrie, Thomas Hurndall, and James Miller, and the maiming of Brian Avery—when both Palestinians and Westerners believed Americans and Europeans were immune to the violence of the Israeli military and indeed could act as protective shields for Palestinian civilians. I felt awkwardly useful that day.

The four of us—I and my companions Margaret, Jeremy, and Ali—all felt a great need to witness as much as we could. We wanted somehow to show support for people whose voices have been nullified in the United States. After making purchases at some of the local businesses and eating a hasty lunch, we decided to do a walking tour of Ramallah, photographing the bombed police station, the smashed house of then Security Chief, Jibril Rajoub, who had only recently been spared in an Israeli assassination attempt, and mats on the ground outside the police barracks where the policemen were sleeping each night—fearing the Israelis would bomb their quarters after dark. It was surreal. We'd done a television interview with a group of students a week earlier at the Amwaj TV station—one of those destroyed less than a year later during the invasion of Ramallah. We wanted to show our solidarity and I believe we all felt equally emboldened and defiant. Outside the police barracks, however, a young officer inquired after us. What were we doing there? Why were we taking pictures? (This was not allowed.) Having been more or less convinced of our sincerity, he suggested we take pictures at another location, not far from there, in Beitunia, a suburb of Ramallah. He hailed a cab for us and gave the driver directions. In a moment, we were off to yet another location, unsure exactly where we were going.

Stepping out of the cab, we found ourselves on a wide open street. To our right were four- and five-story apartment buildings set back a little, some of them abandoned. One of these buildings was considered part of Area C, Israeli controlled territory, and I.D.F. soldiers apparently manned it at night. To our left was mostly open space except for an empty hut, trailer-like in appearance, but more ramshackle with corrugated metal and flimsy wood holding it together, an open doorway and window along its front. This was Area A, Palestinian Authority territory. I remember there was a huge billboard towering above the hut a few feet away. At the top of a large steel red pole was a giant advertisement for Viceroy Cigarettes. The caption read, "The Big Taste of America." For some reason, I photographed it.

Local boys were outside watching us. One of them asked if we wanted a tour. He began to describe where we were, the details of which I confirmed later through news articles and press releases. Early in the morning of May 14, 2001, six Palestinian policemen had been staying in the hut. In fact, they had been coordinating operations with the Israeli military to keep people from entering the area, considered a potential hot-spot. Not long after midnight they were about to sit down and share a meal together. One of them had on his walkman; another was at the table reading a book while the others cooked and talked together. Outside, Israeli soldiers stationed on the top floor of one of the buildings across the street monitored their every action. At around 1:00am they opened fire on the policemen killing five of them instantly with shots fired into their heads and chests. One survived, having leapt into a hole outside the hut that had been dug for their latrine. The killings were brutal and senseless and caused the "Day of Rage" protests across the West Bank. Inside the hut we could see blood stains and the reminders of that horrible night—a cooking pot on the stove, a table and chairs, the mats they had slept on. Neighborhood children had scrawled angry graffiti on the walls inside, but otherwise the place was somberly quiet. Having denied any wrongdoing at first, the Israeli military spokespersons first claimed someone had opened fire on them. Later however, they were forced to issue an apology, tempering it with the usual disingenuous comments that bad things often happen during times of war and conflict. Here was our first encounter with the deliberate breach of trust created by the Israelis against the P.A. and the extent to which they would go to assert their shameless and arbitrary superior military power.

REAPPRAISAL AND RESISTANCE

The latest evidence of Israeli meddling in Palestinian political affairs has been its refusal to allow in arms and ammunition to the Palestinian Authority in order to control Hamas, a superior military force in the Gaza Strip. Sharon's government claims that it will not negotiate with Hamas and that it does not want its participation in the Palestinian Legislative Council or within a newly comprised Palestinian national authority. It charges Abbas' government with failing either to "rein in" or "dismantle" Hamas. But it fully understands that the P.A. is incapable of doing this without well-trained and well-equipped soldiers. One must therefore question its motivations in refusing to allow in the necessary materials for Abbas to regain and hold power. With much of the young leadership of the Palestinian political factions dead, hunted, or imprisoned, the land chopped up and divided, civil society reeling after years of devastation, and the demise of the Palestinian economies, it should be no surprise that the facade of "Palestine" is crumbling in front of our eyes. The question that remains is whether the process has any hope of being reversed. Certainly, the concept of Palestine, the personal consciousness of being Palestinian or of taking up the Palestinian cause, is stronger than ever. Yet there remains a disturbing disjunction between the reality and the idea. What does being a Palestinian mean when all that remains of the actual nation are badly dismembered communities struggling for their very survival? When more than half of the Palestinian people live in exile or as refugees on their own land? When the P.A. is fractured within itself and unable to maintain even the appearance of sovereignty over a people steeped increasingly in chaos? How will understanding the events of the Second Intifada help us resolve these and other related issues?

It is said by some that the seeds of the Second Palestinian Intifada were sown in the late spring of 2000 when the Islamist party Hizbollah succeeded in driving the Israelis out of Southern Lebanon after 22 years of occupation. One can understand how people increasingly disillusioned by the failure of negotiations to achieve a better life would look to the victory of Hizbollah as a model for effective resistance. The summer of 2000 was marked by the fiasco of Camp David in which the failure to reach an overall agreement, particularly over the status of Jerusalem, was laid at Arafat's feet. The media spin machine not only cast this failure as "proof" of Arafat's disingenuousness in seeking a peaceful resolution to the ongoing conflict, it also hatched the myth of the "generous offer," claiming that Barak, with Clinton's support, had offered Arafat more than ever before—without ever providing details or a map to the public to substantiate this erroneous claim. News of arms' build-ups in the Jewish settlements of the West Bank during the same time period barely received coverage. The ongoing closures, settlement building, restrictions on movement, and other features of the occupation (intensified after Oslo) disappeared completely behind the grand spectacle of a Middle East summit in the United States that was supposed to solve once and for all the Israel–Palestine "problem." By late September 2000 the discontent and anger simmering in the Palestinian territories, combined with inspiration from the images of a Hizbollah-David forcing the Israeli Military-Goliath out of South Lebanon, needed but a final precipitating factor to break into open revolt. Ariel Sharon's offensive visit to the Haram al-Sharif in

Jerusalem on September 28, 2000, and the subsequent use of excessive force against demonstrators the following day, unleashed a chain of events that ignited the Second Uprising. What was surprising to some was that it had taken so long for Palestinians to reject Israel's repeated lies and diktats. That the Second Intifada has been characterized as an armed revolt by an array of militias rather than as a popular insurrection in which civil disobedience dominated is not surprising given the level of disaffection following Oslo's failure and the repeated and overwhelming use of force against unarmed civilians especially in the early days of the uprising. Nevertheless, the prevalence of armed attacks against civilians within the Occupied Territories and terror attacks against the civilian population in Israel will ultimately ensure its failure.

Some, including myself, believe that the front line in the battle for Palestine is public opinion in the United States. Only by changing popular attitudes towards Israel and the Palestinians can we hope to end U.S. sponsorship of Israel's ongoing war and "sociocide." Others believe that Israeli policies hold within them the seeds of their own destruction and will ultimately cause the collapse of the Jewish State. The problem is that in the meantime people continue to suffer terribly as a result of policies that are threatening their very existence. We cannot ask an entire people to lie down and accept such a reality. Therefore, resistance—in particular non-violent popular resistance in all its forms—must continue. There have to be local, regional, national, and international levels upon which to foster and enhance understanding, action, and a fundamental refusal to accept the status quo. In the meantime, we should remember that most have not given up despite the circumstances they face.

Indeed, while the principal venue for an effective resistance movement may have shifted, we can draw strength and inspiration from those who embody persistence and defiance in their very lives. At the same time we must not forget that there will be regional ramifications of the Israeli-endorsed U.S. policies, particularly since the invasion and destruction of Iraq. Few recognize the effect that this and some of its consequences are having on the peoples of Palestine and elsewhere. If Hizbollah provided inspiration to a people beaten down by decades of brutal occupation, we can only imagine what the popular response will be to the still distant but inevitable evacuation of U.S. troops from an Iraq overrun by a guerrilla insurgency and internal disintegration. The blind and arrogant U.S. quest for dominance in the Middle East manifested of late in its cruel occupation of Iraq will have repercussions in the region for decades to come. Rebellion in Palestine will be but one facet of a transforming Middle East. In the meantime, however, the Second Palestinian Intifada is not over. It is facing a crucial crossroads, and may follow new and unpredictable paths over the coming years. I only hope the lessons it has taught us—through all the agony of defeat and frustration—have been properly learned.

1
The Intifada Takes Off (2000–01)

This chapter highlights some of the events which take place just months before the outbreak of the Second Palestinian Uprising, as well as the events of its first year. It explores how the Israeli army employs tactics of provocation—from fortifying settlements to invading refugee camps—in an attempt to show the Palestinians that the May 2000 retreat from South Lebanon, after 22 years of uninterrupted occupation, will not be a precedent. Talks at Camp David also commence, where Barak's famous "generous offer" is purportedly presented and subsequently snubbed by the Palestinian delegation. This becomes a monumental turning-point, with the Israelis and Americans jointly declaring that there is no hope for a bilateral peace agreement with Palestinians. Shortly thereafter, Sharon executes his contentious visit to Haram al-Sharif—an event that signifies the breaking point for Palestinians and instigates the onset of the five-year-long Intifada. Sharon is soon elected Prime Minister of Israel and unveils his new plan of targeted assassinations of Palestinian activists, a plan that will claim

Photo 1.1 Palestinian youth smile for the camera as they gather in front of a United Nations-run school.

the lives of hundreds over the next five years. The extradition of Slobodan Milosevic highlights the limitations and double standards of international law, and the question is raised whether Israel will ever be held accountable to the same edicts. Finally, the tragedy of September 11 not only shocks the world, but profoundly changes the political landscape in the Middle East, the ramifications of which are intimately felt among Palestinians.

LESSONS FROM DEFEAT

Some would argue that the birth of the Second Palestinian Uprising was actually rooted in the south of Lebanon. After the long and cruel uprising from 1987–93, empty promises, meaningless summits, and equally barren accords had left Palestinians in a numbing impasse. Rumors circulated and were eventually confirmed when Israeli officials formally disclosed that weapons build-up was taking place within the settlements plaguing the Occupied Territories. Palestinians realized that perilous designs were being crafted in the midst of the stalemate. But to the north, a decades-long skirmish between the Israeli army and the resistance movement Hizbollah was finally coming to an end, with an assured and embarrassing defeat for the Israeli Defense Forces.

It was not until May 2000 that the Israeli army finally abandoned the gains of its precious victory in Lebanon. Nearly two decades of a war of attrition between the Israeli army and a few hundred Hizbollah resistance fighters went mostly unnoticed. It was hardly defined as a war, since it lacked the trappings of traditional combat. Nevertheless, the Lebanese resistance could claim a tangible Arab victory, after decades of humiliating defeats at the hands of the Israeli army—from Israel's so-called War of Independence in 1948, to the Six-Day War in 1967, and the 1982 invasion of Lebanon, to list some primary examples. The Lebanese resistance's triumph on the battlefield is one that Israel still denies.[1]

Israel's then chief of staff, Lieutenant-General Shaul Mofaz, who oversaw Israel's retreat from Lebanon, warned soon after that Israel intended to deploy tanks and helicopters in the occupied West Bank and Gaza. The official claim was that violent clashes with Palestinians were causing the army concern such that the government was persuaded to send additional supplies to Jewish settlers, including sandbags and tear-gas canisters. Considering the injury inflicted on unarmed Palestinians over the years with Israel's conventional "anti-riot" gear (automatic rifles, military jeeps, and tear gas), was this sudden and extreme build-up necessary? Was there any imperative to deploy heavy weaponry to combat youth, women, and children? In the midst of Israel's military build-up, Palestinian Authority officials asserted that Israel was actually targeting the P.A., even though the primary targets were groups that outwardly refused the peace terms prescribed in the Oslo Accords, drafted secretly and without the consent of most Palestinians. The P.A.'s claim to being itself the target seemed unconvincing, if not absurd, considering that joint security coordination between Israeli forces and P.A. police was actively continued, to the indignation of most Palestinians. Such dual loyalty was fully demonstrated in Palestinian protests in May 2000, which were violently suppressed jointly by Israel and the Palestinian Authority. The deliberate killing of six unarmed Palestinians and the injuring of over 1000 was not enough to persuade the P.A. to reassess its allegiances to Israel in favor of an increasingly frustrated Palestinian populace. And while Israel's increasingly violent aggressions failed to persuade the P.A. to rethink its unconditional peace negotiation strategy, it was Israeli Prime Minister Ehud Barak who ordered his negotiation team home, in protest at the wounding of an Israeli toddler.[2]

Concurrently, Barak, who was dubbed a "dove" by Israeli and American political commentators, was putting himself on friendlier terms with radical Jewish settlers who were occupying 145 thriving settlements in the West Bank. These settlers, who had for long been granted participation in suppressing Palestinian protests, had worked alongside Israeli forces for years. A statement issued by Barak's office on June 21 said that Barak instructed his ministers to meet with leaders of the settlement movement regularly, lauding them as "good citizens" with an important role in defending Israel.[3] Barak's softer tone with the settlers was a direct concession to their grievances over his wishy-washy policies, i.e. the policy of dialogue with the Palestinians. But Barak's open disregard for Palestinians' rights, and his insistence on retaining major settlements in the West Bank and Gaza, left little doubt regarding his real intentions. Furthermore, the new alliances which were in the process of being formed, coupled with Barak's growing obsession with fortifying the settlements by deploying heavy military equipment, would likely further expose his not so dove-like demeanor. This military build-up reflected Israel's realization that a Palestinian revolt against the occupation, solidified by the P.A.'s unreserved collaboration, was imminent. The fact that the Israelis were openly pursuing these militaristic policies, at a time when Israel was purportedly eager to produce a framework for a "final status agreement" with the Palestinian leadership, is telling to say the least. However, there was more to Israel's military escalation than just this. Israel's defeat in Lebanon strengthened the Palestinians' faith in armed struggle and shook the confidence of the Israeli army. Israel was, therefore, looking to reassert itself in the West Bank and Gaza. Israeli army officials made statements on various occasions, affirming their concerns regarding Hizbollah's military performance and its impact on Palestinians.[4] The Israeli army also attempted to convey that their humiliating and abrupt retreat from Lebanon would not be repeated in the Occupied Territories. At the same time, they were seeking to redeem their shattered reputation, by taking on unarmed Palestinian youth.

MYTH OF THE GENEROUS OFFER

But there is also a highly relevant political dimension to the Second Palestinian Uprising—that of the failed Camp David II talks between Barak and Palestinian Authority President, Yasser Arafat, in July 2000. Less than two months after the withdrawal from South Lebanon, Israel attempted to force its own conditions on the Palestinian leadership at Camp David. Despite intense pressure from the "honest broker"—a role assumed by former U.S. President Bill Clinton—Arafat stood his ground. The historic narrative as written by the U.S. media often refers to this phase as that of "Barak's generous offer," claiming that Barak offered Palestinians everything they had demanded over the years, only to be refused by the Palestinian delegation, led by obstinate Arafat.

Palestinians hoped that the July talks at Camp David would be more mindful of their national aspirations for statehood than the historic Camp David treaty of 1979, signed between Egypt and Israel under American patronage. For Palestinians, the first Camp David amounted to a catastrophe. It was commonly believed that Israel's chief objective was to marginalize Egypt's role in the Arab–Israeli conflict. And it did so successfully. Not only was Egypt marginalized, but the seemingly united Arab front collapsed soon after. Egypt received harsh criticism from its Arab neighbors and lost its once leading role among Arab nations, making Israel the ultimate beneficiary. Then Israeli Prime Minister, Menachem Begin, refused any proposal for a realistic negotiation framework that could resolve the lingering conflict. Meanwhile, the United States signed a separate agreement with Israel: the Israel–U.S. Memorandum.[5] The agreement provided American guarantees to Israel, should Egypt violate the peace treaty. It also designated a generous annual military and economic aid package to help Israel cope with the cost of peace. The question of Palestine was then shelved for years, though not completely. Israel would now concentrate on suppressing the rebellious Palestinians, while trying to create an alternative leadership to negotiate a peace based on Israeli terms.

Following its exclusive peace deal with Egypt, Israel felt a greater sense of security. Now that the war of attrition—extending from the 1973 war to 1978—was officially over, a bloody campaign could be waged against Lebanon with the aim of altering its political structure, driving Syria out, and above all annihilating the Palestinian resistance. Just three years after the Camp David treaty, Israel's complex scheme led to the invasion of Lebanon, in the summer of 1982, culminating in the massacre of Sabra and Shatilla. The estimates on Lebanese and Palestinian casualties in Israel's war varied. But there is agreement that tens of thousands were killed and wounded.[6] The masterminds of the invasion were the same men who signed the peace treaty with Egypt—Begin, accompanied by the rising star of Israeli politics, Ariel Sharon. And yet, Israel achieved little in its invasion of Lebanon, a lesson that cost Israel hundreds of its soldiers. Barak had the courage to admit that the Israeli presence in Lebanon was costly and futile, and so on an historic night in May 2000, Israeli troops scrambled back to Israel's northern border as their leadership vowed never to return.

Fearing that the Arab military triumph in Lebanon might give the Palestinians a degree of leverage, Barak went to work fortifying settlements and military forces in the West Bank, assuring himself and the Palestinians that he would come to the negotiation table at Camp David with a strong upper hand. It was under these complex circumstances that Israelis and Palestinians set out to Camp David under the mediation of President Clinton. The meetings would indeed prove to be provocative for Palestinians, with Barak supposedly presenting his legendary and much touted "generous offer," and Arafat's negotiation team, as Clinton stated and the media subsequently reiterated, ungratefully discounting it. But a leading Palestinian intellectual, Hanan Ashrawi, has repeatedly affirmed that no written proposal was ever presented to the Palestinians. Palestinians argued that even if there had been such a proposal, Arafat's rejection—of the partitioning of the West Bank into three cantons separated by Israeli military zones and Israeli-only bypass roads, of the continuous presence of illegal settlements, and of Israel's dominion over Occupied East Jerusalem—was nothing less than a sound choice. The declarations uttered by various American and Israeli officials following the plummeting Camp David II summit were wholeheartedly consistent with one another—Arafat has no intention of reaching a final and comprehensive peace agreement with Israel, turning down a very charitable compromise presented by the Israeli negotiation team; Arafat is no peace partner, in fact, no such partner among Palestinians exists; considering this, Israel must now do all it can to protect its citizens from foreseeable Palestinian violence, even if it must seek to achieve peace unilaterally.

But in fact, it unfolded that there was no such generous offer to begin with—according to Robert Malley, Clinton's Special Assistant for Arab–Israeli Affairs and his advisor at Camp David. Barak never unveiled his proposal, not in writing, not verbally, not even to the United States itself, Malley indicated: "It is hard to state with confidence how far Barak was actually prepared to go," the U.S. official wrote in an article published by the *New York Review of Books*.[7] "His strategy was predicated on the belief that Israel ought not reveal its final position—not even to the United States—until the endgame was in sight." But there is more to this charade. There was one lone ranger behind the entire edifice of false depictions, according to the former chief of Israeli Military Intelligence, General Amos Malka. That man is Amos Gilad, the head of the research section at the MI office. Gilad's tall tale (that the Palestinians were not a partner in the peace process, and that Arafat was hell-bent on the destruction of Israel, compounded by the "generous offer" rhetoric) was so widespread it was still cited by political and media pundits in the Western media even after Malka's revealing interview with the Israeli daily newspaper *Haaretz*.[8] According to Malka, Gilad had no basis whatsoever for his assertions, save his own personal views: Gilad was "a very significant factor in persuading a great many people. [Yet] in all the time that I served as head of MI, the research division did not produce so much as a single document expressing the assessment that Gilad claims to have presented to the Prime Minister." That episode had therefore presented an "erroneous view of the cause of the violence [which followed two months later], and hence the mistaken conclusion that there is no Palestinian partner for peace," *Haaretz* concluded, elaborating on Malka's comments. Nonetheless, the Clinton Administration and mainstream media seemed to overlook what should have been a ground-shaking revelation, a scandal even. In their taking no notice, Israel was able to continue its relentless violence against the Palestinians. Its extended campaign of terror would proceed unchecked as long as Palestinians and their leadership were viewed as the source of discord, having supposedly succeeded in their diabolical scheme that began when Barak's "generous offer" was shunned at Camp David.

VIOLENCE SUMMONED

The breakdown at Camp David was exactly what the then right-wing party opposition leader, Ariel Sharon, needed to demonstrate to the Israeli public that Barak could not provide the security they deserved. To strengthen his case further, Sharon devised a plan for an historic "visit" to the Temple Mount, ironically calling it a gesture of "peace." But from the moment his plans were declared, Palestinians and others warned that stepping foot in the sacred shrine of Haram al-Sharif—the third most revered holy site for Muslims— would almost certainly ignite uncontainable violence. Thus, Sharon, accompanied by over 1000 Israeli troops and police, instigated the Middle East upheaval with his forced visit to the holy Muslim shrine in Jerusalem—particularly to the Al-Aqsa Mosque, from which the

Photo 1.2   Palestinian worshippers pray before an Israeli police barricade denying them entry to the Al-Aqsa Mosque in Occupied East Jerusalem.

Second Uprising derived its name—on September 28, 2000. As predicted, a volcano of hostilities erupted and scores of Palestinians were killed and wounded on the grounds of the site. The next day, the Israeli army confronted angry Palestinian masses throughout the Occupied Territories, and resorted to nothing less than traditional war tactics. The Second Palestinian Uprising was born. In the early months of Al-Aqsa Intifada, Israeli tanks rolled back into the West Bank. Sharon's contrived plan to ignite upheaval invited five more long years of bloodshed.

One of the early tragedies to befall the Palestinians was the killing of Mohammed al-Durra in the Gaza Strip, less than one week after the Intifada's inception. In one of the most enduring images of the conflict, the twelve-year-old boy was shot by Israeli forces as he and his father sought refuge from the gunfire in the city of Gaza.[9] His death sparked international sympathy and drew much deserved attention to the number of children killed by Israeli forces in the Occupied Territories. And yet Sharon's aggressive tactics garnered respect and adoration from a desperate Israeli populace, making the Premier's seat look even more promising. Months later, elections took place in Israel and on February 6, 2001, Ariel Sharon was elected Prime Minister of Israel in a landslide victory. His campaign platform had promised to crack down on Palestinian violence in 100 days.[10] The newly elected Israeli government, led by Sharon and backed by the settlers, would soon unleash a bloody onslaught on the disadvantaged, disappointed, and fed-up Palestinian masses, an onslaught that would last for much more than 100 days. One of the many places to suffer the wrath of Sharon's new and violent policy was the Khan Yunis refugee camp in the Gaza Strip on April 11, 2001.

ASSAULT ON KHAN YUNIS

Over 52 years have passed since the Khan Yunis refugee camp was established as "temporary shelter" for displaced Palestinians. This home of over 60,000 refugees is now one of the most crowded spots on earth. To wander through its narrow alleyways and makeshift houses, past the mounting garbage piles and impoverished streets and markets, is to realize that human misery is not an abstract idea but a living reality. The Israeli assault was said to be the first incident in which Israel had re-entered P.A. controlled territories since the Israeli withdrawal from population centers in the West Bank and Gaza in the mid and late 1990s. A few press reports succeeded in depicting most of the damage, narrating the suffering and emphasizing the sense of loss felt by hundreds of now homeless refugees. But the horror felt by a mother whose house was bulldozed while her children slept inside can never be described with mere words. For over half of my life, I lived in a camp only a few miles to the north of Khan Yunis. Yet, while my camp had its share of despair and resistance, Khan Yunis was always perceived differently, it was a true legend in the eyes of most refugees. "The Castle of Revolution"—as the town of Khan Yunis and its refugee camp were hailed during the 1987 Intifada. But the legend started decades earlier.

On March 11, 1956, the camp was the stage for a gruesome attack perpetrated by the Israeli army during its short-lived occupation of Egypt's Sinai and the Gaza Strip. According to the United Nations Relief and Works Agency (U.N.R.W.A.), who investigated Israel's actions, 275 civilians were killed in one night.[11] For days, Israel refused to allow the burial of the bodies scattered about the camp. Finally, under "international pressure," the victims of the massacre were buried in a mass grave. While the Israeli onslaught was aimed at suppressing the camp's resistance, it had the opposite result. The camp's survivors pioneered the Palestinian revolution, which took its toll following the occupation of the Gaza Strip in 1967. Khan Yunis refugee camp then became the home of armed resistance and a town where poets and intellectuals thrived. Israel, aware of the danger that the impoverished camp posed, made Khan Yunis one of its top priorities during the first Intifada. Dozens of people were killed, thousands injured, maimed, and arrested. But their resistance never faded. Years after the signing of the Oslo Accords in 1993, the only change experienced by the residents of the camp was the growth of their disparity. Neighboring Jewish settlements became a further source of anger for the refugees. Living in fancy villas and enjoying their private swimming pools, Jewish settlers continued their never-ending episode of harassment. Palestinian land continued to be seized, and roads separating Gaza's north and south were repeatedly cut off, in addition to the occasional yet never investigated shootings of Palestinians. It was within this context that the Second Uprising emerged. While the role of Khan Yunis in the resistance remained within the boundaries of self-defense, Israel's assaults crossed all boundaries of civility, human rights, and international law.

Three months after the outbreak of the Intifada, Israel began using illegal and unknown chemical agents against Palestinians, particularly in the Khan Yunis area. Sixty cases of unexplained symptoms such as uncontrollable hysteria were reported.[12] The P.A. stood helpless, sought European help, and appealed to the U.N. to intervene. But nothing was done. Then the camp was cut off and savagely attacked, often by guided missiles and helicopter gunships. Scores of homes were destroyed, people killed, including children, and fear once again prevailed. A strong believer in ruthless military strategy, Sharon finally decided to "go in and destroy the same posts from which our communities [illegal Jewish settlements] were shelled," as stated by Israel's Defense Minister, Ben-Eliezer in April, 2001.[13] Eliezer told reporters following the destruction in the camp: "There are points we don't want Palestinians to return to." "This is a clear act of defense," he added. But Eliezer's self-defense strategy was contended by Imad Abu Namous, a long-time resident of the camp. His home was leveled to the ground an hour after midnight. "We started running from our homes, while they were firing toward us and bulldozers started destroying our homes without giving us warning, without giving us a chance to take out some clothes and furniture," he lamented.[14] A nine-year-old boy, Osama Hassouneh, wept as he stood by the rubble of his home. "I lost my toy car. I hate the Israelis," he sobbed as he held to a melted piece of red plastic. More than 30 homes were destroyed that night, two people were killed and dozens were injured. Yet the residents of the camp returned the next morning, salvaging half-burnt blankets, pots, pans, and pillows. Some gazed at the wreckage, pondering how they could find the strength to start all over, and others cried in fright of a nightmare from which they may never recover. Israel labored to devastate the camp that night. The collective efforts of dedicated soldiers and settlers succeeded in obliterating an entire neighborhood. But in the midst of the ruins, a solitary wall remained standing, covered with colorful graffiti and images drawn with the colors of the Palestinian flag. There was a picture of a fist, breaking chains and bursting out of the ground. The trunk of a tree had the shape of the face of a little boy, and the roots were human hands holding tight to the soil. And below, a short statement in Arabic read, "like the trees we die standing."

THE HIT LISTS

Israel's targets were not always so arbitrary, and from its early months the uprising witnessed a fierce and calculated assassination policy carried out by the Sharon government. The right-wing leader even went so far as to publicly present the Israeli Parliament (the Knesset) with an exhaustive list of names, of Palestinian leaders and activists, all marked for assassination. Yet, like the Sharon government, Western governments, led by the U.S., never referred to the policy as one of "assassination," coining instead the term "targeted killings," in an attempt to smooth over the rough edges of the bitter policy. During the five years of upheaval, hundreds of Palestinians would fall victim to Sharon's unabashed assassination policy.

On July 30 and 31, 2001, Sharon's policy was realized with the assassination of 16 Palestinians in the West Bank and Gaza.[15] But the news hardly shocked the Western media. Various White House officials scrambled to find a justification for Israel's killings, and U.S. lawmakers blamed Arafat squarely for the violence. A few days later, on August 9, 2001, a young Palestinian man blew himself up in a crowded pizza parlor in Jerusalem, killing 15 people, mostly innocent civilians.[16] Somehow that was different. Ironically, the two numbers seemed to correspond to entirely different values. The Western mainstream media reacted to the killing of the Israelis with horror. But few asked the question, what would drive a young man to blow himself up? Many media pundits conveniently forgot to link the Jerusalem bombing to earlier events. There was a deliberate failure to admit that when a nation is under siege—when a policy

Photo 1.3   Palestinians gather in the West Bank city of Ramallah to mourn the death of assassinated Palestinian Front for the Liberation of Palestine leader, Abu Ali Mustafa. He was killed August 27, 2001 by two missiles fired from Israeli helicopters.

of starvation, assassination, and systematic killing is imposed, when people are brutalized in the streets, when schools are raided by Apache helicopters, when F16s erratically bombard villages and towns, when a whole nation is collectively abused and violated with almost no protection, while their occupier is backed by the United States and the rest of the world is largely apathetic to their plight—for those victims driven to the verge of desperation, blowing oneself up might actually seem like a rational way out of a despairing situation.

BEIT IBA

In the two weeks following the Jerusalem bombing, another surge of assassinations was carried out by Israel, targeting Palestinian activists in the West Bank and Gaza. But the killing of dozens of Palestinian men generated little empathy and attention in the Western media. Israel labeled its victims "terrorists" and the media converted the term to "militants." But what must one do to be labeled a "militant"? In the media's perception, almost every Palestinian man is a potential militant. Zahir Ismail, 30, Fadi Samaneh, 25, Jamal Tayeh, 22, and Ahed Faris, 23, were "militants" because they rushed to aid wounded men in the West Bank village of Beit Iba, after Israeli soldiers had ambushed them at dawn on August 22. The old mosque of Beit Iba, northwest of the town of Nablus, had called on local residents to help their wounded near the border of the village. Israeli soldiers denied ambulances entry to the scene, according to eyewitnesses. Locals said that soldiers captured the young men, tortured and then shot them at close range.[17] Jamal Tayeh had a hole in his chest and the rest had deep axe wounds and were filled with bullets. The villagers could only recover three of the mutilated bodies. The fourth, that of Ahed Faris, was taken by Israeli soldiers, a typical practice the army has adopted, in order to further torment the families of "militants" and forewarn others of the price of defying the occupation.[18]

Two days earlier, Samir Abu Zeid was in his home in the Gaza Strip's southern town of Rafah, accompanied by his six-year-old son and seven-year-old daughter. An Israeli missile killed all three instantly. Doctors at a nearby hospital said that the bodies arrived in pieces.[19] Israel claimed that Abu Zeid was a terrorist. The Western media dubbed him a "militant." But when one examines the backgrounds of these individuals, one will find incredibly different faces that neither "terrorist" nor "militant" truthfully portray. One finds dedicated and honest individuals, men and women who represent large segments of

Palestinian society with its wide spectrum of political and ideological affiliations. If every Palestinian who identifies with a political party and embraces such principles as freedom, liberty, and human rights becomes a "terrorist" from an Israeli point of view, and a "militant" in the Western perception, then nearly every Palestinian man, woman, and even child is a terrorist and a militant. Being a Palestinian activist means that you could be targeted in a taxicab, in your office, sipping coffee with your neighbors, or sitting in your home. When you live, you live in poverty, deprived of all freedoms and joys of life. And when you die, it's a horrible death by a surface-to-surface missile, a car bomb, or a sniper's bullet.

Israel's murder campaign continued; with yet more names to be added to Sharon's infamous list; more victims to fall, including many leaders such as Abu Ali Mustafa, the leader of the Popular Front for the Liberation of Palestine, decapitated by an Israeli missile while working in his Ramallah office on August 27.[20] Others would be born out of the tragedy to lead the way for a new generation of activists.

GETTING AWAY WITH MURDER

While the Sharon government was getting away with murder, in other places around the world war crimes were not always overlooked. In the midst of this chaos, Palestinians across the West Bank and Gaza watched intently the breaking news of former Yugoslav President Slobodan Milosevic being handed over to the United Nations International Criminal Tribunal to be tried for war crimes. The once powerful man of Yugoslavia was now in detention and powerless. Milosevic's victims and associates never expected that the "Butcher of Bosnia and Kosovo" would ever see his day in court. Times had apparently changed. But how much? It is true that Milosevic's handover to the War Crimes Tribunal in the Netherlands was an unprecedented and ground-breaking event in the history of international law, for he would be the first head of state to stand trial for war crimes and crimes against humanity.[21] But does international law apply to everyone, including Israeli Prime Minister Ariel Sharon? In theory, international law embodies a clear text that should be sufficient to indict war criminals, including numerous individuals in the current and past Israeli governments. It is according to the Nuremberg Charter, designed to try Nazi war criminals, that Israeli leaders could easily find themselves locked in dark cells for many years to come, since many of them have committed "Crimes Against

Peace." According to the Charter, Crimes Against Peace include: I. Planning, preparation, initiation or waging of a war or aggression in violation of international treaties, agreements or assurances. II. Participation in a common plan or conspiracy for the accomplishment of any of the acts mentioned under (I).

The Nuremberg Charter leaves no room for doubt that numerous Israeli leaders from the old to the young have committed Crimes Against Peace and have for years acted in flagrant violation of international law. But Israel's acts of aggression were hardly confined to its initiation of wars. They went beyond the battlefield to include the killing of civilians. The Hague Convention of 1907 and the Geneva Conventions of 1949 provide an abundance of text that is enough to indict Israeli leaders for War Crimes and Crimes Against Humanity. Several cases filed in a Belgian court tested the decency of international law, as representatives of 28 survivors of the Sabra and Shatilla massacre strove to indict Ariel Sharon as a war criminal. The efforts of these individuals received a moral and public boost when the television reporter, Fergal Keane, articulated and further exposed Sharon's role in the 1982 Sabra and Shatilla massacre in a B.B.C. segment entitled "The Accused," aired on June 17, 2001.[22] International law experts, plenty of evidence, and eyewitness accounts lead to the simple conclusion that Sharon is perhaps a more vile war criminal than Milosevic ever was; for the latter's career in war crimes was relatively short. Sharon, on other hand, spent the greater part of his career committing well-documented atrocities, to the point that various Israeli governments have lashed out at him on several occasions; most notably when the Knesset-appointed Kahan Commission indicted him for his "shared responsibility" in the massacres of Sabra and Shatilla.[23]

Unlike the image propagated by his popular autobiography of 1989, entitled "Warrior," Sharon was not a heroic warrior, but in fact based his war strategy on the killing of defenseless men, women, and children. While history narrates two bloody stories from his past, the Qibiya massacre of 1953 and that of Sabra and Shatilla nearly 30 years later, the man's crimes number many more. When Sharon led the infamous 101 Unit allegedly to locate and destroy Arab "terrorists," he ravaged villages and refugee camps throughout Palestine. Bureij refugee camp, located on the eastern part of the Gaza Strip, was a place blossoming with defiance. Refugees who were driven out of their villages in the southern part of Palestine in 1948 were never inclined to submit to the Israeli occupation. In

August of 1953, Sharon decided to put an end to their contempt. U.N. Commander, Major General Vagan Bennike, who witnessed the massacre committed by Sharon's unit in the refugee camp, described an abhorrent scene: "Bombs were thrown through the windows of huts in which the refugees were sleeping and, as they fled they were attacked by small arms and automatic weapons," he said. The 101 Unit attack that day resulted in the killing of 50 refugees, according to modest estimates.[24]

Sharon continued with his onslaught for the next three years and then played a chief role in the aggression against Egypt in 1956, in which Britain and France were joint accomplices. Israeli forces led by Sharon and Rafael Eytan were found responsible, 40 years later, for the killing of 270 Egyptian and Sudanese prisoners of war. The *Daily Telegraph* reported on the findings on August 16, 1995, as Israeli soldiers and generals involved in the slaughter spoke candidly of the Sinai killing fields.[25] Years later, in August of 1971, in the Gaza Shati refugee camp, Sharon truly earned his title "the Bulldozer" when he destroyed some 2000 houses, uprooted, displaced, and deported 16,000 Palestinian refugees, and killed an unknown number of civilians and fighters.[26] It was following horrific accounts such as these that Sharon's expertise in war crimes culminated in the horrifying Sabra and Shatilla massacre. Christian Phalangists carried out much of the slaughter, orchestrated and clearly ordered by Sharon, who then earned yet another title: "the Butcher of Beirut."[27] An estimated 2200 people were slaughtered between 6pm, September 16, 1982 and 8am, September 18, 1982. The two camps, located in West Beirut, which fell under Sharon's command, were surrounded by Israeli troops who sent back refugees trying to escape the horror of the butchery.

It becomes indisputable that the international laws which applied to Milosevic are suited for Sharon. However, the political circumstances are different. Two days before Milosevic was flown to The Hague Tribunal, Sharon was warmly received by British Prime Minister Tony Blair and U.S. President George W. Bush. Shortly thereafter, the same two leaders commended the Yugoslav government for extraditing Milosevic. With this in mind, Sharon was a much more dangerous man than Milosevic, for the latter was not immune to the world's scrutiny. Sharon, however, was in complete command of Israel for the first time, his war machine was on the move, and the Palestinians in the West Bank and Gaza continued to count their dead, victims of the Israeli Army and special assassin units.

SEPTEMBER 11

The handing over of the Yugoslav leader was a critical international event, for it illuminated the double standards according to which international law is interpreted and, furthermore, how the foreign policies of great nations are drafted. However, the horrific terrorist attacks in New York, Washington D.C. and Pennsylvania, on September 11, 2001, proved of greater consequence to the Middle East and its core Palestinian–Israeli conflict than a mere opportunity to draw parallels and extract lessons.

People sat breathless before their television screens, watching the Twin Towers crumble, witnessing the horror of people jumping to their deaths from one hundred flights up. Prayers were uttered and vigils were held the world over, even in the Occupied Territories. A six-year-old Palestinian girl knelt and nervously yet gently laid a flower to join hundreds of other flowers, banners, and candles in a small vigil held in Jerusalem to commemorate the death of thousands of Americans. Few reporters gathered and none of them represented foreign agencies. But Americans who witnessed the world weeping for their victims never knew of the deep sympathy felt by many Palestinians around the world. What they did see, however, with horror and dismay, was a few Palestinian children dancing on an old car, two men shooting in the air, and an old woman waving her arms in celebration of the attacks, so we were told. A quick conclusion was drawn: Palestinians dance on the graves of Americans. Even if the report was accurate, a few kids and an old woman don't represent the Palestinian population, which consists of millions of people; tens of thousands of them American citizens themselves.

To add some historic perspective, let's go back to New York City following the Gulf War in 1991. The American army had just returned from a mission in the Middle East. Former President George Bush Sr. described the intent of the mission as being to "bomb Iraq back to the Stone Age."[28] Mission accomplished. The U.S. Army led the allied forces in the region. They bombed Iraq for months and killed with no remorse as the whole world watched, the same way they would later watch the World Trade Center collapse to the ground. Those killed in Iraq were mostly civilians, innocent men and women, not any more or less innocent than the New Yorkers who fell to their deaths on a seemingly beautiful morning. As far as America was concerned, "our boys and girls" were heroes. And right in New York, where much of the city would soon stand in dust and rubble, thousands took to the streets, lining up with happy faces, cheering and chanting, "U.S.A,

U.S.A." The attack on the United States was horrid. It lasted for several hours. Three days later, the U.S. Congress assigned $40 billion for emergency funds to rebuild, to aid the many victims, and to secure the country against future attacks. But the Palestinian tragedy has lasted much longer than a few hours; it has lasted for generations. For nearly 60 years now, Palestinians have been subjected to some of the most notorious cruelties ever inflicted. They have been forced to live in concentration camps, to drink polluted water, to have their homes razed, their futures shattered, deprived of all God-given rights, even United Nations-given rights. They go to the streets to protest the killing of a child, and they return home carrying another shot while protesting. Grief evolves into rage, and that rage is not only directed at Israel but equally at the U.S., for many of the bullets that killed Palestinians were "Made in the U.S.A"—shells, missiles, and tanks, all subsidized by the U.S. government.

When thousands of Palestinians were killed in the Beirut massacre of 1982, their killers left the camps with piles of decomposing bodies, butchered and raped women, and thousands of empty bullet shells, also manufactured in the U.S.A. Even the bulldozers that tried to hide the crimes in mass graves were supplied by the United States. Since the creation of the State of Israel, the United States has paid more than $125 billion to finance the Israeli army and help construct its illegal settlements.[29] The U.S. government continues to insist that Israel's use of U.S.-made weapons against Palestinians doesn't violate U.S. policy on arms exports. After all this, in contrast to what one would expect, only a dozen children rushed to the streets to celebrate the deaths of Americans. Despite all this, most Palestinians mourned the deaths of Americans and were able to comprehend the tragedy, for they have been living the tragedy for decades. Unlike the millions who celebrated the "victory" against Iraq in 1991, Palestinians didn't parade in the streets, they didn't chant "Palestine, Palestine," they didn't carry colored balloons and break champagne bottles. But they stood in lines in Ramallah, Jerusalem, and Gaza, cities that have been devastated by American-made weapons, and donated blood. The six-year-old Palestinian girl at the vigil finally went home with her mother. Their trip to Ramallah from Jerusalem, a trip that should take half an hour, would take hours because of Israeli military checkpoints. Meanwhile, back in the West Bank town of Jenin, the Israeli army executed another attack, bombarding homes and killing 11 people in a raid that would last several days. "The helicopters are back," screamed a Palestinian teenager armed with a slingshot and a pocket full of rocks. People ran in a panic to seek the refuge of nearby alleyways. Two American-made Apache helicopters emerged from behind a hill and showered the fleeing residents with bullets—all made in the U.S.A.

INSTITUTIONALIZED OPPRESSION

Many lessons can be extracted from the first year of the Second Intifada; most notably concerning the audacious mandate of institutionalized violence. Even more alarming than the crimes themselves, that legislation can be passed through the Knesset in willful and blatant violation of international law, while Israel remains in the safety of the fold of the international community, seems to be one of the most outrageous lessons of all. Perhaps the Sharon government gleaned its wisdom from *The Prince* rather than the Geneva Conventions. Consider the model strategy outlined below as a paradigm of the Machiavellian philosophy applied to the Palestinian struggle:

The fall of the classic theory and practice of imperialism compels us modern imperialists, who are keenly interested in maintaining control of our remaining settlements, to develop an advanced strategy that will protect our interests. Consolidating our power over indigenous populations

Photo 1.4   A Palestinian man passes through an Israeli military checkpoint with his young child as a crowd of Palestinians wait to be screened by Israeli military forces, before being allowed to exit the West Bank.

may be difficult, but if done the right way, the Israeli way, that is, our settlements can be successfully sustained while our subjects are effectively subdued. An important factor in institutionalizing oppression involves the utilization of the legal system. Israel has successfully passed laws, such as the Law of Return, which allow Jews, and only Jews, to immigrate to Israel based on their race, while Palestinians are denied the right to live in their homeland and on their own property because they don't fit into this category.[30] Moreover, the Absentee Law of 1950 allows the state to confiscate the property of dispossessed Palestinians and claim it as state property.[31] These laws have proven quite successful, since they make race the determining factor in attaining rights in Israel, with Jews as first-class citizens and Arabs second class. They also rid Israel of some five million refugees, scattered elsewhere.

Another important element of institutionalized oppression is military occupation. Israel has occupied Palestine and other Arab lands for decades. This way, although condemned by futile United Nations resolutions, Israel has successfully achieved the upper hand over its subjects. The modern imperialist must understand that a strong army remains essential in controlling the settlements and their people. Thanks to the sheer strength of Israel's invincible army, Palestinian rebellions have been suppressed through massive applications of force. It doesn't matter whether force is used against armed or unarmed individuals, children, women, or the elderly. What matters most is conveying a message that subjects have no chance of gaining the rights for which they fight, and if they want to live, they must surrender to whatever the State demands. Today's imperialists must use the mass media, for it is unquestionably the most effective tool in winning today's wars. It is important that the message conveyed through the media highlights the losses of the colonialist, not the colonized. The media must portray us as civilized and our enemies as savage; it must show us as righteous and our enemies as wicked; it must show us as peaceful and our enemies as terrorists. If the media is tightly controlled, we can fashion our own reality. We can cause the world to blame our enemy when we kill their children, and we can make our soldiers heroes while their fighters are branded as criminals. Israel has indeed mastered the art of media control, to the point that we can even blame Palestinian parents for sending their children to be killed to grab media attention. Interestingly enough, many believe us.[32]

Killing your enemies, torturing prisoners, occupying land, and confiscating properties are very important, but not enough. You must humble your enemies while you carry out your policies. The tactic of humiliation is indeed a winning stratagem, for through its employment, you can destroy the spirit of your enemy.[33] Yes you can kill a man, but slaying him as his family watches and then stealing his dead body is more effective. You can beat a defiant young man who refuses to plead for mercy, but if you strip him naked first, you will certainly break his defiant spirit and make him wish for death.

Yes you can torture a prisoner by beating him, but imagine how successful it will be if you threaten to rape, or if you do in fact rape, his wife or sister. We've done it, and it was often quite successful. If your subjects submit, reward them with partial freedom and allow them to get low-paying jobs. But if they defy you, clamp down and have no mercy. Otherwise they will rebel too often. If you push them until they rise up against you, don't back down. Fight back. Close down their schools, uproot their trees, burn down their farms, block their streets, isolate their cities, demolish their homes, throw them in jail, keep them under curfew for weeks, deny them clean water, electricity, and basic supplies. If they increase their defiance by using firearms, then feel free to do all that can be done. In Israel, for example, we are using our best high-tech weapons against them: F15s, F16s, Apache helicopters, missiles—and more. Destroy their symbols and deny them an identity. In Israel we have destroyed numerous mosques and have attacked and desecrated many churches. Imagine what that made them feel? Even God cannot protect them now.[34] If you issue them with identification cards, designate their nationality as "undefined.".[35] Burn their flags, ban their books, forbid them from learning their own history; call their intellectuals "militants" and their religious leaders "fanatics." Make them always feel trapped with nowhere to escape. Besiege their land, their air and water. Make them feel like a wild animal trapped in a net. Terrorize them. Give them ultimatums. Force them to accept their fate, which of course you ordain. Try to make them turn against each other whenever possible. Some of them might be weak, easy to manipulate. Use these to spy on the others. If such traitors become known, they'll be jailed or even executed. That's good, because then, like we do here in Israel, you can tell the world that your enemies violate human rights. Both ways, you win. Build trenches around their fertile land like we did throughout the West Bank. We said it was a security measure. The world believed us, and the people lost thousands of hectares of fertile land that is now useless.[36] Eradicate their forests and woodlands. Dump your toxic waste on their land and destroy their environment.[37] In short, imprison their men, rape their land, murder their youth, and push them to the brink of desperation, to the point of suicide. You will then have succeeded in the complete dehumanization and defeat of your enemy, while through the media you will have convinced the world that you are actually the victim.

2
Intifada International (2002)

This chapter explores how the Second Palestinian Uprising garnered international attention and support from people and organizations the world over, chiefly through the inception of the International Solidarity Movement (I.S.M.). It details the identification of Israel's assault, citing the April invasion of the Jenin refugee camp, where scores of Palestinians are killed. Shortly thereafter, United Nations worker, Ian Hook, is shot and killed by the Israeli army, and 23-year-old international activist, Caoimhe Butterly, is wounded but survives what appears to be a premeditated attempted killing by the Israelis. The chapter also investigates issues surrounding the highly controversial Separation Wall, which is still under construction. While Israel claims that the intent of the wall is to prevent Palestinian terrorists from penetrating Israeli cities, the reality is that thousands of Palestinian homes and farms, and thousands of acres of land, have been stolen to make way for the monolith. It is also the year when Russian

Photo 2.1 A Palestinian man digs a new grave at the crowded Balata refugee camp cemetery in the West Bank. Most of the graves in the cemetery belong to Palestinians killed during the uprising (January 2005).

President Vladimir Putin orders Russian troops to attack a Moscow theater overtaken by Chechen fighters. The attack results in the deaths of hundreds. Again, parallels are drawn between these two unique struggles, and armed resistance is once again at the forefront of the debate.

INTIFADA INTERNATIONAL

The international support garnered by Palestinians pinnacled in the phenomenon of the International Solidarity Movement (I.S.M.), which came to fruition in full force with the onset of the Second Palestinian Uprising. Founded in August of 2001, the organization of activists came to support Palestinian resistance through two means: international protection and a voice with which to non-violently resist the Israeli military occupation. The audacious members of this organization confronted Israeli tanks, armed with kuffiyas and loud voices, demanding freedom and justice for a besieged nation. Israeli forces labored to intimidate them. The process of intimidation quickly evolved to that of physical harm as many were wounded, or even killed, while many more were deported or jailed.[1] But they refused to desert the battlefield. Members of the movement spoke many tongues, held different passports, and came from towns and cities that were oceans apart. They were Americans, French, British, Italians, and internationals from many countries around the world, who, with their simple means, came to Palestine offering protection to those whom the United Nations had failed to protect. At the Security Council, the United States repeatedly used its power of veto to prevent even minimal protection for the Palestinian people in the West Bank and Gaza.[2] But the I.S.M. needed no vetoes nor American government approval to bear witness to the atrocities faced daily by Palestinians.

In December 2001, in the Palestinian town of Ramallah, a group of activists faced Israeli tanks; they conveyed a message of peace, but Israeli troops fired anyway, creating clouds of gas and dust, giving the activists a glimpse of what the life of Palestinians is really like. An illustrative photo captured the scene in Ramallah as an Israeli tank rolled over a banner while the person holding the banner, a European demonstrator, struggled to salvage it from beneath the obstinate tank. The banner clearly bore the word "peace," as it was slowly crushed under the chains of the reckless vehicle. In late December, several groups visited refugee camps, schools, and houses throughout the Occupied Territories. Some Palestinian homes were barely standing while others were completely leveled by Israeli bombs and bulldozers. Israeli soldiers, whose government was beginning to realize the potential danger of being further exposed before the international community, prevented one of the delegations from entering Gaza. Members of the group were adamant about crossing the checkpoint, for it was their right, in fact their duty, so they argued. Fed up with the contention, the troops began beating the activists, dragging some back onto the buses. On the other side of the Israeli checkpoint, soldiers also abused members of a Palestinian delegation that had come to receive the internationals. A few Palestinians were detained, in an Israeli attempt to send out the message that such activities would no longer be tolerated. Israel may have hoped that its crackdown on peace activists would discourage the movement from carrying out more protests. Yet following each violent clampdown, more Americans, French, British, Italians, and volunteers from a plethora of nations around the world gathered somewhere in the West Bank, laying down before tanks and breaking curfews. In the early months of the Intifada, as Israel upgraded its violent measures to include random bombings and shelling of residential neighborhoods, internationals "deployed" themselves in Palestinian homes around the West Bank. At first they hoped that Israel would refrain from bombing homes if they knew that internationals were lodging there. But when Israel's bombardment did not cease, neither did the persistence of the volunteers in using themselves as "human shields." Various groups continued to cooperate, crossing national boundaries and ideologies: "more internationals are needed as human shields in Beit Jala," conveyed an urgent message emailed to thousands, calling on more Americans and Europeans to join them in their fight for justice.

Israel wrote off their efforts, referring to them as "anti-Israeli radicals," and the United Nations gave them no legitimacy, for they were not the "unarmed observers" Palestinians continued to seek.[3] They were members of a popular international movement, whose mere existence was a clear indication of the incompetence of the United Nations and of Western governments. British activist Malanie Jerman, 30, suffered her fair share of Israeli tear gas, yet she continued to lead, with hundreds of her peers, the international struggle. She told a journalist, as she was blinded by the tear gas: "it's important to challenge the [Israeli] occupation and to say that the occupation is killing Palestinians and cannot continue." Jerman's message managed to break through all Israeli checkpoints and made it into the British *Daily Telegraph* the following day.[4]

WOUND OF JENIN

In spite of the growing popular movement, Israel's brutal treatment of refugees continued unabated, and came to a head in early April 2002 with the invasion of the Jenin refugee camp. As I interviewed a young wounded man from Jenin, he explained the perception the Israelis hold of the Jenin refugee camp and its inhabitants: "Israel calls us the house of bees, but we think of our camp as the home of resistance."[5] In fact, for quite some time, Israel claimed that Jenin was a breeding-ground for terrorists. The Israeli invasion of Jenin, however, is not an isolated episode aimed at "taming bees" or cracking down on "terrorists." Erected in 1953 as a makeshift tent city to host thousands of Palestinian refugees, this small camp bred tenacity and defiance. Many of those Palestinians who were uprooted from their villages in 1948 to live in the most humiliating conditions were still able to see the land that once was theirs, simply by looking to the west. For nearly five decades they looked west to their home. For years and years, they were told stories by aging grandmothers of how wonderful life once was. It was a reminder of their dire hardship and life under occupation. In all, 13,000 displaced Palestinians lived in the Jenin refugee camp, located near the city of Jenin in the northern West Bank. Their dream went beyond paved roads, functioning sewer systems, and good schools. Their dream was returning home. Many held the deeds to their land in Palestine, some even held the rusty keys to their vanished homes, and most of them knew too well what U.N. Resolution 194 meant: It was the world legitimizing their right to return.[6] But for decades those refugees remained without homes, without rights, and for decades they were subjected to never-ending cruelty. In the war of 1967, which is referred to by Palestinians as the "second catastrophe" (the first being the war of 1948), Israel added insult to injury when it invaded the West Bank and Gaza; the refugees were now under military occupation.

In recent years, the proportion of young people in the camps had grown to reach 44 percent. With little means, many managed to attain a proper education at nearby universities, such as Bir Zeit, Bethlehem, and Najah University in Nablus. In September 2000, when Palestinian streets exploded and the uprising was just getting started, Jenin was there, leading the crowd, demanding justice, human

Photo 2.2   Bodies of victims of the Israeli attack on the refugee camp of Jenin in April 2002 are laid to rest in a mass grave.

rights, and return for Palestinian refugees. Israel knew what Jenin meant for its military aspirations—that particular refugee camp was a deal-breaker for Israel's attempt to subdue the Palestinian population and to break its spirit. In March 2002, Israel carried out "Operation Colorful Journey" against the Jenin and Balata refugee camps. Scores of Palestinians were killed and hundreds wounded. Many homes were destroyed, but the refugees' spirit remained strong. Israeli officials said that their mission in Jenin was like "picking up terrorists with tweezers." But even the might of one of the strongest armies in the world, one of the greatest nuclear powers, was hardly enough to bend the will of Jenin. Jenin fought hard, and, as the soldiers were pulling out, Palestinians emerged from their homes, carrying their dead, and chanting for freedom. But Sharon never forgot his unfinished battles. His army was in the process of conducting one of the largest military operations in the Occupied Territories since the signing of the Oslo Accords and the subsequent redeployment of Israeli forces from Palestinian Territories. This full-blown attack on dozens of towns, villages, and cities claimed more than 500 Palestinian lives. But during this historic operation, Sharon set aside hundreds of tanks, hundreds of soldiers, and many Apaches to invade Jenin.[7] Frustrated by the resilience of this small and impoverished camp, Israeli tanks began tearing down everything in their way—homes, mosques, and even schools—to open a new battlefront. But after nearly two weeks, the camp had still not fallen.

The man in charge of the Israeli military, Shaul Mofaz, publicly embarrassed by the blunder, led the operation himself.[8] The residents of Jenin alone battled the tanks and fought the Apaches. Within the first hour, scores of missiles were fired into the camp and bodies were scattered throughout the streets. As the systematic bombardment continued, the wounded bled to death with no medical attention.[9] With little means, the small camp not only resisted, but inflicted losses on the Israeli army that once claimed to be "invincible." From inside the camp, using a cell phone with a dying battery, a Palestinian fighter reached Al-Jazeera satellite television. "I just wanted to tell the proud people of world not to worry, we are resisting and will fight to the last drop of blood." In the background, a proud population stood listening to the speaker, maybe thinking that the world really listened or cared. They all chanted in one voice for freedom, before the phone's battery died.

MAHMOUD

One of the many wounded fighters of Jenin was a young man named Mahmoud Amr Turkman. He never uttered a word to me, since a bullet had left a hole in his throat, depriving him of speech. He was forced to gesture, but with only his hands and eyes he could do miracles. He was jammed with several other Palestinians in a Jordanian hospital room. He and one other young man were the only two wounded from the Jenin refugee camp who were allowed to leave the Occupied Territories for medical treatment. Even though the distance between Jenin and Amman is a few hours' drive, it took Mahmoud 22 days to finally reach his destination. His resilient ambulance driver carried him from a tiny Jericho clinic in the West Bank to the border with Jordan, now controlled by Israel, 22 times. Each time, the Israelis would interrogate Mahmoud, trying to drag words out of a muted boy. Finally he was allowed entry. By the time he arrived in Jordan he had lost half his body weight while waiting at the border. He slept on his hospital bed, as light as a feather, lost in what seemed to be a massive hospital gown. His doctors said that the bullet had destroyed much of his lungs, broke its way to his back, and left him almost completely paralyzed. They said that advanced medical technology in Europe could help save his life.

I met Mahmoud when I was on my way back to the United States— a month after Israeli border police had told me I was not allowed entry into my homeland. It was after a month of almost daily trips to the border that I decided to return to the States. Only two weeks had passed since the Israeli invasion of Jenin, in early April 2002. The purpose of my West Bank trip was to conduct an eyewitness enquiry into the atrocities reported there. I was motivated by my worries that the Jenin story might never be told the way it ought to have been, by the victims. I waited at the border and watched many ambulances from the West Bank, carrying wounded Palestinians, all being ordered to return, amid cries of pain from the injured and futile pleas from ambulance drivers. Before I boarded my plane back to Seattle, I stopped by an Amman hospital where wounded Palestinians were being treated. I waited in a long line. There were several officials representing various Arab governments who were ahead of me, being escorted by several journalists. But their visits to the Palestinian wounded didn't last long. They were clearly present for a quick and strategic photo opportunity. The wounded youth were fully aware of what was going on, and were little impressed. A man from Balata refugee camp, who had multiple gunshot wounds to the chest, bombarded me with a flood of jokes about the people of Gaza. Born and raised in Gaza, of course I couldn't let this go. "Do you know the one about the man from Balata who was invited to a wedding?" I rebutted. I finished my joke but was hit with another, related by a wounded boy from Hebron on the other side of the room. This gave me even more room to fight back as I plotted beside Mahmoud's bed. My journalistic mission was overshadowed by the laughter of the wounded. Hussein, Mahmoud's older brother, cheered "Mahmoud just smiled!" Some felt inspired that he might even soon eat without the help of tubes. Others went as far as predicting that the young man would one day talk, or maybe even walk again. Mahmoud was wounded during Israel's "Colorful Journey" operation. On one of the first days of the fighting, he was shot in the foot, and although it was very painful and difficult to walk, he was compelled to join the fight the next day. He snuck out of his house to join his comrades, with a bullet still lodged in his foot, only to be shot again, this time with the bullet in the throat that would paralyze him. I told Mahmoud about the book I was writing about Jenin and he listened intently. It mattered a great deal to him that the story of his camp would be detailed, for the world to see. Although feeling a sense of hopelessness for the young man, I ventured to ask him: "What do you want to do when you get out of this hospital?" He struggled to write his ambitious response on a scrap of paper: "I want to go back and fight for Jenin."

Hussein explained to me that Mahmoud had no political affiliations, and that up until the Israeli attack he had shown no interest in participating in the resistance. As a young man he had had to drop out of school to help his ailing father take care of the family. During the April invasion, their home was demolished. A few short months after meeting Mahmoud, I called him to tell him that his story was finally published. With anticipation I greeted Hussein on the phone. Between tears, Hussein told me that on that very morning, Mahmoud had died in a decrepit Jenin hospital. His family had given up on the dream of getting Mahmoud the medical attention he needed in the West. All they hoped for was to get him to a Ramallah hospital just a few miles away from their home. But Israeli army blockades snuffed out even that simple wish. I wish I could say that Mahmoud died with a smile on his face, but he clearly didn't, as his pain was unbearable. Moments after his death, when other residents of Jenin learned of his passing, hundreds broke the siege and rushed to his family's home. They wept, chanted, and wrote Mahmoud's name all over the walls of the torn-down camp: "Jenin mourns its latest martyr, Mahmoud Amr Turkman." On that same day, Jenin witnessed a fierce four-hour battle with Israeli troops, tanks, and Apache helicopters. Once again, they attacked the camp in search of fighters whose names were inscribed on their endless list of "wanted" Palestinians. But the Israeli army was forced to retreat. Jenin celebrated the victory and mourned the burial of its fallen hero. A mix of chants occupied the misty air of the demolished refugee camp, honoring 22-year-old Mahmoud, and vowing to continue the fight for his sake and for the sake of their long-awaited freedom. As to be expected, the Western media covered the episode under the ever-predictable headline of "Israel rooting out terrorist infrastructure in West Bank."

PEACE UNDER FIRE

As in the case of Jenin, few in the "international community" have failed to condemn Palestinian attacks against Israeli targets, whether they be civilians, soldiers, or armed settlers. But there are many who find it less urgent and compelling to condemn the killing of Palestinians, whether they be civilians, police officers, armed or unarmed activists. Sadly this couldn't have been truer in the case of Jenin. Equally outrageous was the utter disregard for the killing of Ian Hook, a United Nations coordinator who was dispatched to help the refugees put their lives back together after the invasion of the camp in April. In November of the same year, Hook was shot three times and killed by an Israeli sniper in the Jenin refugee camp. An Israeli army spokesperson claimed that it appeared as if Hook had a gun in his hand, not a cell phone. But they failed to explain why they left the British worker to bleed to death, as his Palestinian colleagues struggled to save his life.

Caoimhe Butterly was shot and wounded on the same day that Hook was murdered. Butterly, a 23-year-old Irish activist, garnered much deserved attention for her unrelenting efforts to save innocent lives. "Footage of her blocking Israel Defense Force tanks as they fired over her head, and stories of her standing in the line of fire between soldiers and Palestinian children,"[10] turned her story of valor and graciousness into that of a Palestinian folk hero. Mockingly, Israeli soldiers threatened to "make her a hero"[11] for Palestinians as well, a warning of their intent to kill her. On the day of Hook's murder, in what seemed a premeditated plan, Butterly was also shot. The

Photo 2.3   A young Palestinian boy stands in front of the remains of homes that once formed the al-Damaj neighborhood in the Jenin refugee camp, destroyed during the Israeli invasion of April 2002.

bullet struck her in the left thigh as she reportedly stood between firing soldiers and three young boys in the street. The young activist explained that she "had been trying to persuade the I.D.F., after they shot dead a nine-year-old boy, to stop shooting at the children." A journalist for the British *Guardian* elaborates: "they had told her to get out of their way or they would shoot her. It was while she was clearing the children off the streets that she was shot. She is sure she was a direct target; the tank was close by, the soldier pointed his gun at her and fired, and continued to do so as she crawled to an alleyway for shelter."[12] An Israeli army spokesman had a different, albeit bizarre explanation:

We are in the middle of a war and we cannot be responsible for the safety of anyone who has not been coordinated by the I.D.F. to be in the Occupied Territories right now. We are trying to ensure the safety of the Israelis and we will not tolerate internationals interfering with I.D.F. operations. It is not the job of internationals to stand in the line of fire, unless they are the son of God, but he hasn't come yet.

Along with Hook, Butterly had negotiated with the Israelis earlier that day to allow sick Palestinian children to the hospital. Their efforts to save the children's lives culminated into their own personal tragedy.

Hook was shot in the stomach and bled to death as soldiers refused to allow him to reach a hospital. Butterly survived the apparent attempt on her life with her head held high and enduring determination: "I'm going nowhere. I am staying until this occupation ends. I have the right to be here, a responsibility to be here. So does anyone who knows what is going on here," she announced from her hospital bed.[13]

The killing of Hook was hushed up, if not swept under the carpet altogether. Less than one month later, in December, a draft resolution criticizing the killing by Israeli forces of several United Nations employees, including Hook, as well as the destruction of the World Food Program warehouse, was vetoed by the U.S. in the Security Council. Once again, the priority for the U.S. was the "special relationship with Israel" and not the safety and security of civilians, even United Nations personnel.

"ENEMIES OF PEACE"

The U.S. Administration and Congress are well-versed, to say the least, in sophisticated terminology condemning "Palestinian terror." Indeed, words like "Palestinian terror" and "Palestinian terrorism" are taken at face value and without question. Israel determines and therefore defines the term "terrorism," and equally determines what acts are to receive this designation, based on its own political ambitions. And strangely, the mainstream U.S. media and U.S. government spokesmen abide by the official Israeli positions on the matter to a more faithful degree than do even the Israeli left-wing opposition and media themselves. Even in some European countries, which are reputed to take a more balanced view of the issue than does the United States government, words such as "terrorism" or "state terrorism" are hardly ever associated with Israel. The American Heritage Dictionary of the English Language clarifies a great deal in the way it defines the term: "Terrorism," is "the unlawful use or threatened use of force or violence by a person or an organized group against people or property with the intention of intimidating or coercing societies or governments, often for ideological or political reasons."[14]

Nothing can be more menacing than state terrorism, and no army in the Middle East will ever reach the degree of efficiency attained by the Israeli army. In the past, when Israel has suffered a blow through Palestinian attacks, heads of state of leading world governments have almost battled to come out with the first words of denunciation. Such was the case when an 18-year-old girl, Ayat al-Akhras, blew herself up in Jerusalem on March 29, 2002.[15] But the killing of innocent Palestinians often evokes nothing more than dead silence. In the months of August and September of 2002, it was widely reported in the mainstream U.S. media that Palestinians and Israelis had finally enjoyed a month of "calm," free of violence. But strangely, while no suicide bombings took place during that span of 30 days, scores of Palestinians were killed by Israeli forces and armed Israeli settlers. The lull of Palestinian attacks was the outcome of ongoing deliberations among Palestinian factions regarding the morality, necessity, and political wisdom of the suicide bombings. It was also the result of a suffocating curfew throughout the Occupied Territories. During the halt in Palestinian attacks, some political "achievements" were claimed between Israel and the P.A., as officials from both sides indicated. Moreover, European diplomats took advantage of the "calm" to visit the region, promoting the E.U.'s latest peace proposal.

If the international community genuinely took an interest in peace in the Middle East, it would have strongly condemned and vehemently opposed any attempt to jeopardize this promising period of relative quiet in the region. But the United States government and European leaders turned a blind eye as the Israeli government, led by Prime Minister Sharon, toiled to thwart any opportunity for calm in the West Bank and Gaza. Sixty-one Palestinians were killed by the Israeli army and armed settlers from mid-August to mid-September 2002 alone. Those included Nivin Salmi, 6 years old, Aymen Faris, 5, Asma Ahmed, 9, Hamzeh Al-Badwi, 15, Ateih Abu Mgheiseb, 13, Mahmoud Abu Audeh, 14, Abdul Hadi Hamyeh, 14, Abdul Karim Al-Sa'di, 16. They also included four members of the same family—Ruedah Al-Hjain, 55, both of her sons, and their cousin—near Jabaliya in Gaza. They also included the killing of five people who were blown to pieces after a missile attack on civilian cars in Tubas near Jenin. Burham and Osama Daraghmeh, aged 6 and 12, were among those killed.[16] They also included the ambushing and murder of four Palestinian laborers in the village of Bani Naem near Hebron, who were killed on their way home from work. It's the same dreadful scenario repeated incessantly. Israel murders many innocent civilians; the international community hears nothing, sees nothing, and does nothing; Palestinian officials demand an international response and a meaningful strategy to protect Palestinians as dictated by international law; the call goes unanswered; in anger and desperation, a Palestinian blows himself up in a crowd of Israelis, magnifying even further the carnage and suffering; the Western world is utterly overcome with a wave of condemnations of "Palestinian terrorism," "the enemies of peace," the intrinsic fanaticism of Palestinians, and a long list of accusations.

WALLS

It was at about this time that Israel went public regarding its ambitions to build a large "security fence." The proposition was in many ways analogous to the Berlin Wall, though the fence was to be twice as high and five times longer.[17] Not once has an Israeli official appeared on television or addressed a crowd of journalists without speaking of Israel's desire for peace with the Palestinians. But on the ground, the Israelis have carried out every brutal policy imaginable to eliminate the possibility of coexistence. Yet, in most of its wars against the Arabs, Israel has managed to enjoy relative calm in its own territory. Thus while parts of Egypt, Syria, and most of Lebanon were ravaged by Israeli bombs, Tel Aviv was still a great spot for shoppers and tourists. Even the illegal settlements in the West Bank and Gaza were safe havens in the midst of devastated Palestinian land. While the refugees fought for daily survival, between an occupying army and dire economic conditions, settlers enjoyed a lavish lifestyle—large swimming pools, tennis courts, and inexpensive yet fine housing.

Photo 2.4   Palestinian children in Qalqilya. The West Bank town will be completely encircled by the Israeli Separation Wall once finished (August 2005).

Pushed to the brink, following years of subjugation under Israel's policies, Palestinian resistance groups adopted a strategy that inflicted significant harm on the Israeli army, settlers, and societies outside the Occupied Territories. The Israelis, unaccustomed to such heavy casualties, lined up behind Sharon, angry and desperate. Peace movements in Israel were almost completely mute, and if they spoke out at all, they remained reserved and careful not to upset the consensus surrounding Sharon's so-called national unity government. Violent Palestinian retaliation should have been a wake-up call for the Israeli government, making it clear that violence begets nothing but violence and that accused war criminals like Sharon have brought nothing but a violent present and an uncertain future; that a solution to the conflict would only come through the implementation of international law, not Apache helicopters and missiles.

The Israeli Knesset turned mafia when it endorsed the assassination of top Palestinian leaders and applauded the murder of refugees. Starting with the shooting of kids like Mohammed al-Durra in Gaza, to bloodier episodes like those of Jenin, Balata, Nablus, and Ramallah, Israel used every card in an attempt to crush Palestinian resistance, including new duration standards for curfews. During this time, cities like Nablus were put under curfew for many long months.[18] The army lifted the curfew every few days for a short period for people to get food and necessary supplies, which were most often not even available. The Israeli government, backed by a large majority of Israelis, made it clear that it was only interested in pursuing a military solution,[19] which resulted in a deadly campaign targeting every Palestinian in the West Bank and Gaza. Just weeks after the temporary halting of the Israeli attacks on the West Bank, bombings inside Israel and against soldiers and settlers in the West Bank reached record highs. Despite an unprecedented security arrangement that sealed off Israel from all directions, young Palestinian men and women penetrated Israeli towns, exploding themselves along with the myth that peace can be achieved with an iron fist.[20] So Israel devised a new strategy: the erection of a "security fence" inside the West Bank, that would eventually stretch more than 600 kilometers and completely cage in West Bank Palestinians, while robbing thousands of acres of fertile land from Palestinian farmers. Of course the notion itself defied international law, the Fourth Geneva Convention, and the most basic standards of human rights. But according to Sharon and his right-wing government, terrorism would be snuffed out by any means necessary.

MANUFACTURING TERROR

Though Israeli defiance of international law as applied to its conflict with the Palestinians is nothing new, the Israeli government's boldness in violating or misinterpreting these laws was fortified by the United States' so-called "war on terror." The U.S. campaign supposedly to eradicate international terrorism gave the Bush Administration free rein to pursue its strategic policies around the globe, under the guise of "hunting terrorists" and destroying their infrastructure. The unwarranted war on Afghanistan and the invasion of Iraq, in addition to numerous military interventions elsewhere, all proceeded according to that prevailing logic. But America's wars, which blatantly defied international law and the constraints to the use of military force as articulated by United Nations edicts, have also freed the hands of other militant governments around the world to rein in their own oppositional forces, no matter how legitimate their struggles might be. Governments all around the world were infused with this new spirit of "fighting terrorism," with democratically elected governments at the forefront of the evasively coined mantra. The disheartening development of the Russia–Chechnya conflict was a prime example of this shift in the interpretation of international violence. Like the Palestinians, the Chechens were growing desperate, and this was reflected in their resistance tactics. Like the Israeli government, Russia saw little harm in oppressing the Chechens to win the "war on terror" at any cost. The world witnessed the outcome of this in a most powerful way on October 23, 2002, when 40 Chechen fighters took over a Moscow theater, taking 700 hostages and demanding the withdrawal of Russian forces from Chechnya. After a siege of two and a half days, the Russian government raided the building and retaliated with lethal knockout gas. All of the terrorists were killed, along with about 120 of the hostages.

I sank into my chair in disbelief when I learned of how many people were poisoned by Russia's use of gas in retaking the theater. But I also grieved the death of the 40 rebels. I cannot escape the images of more than ten Chechen women, clearly young, slouched over in their chairs, some gazing heavenward, all dead. Needless to say, growing up to become a suicide bomber is simply not the course of normal human behavior. Leaving one's children behind in Grozny, going to Moscow and seizing hundreds of people at gunpoint in a theater is not an act born out of some ingrained Chechen hatred for Russians. Nor have the Kurds fought for more than 15 years simply because they are, in some mysterious way, bad folk, full of unexplainable hostility toward Turkey. We are not programmed to pity such people: They are the ones who initiated the violence; they are the insurgents, the rebels, the terrorists, the militants, we are told. All we owe them is unquestioning condemnation. But when groups such as Human Rights Watch and Amnesty International call for an international investigation of Russia's actions in Chechnya,[21] why have the United Nations, the U.S. Administration, and other Western governments not pressed the issue? Why is Russia allowed a free hand in Chechnya? Why have the Chechens endured so many painful and bloody onslaughts at the hands of the Russian army? Moscow has recovered from its nightmare and has returned to normality. We can hold out no such hopes for Grozny, though. The Russian army is still there. The fighting, the occupation, the puppet government, the daily terror, mass arrests, rape, and torture are all amply reported and will likely carry on. Human Rights Watch continues, largely alone, with its routine updates on crimes against the civilian population. But who has time to read?

The suffering of the Chechens doesn't excuse the violent hostage taking, but it explains it. We can evade the facts, our sense of reason, and even our humanity, accusing those who disagree with us of being sympathetic with the terrorists; even of being traitors themselves. But that will change nothing. The Russians have since faced more tragic and deadly attacks by the Chechens. The unilateral ceasefire of the Kurds in Turkey will likely be ended by the Turkish army's continuing violence against the Kurdish population. Suicide bombings in the Occupied Territories and Israel will subside or change style or targets, but it is unlikely that they will come to a halt.

Fighting terror is the new trend; whereby aggressive, powerful countries crush their weaker foes, deprive them of freedom, while continuing to blame them for all the woes of the world. And we, the people of this world who mean well but fail to act, are expected to believe everything we are told. Israel is defending itself as though it were the Palestinians who occupy Israeli territories, besiege the Israeli people, blow up their homes, steal their land, and gun down their children. We are expected to hate the Kurdish rebels and deny any feelings of sympathy toward the Chechens, because the powerful set the terms of the battle, make the definitions—what deserves to be damned and what is regarded as a victory. When will we treasure the lives of people of all nations on an equal level, whether they be American, Afghani, Iraqi, Israeli, Palestinian, Turkish, Kurdish, Russian, Chechen, or any other? How long will we remain blinded by empty slogans, unexplained hatred, and pretentious condemnations?

Sharon was not content just to condemn the Chechen hostage-takers; he also praised the Russian victory and its "perfect military operation."[22] For Palestinians, his remarks came as no surprise.

3
Calls for Reform (2003)

The year of 2003 witnesses an escalation in Israeli assassinations of Palestinian activists—or "targeted killings" as parroted by the mainstream Western media—which results in the murder of hundreds of Palestinians during the five-year-long uprising. The escalation provokes a bitter Palestinian retaliation, with suicide bombings targeting non-military personnel rising at an alarming rate. Moreover, ongoing strife becomes apparent between P.A. President, Yasser Arafat, and his Prime Minister, Mahmoud Abbas, amidst debilitating corruption and continuing calls for reform within the ranks of the P.A. After months of violence, a months-long "hudna," or ceasefire agreement, is endorsed by Palestinian resistance groups, and Israel agrees to honor the effort as well—until ever-continuing house demolitions, assassinations of Palestinian activists, and land confiscation render the ceasefire null and void. In this year, the International Solidarity Movement suffers the loss of 23-year-old Rachel Corrie, a young American woman who is crushed to death under the chains of an Israeli bulldozer, in what

Photo 3.1   Palestinians in Qalqilya demonstrate in support of thousands of political prisoners on hunger strike in Israeli prisons (August 2004).

eyewitnesses call an intentional killing. The author of this book also suffers the loss of two relatives, both killed by the Israelis, and both officers in the P.A. police force.

MY COUSINS, THE TERRORISTS

On the first day of the Muslim feast, Eid al-Fitr, I received a disturbing telephone call. On the answering machine, there was a message: "Both of your cousins were killed in the Bureij attack today. The third is seriously wounded and is in the hospital." Dumbfounded, I sat at my computer in my tiny office in Seattle. An annoying screensaver image circled the dark screen, pointlessly. I gazed at the screen thinking of how thin the line can be between life and death, happiness and tears, feasts and funerals. On my desk sat a letter, fresh from the printer. It was decked with the logo of the "Anti-Defamation League" (A.D.L.), one of the strongest and most influential pro-Israel lobbies in the United States. The letter was written by Christopher Wolf, the chair of the group's regional board in Washington D.C., in response to my article in the *Washington Post* entitled "Condemned to Violence," on December 2, 2002.[1] In the article I argued that pretentious condemnations of violence and of "terrorism," which fail to go to the roots of the problem in the injustices imposed on poor nations, will backfire. I urged that all human life should be treasured, whether be it an Israeli or Palestinian life, an American or an Iraqi life. I insisted that we challenge the empty slogans and condemnations, and ask questions about why terrorism is shunned when carried out by the oppressed, yet discounted if carried out by the strong and powerful? But Mr. Wolf wrote the *Post* saying: "Ramzy Baroud ignores the real roots of terrorism, which are the societies that preach hate and intolerance." He said terrorists "are taught from birth that violence and murder are an acceptable means in which to achieve their goals." He went further, elaborating on the generous offers made to the Palestinians. He accused Palestinian mothers and fathers of praising the "murderous actions of their children." He concluded, "terrorism will not go away until societies that breed terrorists reevaluate what they are teaching their children."[2]

Finally, my call to Gaza went through. I managed to reach my relatives. The details were unbearable. Abdul-Hamid, 28, and Mohammed, 24, were Palestinian Authority police officers. They had no explosive belts, nor did they intend to blow themselves up. They lived in a refugee camp along with their families. They had dreams of prosperous lives that the besieged camp, crowded with refugees and bitter memories, failed to deliver. On the day they died, both young men were joyously celebrating the Muslim feast in their neighborhood, free of their uniforms, night shifts, and overbearing officers. They were always handsomely dressed. While Mohammed liked to impress the neighbors with his sunglasses, which he often wore, even at night, Abdul-Hamid defined fun as cigarettes, sodas, and out-dated western movies. In the camp such pleasures were easily met. Yet in the midst of the Eid euphoria, Israeli tanks invaded Bureij.[3] A mosque loudspeaker screamed in vain, "people of Bureij, protect your families, save your wounded." The voice from the minaret faded as some of the wounded, mostly civilians, bled to death in the streets. I spoke with a friend after he had attended the funeral of my cousins. He explained: "The key to ending the attack was to block the movement of the tanks. Abdul-Hamid, Imad, and Mohammed rushed to their post and ran back with their rifles to face the Israeli tanks. They put up a good fight, allowing hundreds of people to flee, before a tank shell exploded in their midst." Not all the body parts of my two cousins were recovered, I was told. But thousands escorted what remained of them to the refugee-camp's graveyard, packed with daring souls who died fighting for their right to live freely, many of whom were either killed by the army or crushed under the wheels of poverty and fading dreams.

The word "Bureij" is now ingrained in my mind. Not only because the camp was my mother's first home as a refugee, or because my grandmother's house in Bureij was my only escape to the other side of the Israeli army post as a child. Bureij is special because my cousins died there, holding on to old rifles while defending a falling refugee-camp, wearing brand-new cloths to celebrate a feast that ended with a funeral procession. I hung up the phone to face that letter with the A.D.L. logo, accusing Palestinian parents of teaching murder to their children. For some reason the strong urge to counter Mr. Wolf's letter faded. Does he need my explanation of why Abdul-Hamid and Mohammed were heroes, not terrorists; that their parents indeed taught them something: the value of courage and sacrifice, not hate and murder? There are many ironies in this story, the strongest one being my cousins' role reversal in the whole event. Even though they were officers in the P.A.'s police force, the moment they took up arms to defend their neighbors, they were branded "militants." Creating this distinction makes it all the more easy to deny someone the dignity and respect that all human beings deserve. Humanity is no longer so critical when one is dealing with "lesser-humans." Sadly, this scenario has been repeated throughout history, where the weaker party takes up arms as a means of self-defense, and hence, because he does not simply surrender, he becomes a "savage." The story of the native peoples of North America is by far one of the strongest cases in point.

LEGACY OF DENIAL

Few can have been as blunt regarding the legacy of the United States toward the native peoples as the 26th President of the United States, Theodore Roosevelt. In his narrative, *The Winning of the West*, Roosevelt spoke about the "spread of the English-speaking peoples over the world's wasted spaces." He wrote: "The European settlers moved into an uninhabited waste ... the land is really owned by no one. ... The settler ousts no one from the land. The truth is, the Indians never had any real title to the soil."[4] Reiterating a very similar philosophy, in an interview with the British *Sunday Times* on June 15, 1969, former Israeli Prime Minister, Golda Meir, made similar claims, stating: "There was no such thing as Palestinians. It was not as though there was a Palestinian people in Palestine considering

Photo 3.2   Israeli military bulldozers demolish a Palestinian home near Occupied East Jerusalem, one of several thousand Palestinian homes destroyed during the Second Palestinian Uprising.

itself as a Palestinian people and we came and threw them out and took their country from them. They did not exist."[5] While Native Americans and Palestinians were the ancient indigenous peoples of their lands, this was of little or no relevance to the foreign settlers. What really mattered was "Manifest Destiny," a teaching that in many aspects mirrors Hertzl's "Zionism." Roosevelt goes on: "The world would probably not have gone forward at all, had it not been for the displacement or submersion of savage and barbaric peoples as a consequence of the armed settlement in strange lands of the races who hold in their hands the fate of the years." In the mid forties, David Ben-Gurion declared that Israel was adopting a system of "aggressive defense. With every Arab attack we must respond with a decisive blow: the destruction of the place or the expulsion of the residents along with the seizure of the place."

In 1948, nearly one million people were expelled from their land after the brutal destruction of 418 villages and towns, and the murder of thousands of Palestinians.[6] They spread in all directions, mostly on foot to clear space for the Chosen People. They settled in refugee camps, concentration camps, which are still in existence today. Ben-Gurion retired in 1963, four years before Israel invaded the rest of historic Palestine, the West Bank, Gaza, and East Jerusalem. It created another tragedy, another dispossession, all in the hope of creating a purely Jewish Israel. Israel defied international mandates calling for the right of return for Palestinian refugees. Instead, it instituted its own law, shortly after its establishment in 1948, issuing the right of return for Jews only. Anyone of Jewish race, anywhere in the world, was and still is allowed to come to Palestine, to be granted citizenship, and to live for free in a land that is not theirs, in a place where they did not belong.[7] Amid this "civilizing" savagery and land grabbing, both the United States and Israel have managed to convince themselves that the way they treated their victims was in fact humane and civilized. "No other conquering or colonizing nation has ever treated savage owners of the soil with such generosity as has the United States," Roosevelt said.

During the Israeli attack on the Jenin refugee camp in April 2002, hundreds of Israeli tanks, Apache helicopters, and thousands of soldiers brutalized and terrorized the 13,000 inhabitants of the camp living on barely one square kilometer of land. The people of the camp fought as far as homemade explosives, kitchen knives, and a few bullets could take them. They fought and refused to give up, for they knew that this defeat would be their last.[8] This is what an Israeli army bulldozer driver, known as "Kurdi Bear," said in his testimony on what took place in the camp, as narrated to the Israeli newspaper *Yidiot Ahronot*:

Many people were inside the houses we started to demolish. They would come out of the houses while we where working on them. I found joy with every house that came down, because I knew they didn't mind dying, but they cared for their homes. If you knocked down a house, you bury 40 or 50 people for generations. If I am sorry for anything, it is for not tearing the whole camp down. This is the way I thought in Jenin. I didn't give a damn. If I had been given three weeks, I would have had more fun. That is, if they would let me tear the whole camp down. I have no mercy.[9]

Roosevelt's claim that "No other conquering or colonizing nation has ever treated savage owners of the soil with such generosity as has the United States," resonated once again in the words of the Israeli army commander, General Didi, who oversaw the invasion. The Israeli army has behaved "as the most moral army in the world and the most careful army in the world," he said.[10]

Interestingly enough there is unity in the responses of the colonized as well, although their tragedies may fall years apart. In 1927, at the Grand Council of American Indians, it was boldly declared:

We want freedom from the white man rather than to be integrated. We don't want any part of the establishment, we want to be free to raise our children in our religion, in our ways, to be able to hunt and fish and live in peace. We want to be ourselves. We want to have our heritage, because we are the owners of this land and because we belong here. The white man says there is freedom and justice for all. We have had their "freedom and justice," and that is why we have been almost exterminated. We shall not forget this.[11]

Similar were the sentiments of Abdelrazik Abu al-Hayjah, the Palestinian administrator of the Jenin refugee camp, who told to me with similar defiance:

If they will destroy the camp many times, the people of Jenin will rebuild it, because with each time, the peoples' courage and determination intensify. The more Israel brutalizes Palestinians, the stronger their resistance shall be. Israel cannot resolve its problems by force. They have to understand that Palestinians' quest for freedom cannot be stopped. The people of Jenin do not hate Israelis because their names are different, or because their language is different. Nor do they hate them because they have anything against the Jewish religion, but because they are occupiers, and as long as they are occupiers, the resistance will go on. The Palestinian resistance shall live as long as the occupation lives.[12]

ARMED STRUGGLE

True, the Intifada was a continuation of the Palestinian people's decades-long revolt against Israel's occupation of their land, which was carried out in several stages, most prominently in 1948 and 1967. But one can hardly ignore the fact that the second Intifada was uniquely different from the largely symbolic protests of 1987, or the armed resistance in Lebanon during the Israeli invasion of 1982. The second Intifada stands somewhere in-between, and the struggle, which for the most part was a popular resistance, employed new methods, going beyond the traditional stone-throwing of the past.

Provoking the issue of armed resistance and a people's right to defend themselves in the time of the Second Palestinian Uprising was more significant than ever. Palestinian factions were more actively deliberating a united strategy in their fight against Israel, amid heated discussions on whether they should or should not resort to violence in their resistance against the Israeli army, which had now reoccupied almost completely the areas that had fallen under Palestinian control following the Oslo Accords and related agreements from 1993 onward. Moreover, leading human rights groups, including Amnesty International and Human Rights Watch, recognized suicide bombings as "crimes against humanity," and those who planned or perpetrated them as "war criminals."[13]

I do not want to enter here into the particularities of these claims or of any others, but only attempt to clear away some of the confusion created by the uniqueness of the second Intifada, by the claims and counterclaims made by the parties involved regarding the legitimacy of Palestinian resistance and its legality in accordance with international law. I am simply addressing the issue of the legality—that is, whether armed struggle is permissible under and compatible with international law.

For long, international law remained unclear on the issue of a "people's right to defend themselves," while it clearly granted that right to sovereign states. The use of force is only legitimate under the following two conditions, according to the Charter of the United Nations: As specified in Article 51 of the Charter, the use of force is limited to self-defense, or, according to Chapter VII, when the United Nations itself embarks on an enforcement action where it decides that there is a threat to peace.[14] There were always insinuations in international law, however subtle, that granted an individual or a group the right to self-defense. For example, the preamble to the Universal Declaration of Human Rights (adopted and proclaimed by General Assembly Resolution 217 A (III) of December 10, 1948) reads: "Whereas it is essential if man is not compelled as a last resort to rebellion against tyranny and oppression, that human rights should be protected by the rule of law."[15]

However, it was not until the General Assembly's 20th session, in 1965, that, for the first time, "the legitimacy of struggle by the people under colonial rule to exercise their rights to self-determination and independence" was recognized. More, the assembly pressed "all States to provide material and moral assistance to the national liberation movements in colonial territories."[16] The decisive proclamation always applied to the Palestinian people and their struggle for freedom. But again, intentional misinterpretation of that law compelled the passing of Resolution 3236, passed in 1974 by the General Assembly in its 29th session. The resolution recognized that the collective rights of the Palestinian people should be fully and properly recognized. It recognized the Palestinian people's right to self-determination in accordance with the United Nations Charter (which, in retrospect, gives them the same right to self-defense granted to sovereign states). In addition, it granted them the right to national independence, sovereignty, and the right of return to their homes. The resolution further replaced the reference to Palestinians as "refugees" or "the refugee problem," making them a "principal party in the establishment of a just and durable peace in the Middle East."[17] Moreover, in 1975, General Assembly Resolution 3375 recognized the Palestinian Liberation Organization (P.L.O.) as a liberation movement, and its right to represent the Palestinian people in their aspirations for self-determination, in accordance to Resolution 3236.

Those who still found loopholes in international law to deny the Palestinian people the right to defend themselves had to answer to yet another resolution. Additional Protocol I to the Geneva Convention of 1949 (Act 1 C4), passed in 1977, declared that armed struggle can be used, as a last resort, as a method of exercising the right of self-determination.[18] One can hardly deny that Israel's decades-long occupation of Palestinian land—the full-fledged apartheid regime it instituted in the Occupied Territories, the loud violations of the Fourth Geneva Convention, the land theft, the destruction of property, and, most importantly, the refusal to honor nearly 70 United Nations Resolutions amid daily killings and assassinations of Palestinians (acts recognized by the Convention and by leading human rights groups as war crimes)—qualifies the Palestinians, as it always did, to fight back using armed struggle.

This is not an attempt to propagate the idea of violent resistance, but an effort to reconstruct, if briefly, the argument that the Palestinian people's struggle, including their armed struggle, in the Occupied Territories is defended and protected under international law. In fact, "all States [are encouraged] to provide material and moral assistance to the national liberation movements in colonial territories." This issue has been of the essence, since we have seen such an escalation in armed resistance in the Second Palestinian Uprising as compared to the first Intifada. In my exhaustive research of the issue, I focused primarily on the historic invasion of Jenin, since it was one of the most blatant Israeli invasions, the resistance to which was history itself in the making. I haven't found one reference in international law that refers to the Jenin fighters who defended the camp as "terrorists." In fact, I found more than one reference classifying the Israeli army action as "state-terrorism."[19] This is not a selective reading of international law, but a highlighting of relevant resolutions that Israel and its patrons in the United States seem to disregard. And to the United States' utter infamy, these critical issues have been deliberately disregarded even when U.S. citizens have fallen victim to state-sponsored terrorism. The United States' official response regarding the horrific death of 23-year-old Rachel Corrie, a young American woman from the state of Washington who was run-over and crushed to death by an Israeli bulldozer, is a precise albeit dreadful example.

RACHEL

It is the responsibility of the High Contracting Parties to ensure Israel's respect of the Fourth Geneva Convention of 1949, Relative to the Protection of Civilian Persons in Times of War. Part IV, Section I, Article 142 of the Convention states that:

representatives of religious organizations, relief societies, or any other organizations assisting the protected persons, shall receive from these Powers, for themselves or their duly accredited agents, all facilities for visiting the protected persons, for distributing relief supplies and material from any source, intended for educational, recreational or religious purposes, or for assisting them in organizing their leisure time within the places of internment.[20]

The above references to the Fourth Geneva Convention, which remain the most important frame of reference to the conduct of war, mostly dealing with the responsibility of an occupying power, are apparently of no concern to the United States, for the most conspicuous violator of such a law is the state of Israel. Israel has violated a long list of U.N. Resolutions, whether those of the Security Council or the General Assembly. Even the repeated American veto throughout the years was hardly enough to save Israel from its duty before international law. In fact, Israel's legitimacy as a member of the international community was never obtained in the first place. It was actually a conditional member, pending the implementation of U.N. Resolutions 181 and 194, both of which are nowhere near being fulfilled.[21] Of course, the everyday practices of the Israeli government and army are good enough reminders of the failure of the international community to uphold its own principles, and good enough indicators of the continuing violations of international law.

On March 16, 2003, Rachel Corrie, a vibrant American activist, was deliberately run over by an Israeli army bulldozer, in the Rafah refugee camp, south of Gaza City. Rachel, from the small town of Olympia, in Washington State, protested as Israeli bulldozers were about to tear down a building that belonged to a "protected person" because no one else, except Rachel and a few of her fellow activists, dared to confront the Israeli army. There is a bittersweet irony in her tragic death. It was not Rachel's responsibility to be in Palestine, but the responsibility of the U.N. The United Nations should have been blocking the Israeli bulldozers, since they were the institution designated to provide protection to the refugees. After all, as international law states, refugees are "protected persons," and their designated "protector" is the United Nations. Rachel's death not only reflects the depth of her humanity, it also reflects the tremendous failure of the United Nations, or perhaps their indifference, regarding this critical task.

I don't suppose that Rachel was deliberating Geneva Conventions or had a particular U.N. resolution in mind when she defied the Israeli bulldozer, and before the soldier manning the bulldozer ran over her, repeatedly, despite the pleas from people to stop. But I can imagine the rage that went through the young woman's head as she witnessed the monstrous vessel encroaching upon the refugees' homes.

"Rachel was alone in front of the house as we were trying to get them to stop," Greg Schnabel, 28, from Chicago, told the Associated Press. "She waved and waved for the bulldozer to stop. She fell down and the bulldozer kept going. We yelled 'stop, stop', and the bulldozer didn't stop at all. It had completely run over her and then it reversed and ran back over her," he said.[22] Back in the United States, the media coverage of the episode was nothing less than complacent, even though Rachel appeared on the front page of newspapers nationwide, if not worldwide, standing bravely, all 110 pounds of her, with a fluorescent orange vest and a megaphone, just moments before she fell under the chains of the bulldozer. Many commentators added insult to injury, calling Rachel an "idiot," "stupid," and responsible for her own death. On Capitol Hill, the mantra was the same: condemnation of Israel's behavior was mute, but criticism regarding the actions of the 23-year-old college student was harsh and plentiful.[23]

In an article for *American Partisan* entitled "Rachel Corrie: Bravery or Stupidity?" columnist J. Edward Tremlett wrote, concluding his condescending argument: "so, in the end, I have to go with stupid: very, very stupid. Her parents say they're proud of her, and maybe they really are. But if I were them I would be terribly ashamed for not teaching her the difference between being brave and being stupid. Even if the line is sometimes a little blurry, there's something to be said for some basic, common sense—something that was, perhaps, criminally lacking in a certain household."[24] Tremlett, whose bizarre arguments were consistent with the writings of other pro-Israel apologists, was not alone in pinning the "stupidity" label on Rachel. The term was so widespread that any Internet search engine would spit out thousands of search results all confirming the same conclusion. The lead editorial cartoon of the University of Maryland newspaper showed Rachel in front of the Israeli bulldozer. Accompanying the drawing the cartoonist offered his definition of "stupidity": Protecting a "gang of terrorists."[25] The truth is that Rachel Corrie was not offering protection to a gang of terrorists, but to a civilian home marked by the Israeli army for unjustifiable destruction. Moreover, the American activist didn't throw herself in front of the bulldozer as the pro-Israeli crowd claimed, deliberately attempting to misrepresent the event.

The thorough account of Joseph Smith, a peace activist from Kansas who accompanied Rachel in Rafah, was widely available on the Internet and could have easily been consulted by anyone interested in understanding the nature of her tragic death:

One bulldozer, serial number 949623, began to work near the house of a physician who is a friend of ours, and in whose house Rachel and other activists often stayed. While we occupied the other structures directly west (the closest was less than 5 meters away and the furthest was less than 25 meters away), Rachel sat down in the pathway of the bulldozer. I was elevated about 2 meters above the ground, and had a clear view of the action happening about 20 meters away. Still wearing her fluorescent jacket, she sat down at least 15 meters in front of the bulldozer, and began waving her arms and shouting, just as activists had successfully done dozens of times that day.

The bulldozer continued driving forward headed straight for Rachel. When it got so close that it was moving the earth beneath her, she climbed onto the pile of rubble being pushed by the bulldozer. She got so high onto it that she was at eye-level with the cab of the bulldozer. Her head and upper torso were above the bulldozer's blade, and the bulldozer driver and co-operator could clearly see her. Despite this, he continued forward, which pulled her legs into the pile of rubble, and pulled her down out of view of the driver. If he'd stopped at this point, he may have only broken her legs, but he continued forward, which pulled her underneath the bulldozer. We ran towards him, and waved our arms and shouted, one activist with a megaphone. But the bulldozer driver continued forward, until Rachel was underneath the cab of the bulldozer. At this point, it was more than clear that she was nowhere but underneath the bulldozer, there was simply nowhere else she could have been, as she had not appeared on either side of the bulldozer, and could not have stayed in front of it that long without being crushed.

Despite the obviousness of her position, the bulldozer began to reverse, without lifting its blade, and dragged the blade over her body again. He continued to reverse until he was on the border strip, about 100 meters away, and left her crushed body in the sand. Three activists ran to her and began administering first-response medical treatment. Her body was in a mangled position, her face was very bloody, and her skin was turning blue. She said, "My back is broken!" but nothing else. The three activists took care to keep her neck straight, and turned her to her side in case of vomit or blood from the mouth.

She was showing signs of brain hemorrhaging (I found out later from the British medical activist), so they elevated her head in order to allow it to drain blood, as this injury was more serious than simply a spinal injury. They continued to talk to her in attempts to keep her conscious. The other bulldozer, which had been working about 30 meters to the west, abandoned work and withdrew to the border strip, and parked about 10 meters to the west of the murderous bulldozer. The tank came over to see what had happened, and I shouted that they had run over our friend, and that she may die. The soldiers in the tank never spoke to us, nor did they ask us any questions or offer us any help.[26]

TOM

I recall an interview with a Palestinian mother from the northern West Bank, Um Jamal Al-Shalabi, as she relayed her own story about the bulldozers that also refused to stop and demolished her house over her paralyzed son. "We have a schedule to keep," Um Jamal was told by the driver, who along with his colleagues demolished entire neighborhoods and on several occasions did so while people were still inside their homes.[27] Although tragic, this is not out of the ordinary as far as Israeli conduct in the Occupied Territories is concerned. Less than one month after the killing of Rachel, the same scenario was repeated, but this time the victim was a young British man, Tom Hurndall. Tom arrived in the town of Rafah on April 6, 2003 to work with the International Solidarity Movement. This is how the *Guardian* described the episode:

The practice of I.S.M. members in Rafah was, while waving their passports, to accompany Palestinians as they attempted to restore water supplies and telecommunications shot up by the I.D.F., and to prevent the demolition of houses. On April 11, 2003 Tom, dressed in a fluorescent orange I.S.M. vest, was at the end of a Rafah street observing an earthen mound where a score of children were playing. As I.D.F. rifle fire hit the mound, the children fled. But three, aged between four and seven, were paralyzed by fear. Tom, having taken a boy to safety, returned for the girls. He was hit in the head by a single bullet, fired by an I.D.F. soldier. After a two-hour delay on the border, Tom was taken to a specialist hospital in Be'ersheva, and then back to London, where he survived, in a vegetative state, until his death [on January 13, 2004].[28]

But these killings were not a deterrent for international activists. From all over the world, ordinary people, young and old, were flocking to the Occupied Territories, a de facto United Nations of sorts, to provide some kind of protection to the Palestinian people. Like Rachel and Tom, their bodies were their only ammunition confronting the mammoth Israeli Merchava tanks and D-9 bulldozers. They were angry, like many of us, because of the untold hypocrisy of the United States government, and the failure of the "High Contracting Parties," to live up to the law they drafted and to the resolutions for which they voted.

A great deal is revealed about the brutality of an army that doesn't mind running over a young woman for simply protesting the demolishing of a house in Rafah, or a paralyzed man in the West Bank. But stories of courage are also told, not only by the Palestinian people, but also by those courageous individuals from all over the world who have literally put their lives on the line to stand by another people, forgotten by the rest of the world, and deemed irrelevant when laws are implemented.

BATTLE FOR REFORMS

On the political front, the Palestinian Legislative Council (P.L.C.) had just voted in favor of the appointment of Mahmoud Abbas' government on April 29, 2003. It was an historic moment, for Palestinians finally had their own Prime Minister. As a result, Palestinian society was consumed with an intense debate. At the forefront of the debate, which was revealed through the local Palestinian and Arab media, and on the street, was the personal legacy of Abbas himself, a man who was seen as the first challenge to the authority of P.A. President, Yasser Arafat. Arafat had rarely been challenged from within his own ranks. For years, Israel schemed to undermine Arafat's influence among his people, but failed miserably. In fact, opinion polls have shown that Arafat's popularity actually surged during Israeli assaults on the Palestinians, especially when the aging leader became a target himself.

Opposition groups such as Hamas, and independent politicians, continued to be regarded with respect by various segments of Palestinian society, but they too failed to present a challenge to Arafat. Some were not interested in presenting themselves as alternatives, and others, although popular among large segments of Palestinian society, weren't given the chance to prove their ability to lead the Palestinian people. But within Arafat's circle, the Abbas challenge was atypical. True, during the Lebanon war, where Arafat was an important player, there were those who defied his political and military philosophies, but they were either discredited or quickly marginalized. But Abbas, who was also the P.L.O.'s secretary general, was exceptional compared to past contenders. Abbas was different because he came to prominence as a result of two simultaneous movements, one genuine and the other purely political. The genuine movement was that of the Palestinian people's desire for true reforms and democracy. The other presented itself in the form of the so-called Middle East Quartet for peace, designed to forge a peace agreement between Israel and the Palestinians on the basis of the U.S.-devised Road Map for Peace Initiative.[29] The Palestinian people's call for reforms emerged shortly after the birth of the P.A., but was strongly emphasized following the Israeli reoccupation of major urban centers in the West Bank in March 2002, then again in June 2002. While the Palestinian resistance put up a good fight, the P.A. struggled on in uncertainty and apparently without a plan B, with accusations exchanged among various Palestinian officials, some vowing to "resist until the end" and others willing to talk with Israel unconditionally and openly willing to "compromise," even though virtually nothing with which to compromise was left. A split took place in the P.A., reflecting a reality that was always present but never displayed so openly, so vividly. That split subsequently reappeared in the Fatah movement, the largest P.L.O. faction and the leadership base for the P.A.

There was a portion within Fatah that was concerned more about national unity among various Palestinian factions, and refused to negotiate under military assaults and settlement expansion. It also demanded an end to the assassination policy of Israel, believed in the continuing attacks targeting Israeli forces and armed settlers, yet affirmed Israel's right to exist and candidly preached coexistence under a just and peaceful formula. The leaders of this segment were either assassinated, arrested and sent to Israeli prisons, or placed on Israel's wanted list. Marwan Barghouti, an elected P.L.C. member who is now in an Israeli prison, was and is still regarded as the leader of this movement.

Then there was another segment, which was emerging more forcefully than ever before, represented by Abbas. Described by the late Professor Edward Said as "moderately corrupt,"[30] Abbas made himself few friends upon his return to the Occupied Territories from exile, following the signing of the Oslo Accords. For a start, he was one of the engineers of that agreement, which many Palestinians now regard as king amongst the worst decisions made by their leadership. Furthermore, the man's outward expressions of his wealth often evoked objection and bitter questioning from many. The Intifada was a direct response to the unfairness of Oslo, and understandably led to the marginalization of Abbas during its first year. Later in the second year, Abbas was once again back on the scene, demanding an end to all violent expressions of the Intifada,[31] calling for Palestinian groups to disarm and for an unconditional return to the negotiation table. Furthermore, Abbas indicated his willingness to "compromise" on fundamental issues that had ignited the Palestinian struggle for decades, especially on discounting historic Palestinian rights in Jerusalem. Meanwhile, the Palestinian people increasingly demanded reforms that would create accountability on all levels, reforms that would achieve equitable political governance, representing all Palestinians.

Palestinian demands for reform echoed in Israel and the United States, both of which eagerly followed suit and pressed for reforms as well. But Israel's call was primarily aimed at fighting the Intifada with Palestinian resources, through the unification of the P.A.'s military apparatus to crush Palestinian resistance once and for all. The Americans nodded in agreement.[32] From the Oslo Accords up until the Second Uprising, Israel had considerable success in utilizing the P.A. to police the Occupied Territories. Yet despite all of this, the objectives of the Palestinian people remained as clear as they always had: an end to the Israeli occupation and the dismantling of settlements erected illegally on their land. They were neither interested in ending their Intifada nor in subscribing to the political system of imposed democracies. Their indifference to, or indeed rejection of, Abbas represented their rejection of the political legacy brought about by his re-emergence, which as far as Palestinians were concerned was a continuation of the dreadful Oslo legacy, for which they had paid a very costly price.

OFFICIAL HYPOCRISY

On May 23, 2003, amidst internal and external calls for reforms, United Nations Envoy, Terje Roed-Larsen, paid a visit to Israel and the Occupied Territories. For many Palestinians, his visit was a monumental disappointment, as he exhorted them to reform their political institutions and to halt terrorism, while pressing the Israelis to merely "ease travel restrictions." Following a suicide bombing in northern Israel, where four Israelis were reportedly killed, Roed-Larsen described suicide bombings as "senseless acts that are unjustified on any moral or political grounds."[33] Sure, no one expected the U.N. Special Coordinator to distance himself from the line of thinking that sees such acts as if they were born in a vacuum, without any relation whatsoever to the desperate, often bloody reality under which Palestinians are forced to live. But why shouldn't we expect Roed-Larsen, or any other U.N. representative, to speak out with the same clarity against state-sponsored Israeli terrorism? Once he had finished outlining his position on the deadly bombings in Israel, Roed-Larsen did turn the heat on Israel, but just a little. He said that Israeli roadblocks and checkpoints were "the single largest impediment to the Palestinian economy." To those who most often receive only half of the news from the Middle East, Israel's checkpoints must make good sense. What else can the violated state of Israel do in the face of these heinous crimes but restrict the movement of Palestinians in the hope that such limitations will reduce the frequency of the bombers' penetration of the hapless and vulnerable state?

Photo 3.3   A Palestinian funeral procession mourns the killing of 45-year-old Nazeh Darwazeh, a journalist and a father of five. Darwazeh was shot and killed by Israeli forces in April 2003.

In the first two weeks of May 2003, up until a deadly bombing in northern Israel on May 19, 2003, the Israeli army killed 47 Palestinians; that's over ten times the number of Israeli victims in the suicide bombing. A few of those Palestinians killed, as we were informed, had attacked Israeli army or civilian targets, including my former neighbor in the Nuseirat refugee camp in Gaza, Mahmoud Annani. He was killed on May 8, 2003. I hold out no expectation that experts or officials will examine the years of suffering endured by Mahmoud, to study the reasons that led a promising young man to blow himself up, wounding four Israeli soldiers in the Gaza Strip, while he was just stepping into manhood at the age of 21. But it pained me to see that those who felt no hesitation in condemning Mahmoud's senseless, heinous, and abhorrent crime, stayed silent while scores of Palestinians were killed, including eight children, in the first two weeks of May alone. Kofi Annan, the U.N.'s chief, is a prime example of how officials around the world labor to undermine Palestinian suffering while emphasizing that of the Israelis. The three months of March, April, and May 2003 witnessed a killing extravaganza by the Israeli army, mostly focused in the Gaza Strip.[34] March 7 was a day in which eight Palestinians, including a one-year-old baby girl (Hanan al-Assar) were killed in Nuseirat refugee camp; March 31, four were killed in the village of Beit Hanoun; April 3, four were killed in Rafah; April 8, seven were killed in Gaza; April 9, five were killed in the refugee camp of Jabaliya; April 19, three were killed in Rafah; May 1, 13 were killed in a crowded neighborhood in Gaza City; May 14, three were killed in the Nuseirat refugee camp; May 15, five were killed in Gaza ...

During the period extending from the beginning of March to May 19, 2003, 196 Palestinians were killed in the Occupied Territories. The great majority were civilians.[35] The world's general indifference to the killing of Palestinians shows how human life is measured in terms of politics, not in terms of numbers or by the basic principle of the sanctity of human life. But while many understand the approach of the mainstream media, which either ignores Palestinian losses altogether or packages the news carefully, so as to absolve Israel from any liability, a greater number fail to see where someone like Kofi Annan fits in to all of this. Annan, whose credibility dwindled to unprecedented levels following the botched Jenin war-crimes investigation and the Iraq war, utters little when Palestinians are the victims. Cornered by the embarrassingly high number of casualties in the Gaza carnage, he expressed deep concern regarding violence in the region, and simply urged both sides to adhere to the Road Map as a way out. His words were generic and his blame included both sides. However, his touching sermons following the killing of Israelis, even illegal Jewish settlers who are armed to the teeth, are often the bolded headlines of the United Nations news service. But the most troubling aspect of it all was the method that these supposedly even-handed politicians chose to call on both sides to adhere to peace: Palestinians must end their terror campaign and Israelis must ease travel restrictions. So this is what the Middle East's conflict boils down to: the removal of a few checkpoints? Checkpoints are indeed provocative and frustrating, but Mahmoud Annani didn't choose to blow himself up near an Israeli military base in Gaza because he couldn't stand the long wait in a taxi near an Israeli army checkpoint.

Many problems are indeed plaguing the Middle East, but lack of conscience is undoubtedly the greatest.

CEASEFIRE!

On August 6, Palestinian factions concluded a meeting with Abbas in Gaza. Although the meeting was described as "positive" by various Palestinian media, it had been full of grievances expressed by Hamas, the Islamic Jihad, and others. These groups had previously agreed to a three-month "hudna," or ceasefire, starting on June 29, 2003, as requested by Abbas, on the condition that Israel would reciprocate, ceasing violent activities in the Occupied Territories. The hudna wasn't over yet, but a list of reported Israeli violations of the ceasefire, presented to Abbas, was too long to ignore, including as it did assassinations, land confiscation, arrests, and incitement.

The Sharon government did not march behind the U.S. initiative without receiving the administration's assurances that a list of 14 conditions presented to U.S. Secretary of State Colin Powell would be honored. Powell pacified the Israelis when he promised to study the conditions "seriously."[36] Israel claimed that the ceasefire agreement struck between Palestinian factions and Abbas by no means placed an obligation on Sharon's government. In fact, Israel was pushing Abbas and his men to go after these groups, which were collectively far more popular than the P.A. and its discredited political apparatus. If the Israeli vision were to be realized in full, Palestinians would certainly have been standing at the threshold of civil war. The "Road Map" peace initiative was now confronted with many questions: How long could the ceasefire hold if Israel didn't satisfy even a fragment of Palestinian aspirations? How long could Abbas stand his ground with so little to show for it, in terms of progress in the peace process? And would the United States continue to pressure Palestinians while vacillating about applying due pressure on the Israeli government? The probability of the U.S. shifting its approach in handling the Middle East conflict was unlikely, even when, after an historic meeting with Abbas on July 25, 2003, U.S. President George W. Bush referred to Israel's Separation Wall in the West Bank as a "problem."[37] P.A. officials brimmed with confidence that the expression signaled a major shift in Washington's policy, which was regarded as fundamentally biased toward Israel by most Arabs.

But only a few days later, this momentous shift seemed to be nothing more than a poor choice of words. Bush, standing by a smiling Sharon, told reporters that he understood that the "fence" was a "sensitive issue" to Israel, and merely sought to ensure that the "fence sends the right signals."[38] Palestinians, of course, were looking for more than a pleasant justification of why large chunks of the West Bank would be cut off by Israel, or why scores of villages and thousands of Palestinians would now find themselves encircled by a giant fortified wall much longer than that of Berlin. As the U.S. continued to snub the idea of taking a strong stance against Israel's failure to abide by the demands of the Road Map, the once promising peace initiative was likely to be remembered, at best, as a ceasefire that never lasted.

Photo 3.4   Palestinian families in Ramallah demonstrate in support of their sons and daughters in Israeli prisons (April 2005).

The release of a few hundred Palestinian prisoners, many of whom were due to be released within a very short period of time anyway, was accompanied by arrest campaigns. On August 6, 2003, even Palestinian security officers fell victim to the Israeli sweep, as 18 were apprehended in the town of Jericho. Palestinians, although cheerful at seeing busloads of freed prisoners, were growing uneasy over what some believed to be an "Israeli ruse," accusing Sharon's government of using the 6000 prisoners as a bargaining chip. Palestinian uneasiness was growing much more rapidly over the delicate issue of settlements. Although the Road Map forbade Israel from building more settlements, Israel broke new ground every day. The Israeli government is not even secretive about the violation, as it solicited construction bids, using large ads in local newspapers.

THE ROAD MAP IS DEAD

In the midst of these blatant violations of the U.S. drafted Road Map, Powell delivered a speech: "We've already seen reports on television that say, well, the Road Map is now finished, or the ceasefire is over, or this is all off-track. No, it is not," he told a group of Arab and Israeli kids in the State of Maine, who had gathered for a three-week summer camp in mid-August.[39] Powell's words defied reality. Setting aside the violations of the Road Map by Israel, he singled out the only violent Palestinian act of retaliation, stating: "We will not be stopped by bombs, we will not be stopped by this kind of violence." I cannot confirm, but I have a feeling that Powell's courageous exclamation won him lengthy applause from the kids and their mentors at the camp.

I only wish that Powell's courage had been great enough to acknowledge the multiple Israeli violations of the Road Map. Wouldn't it have been equally appropriate to exclaim: "We will not be stopped by assassinations, home demolitions, military checkpoints, the building of illegal settlements, the uprooting of trees, the seizure of land, and the deteriorating health of most Palestinian children as a result of Israel's deadly blockade"? But on the other hand, maybe such a lengthy statement would not have been as eloquent as Powell's original. Indeed, listing Israel's violations was unlikely to win the respected Secretary applause from the crowd of children.

But even these sarcastic remarks are insufficient to convey the frustration felt by many Palestinians, a rage that gave birth to two bombings in Israel, on August 12, 2003, after a lull in Palestinian retaliation that had lasted for weeks. The ceasefire agreement of June 29, 2003 created a different reality on the ground, since, for the first time in years, Palestinians refrained from attacking Israeli targets, military or otherwise. Even Palestinians themselves were astonished at how various factions abided by the ceasefire. But Israel did not reciprocate. Land confiscation continued. Bids to build new illegal settlements, commissioned by the Israeli government, continued to be published in Israeli newspapers. Raids on West Bank towns and villages continued. Threats, incitement, and provocative schemes by Israeli officials—such as attempts by a Knesset member to force his way into Al-Aqsa Mosque—are just a few examples of how Israel breached the agreement. Moreover, Sharon made it clear that he was little concerned with the Palestinian ceasefire. Rather than using the opportunity to rebuild the battered mutual trust between Palestinians and Israelis, he demanded that every Palestinian resistance group be dismantled.

THE HONEST BROKER

Shortly thereafter, a resolution was presented to the U.N. Security Council, calling on Israel not to harm Yasser Arafat—a response to many suggestions, some covert and others overt, that "removing" Arafat was a viable option for Israel.[40] The U.S. government chose to veto the resolution on September 16, 2003, which pressed Israel not to "remove" the Palestinian leader. It was the U.S. Ambassador to the United Nations, John Negroponte, who once again raised his hand conveying his country's objection. Soon after Negroponte had the honor of bending international will through the American veto for the 77th time since the creation of the United Nations in 1948, he rushed to make sense of his government's insensible act. The draft was "flawed," Negroponte exclaimed, for it failed to include a "robust condemnation of acts of terrorism, an explicit condemnation of Hamas, the Palestinian Islamic Jihad, and Al-Aqsa Martyrs Brigades."[41] But Negroponte, as well as every other member state of the United Nations, knew too well that even with an "explicit" condemnation of Hamas, an American veto was likely to be unleashed anyway. To its credit, the draft resolution did in fact condemn violence and terrorism, demanding "complete cessation of all acts of violence, including all acts of terrorism, provocation, incitement and destruction." It further hailed the U.S.-proposed initiative, the Roadmap for Peace, perhaps in the hope that such praise would tickle a soft spot in the U.S. Administration's heart. Nonetheless, Negroponte looked as callous as he had appeared the previous time, when he vetoed an earlier resolution condemning Israel's killings of three U.N. workers in the West Bank and Gaza, including the British relief worker, Ian Hook, killed on November 22, 2002. Negroponte justified his objection to the resolution on December 20, 2002, criticizing the text as being "one-sided" and not "conducive" to Middle East peace efforts.

If condemning the murder of U.N. workers is not "conducive" to peace, why did every U.N. member, at the Security Council and General Assembly, "strongly" condemn the "terrorist" and "criminal" attack on the U.N. headquarters in Baghdad on August 19, 2003? Is there a time when the killing of U.N. personnel is permitted and a time when it is tabooed? If Negroponte was indeed critical of the resolution, which called on a sovereign country to refrain from deporting or physically harming an elected leader of another nation, and if it were true that condemning the killings of U.N. workers is "not conducive" to peace, then why did the U.S. veto the December 2001 resolution that called for the deployment of unarmed international observers to end the Middle East bloodshed?[42] The draft was put to a vote nearly a year after the eruption of the Palestinian Uprising and was aimed solely at creating a barrier between both sides as a first step before resuming peace talks. Then, the number of people killed from both parties was relatively small. Without the needed international intervention, the death toll grew tremendously. If the U.S. had refrained for once from abusing the sacred right it possessed in the Council, one has to wonder how many lives could have been saved.

From the 77 vetoes unleashed by the U.S. at the Security Council, 26 have been an attempt to abort any tangible international role in the ongoing Middle East dilemma. The U.S. government has often sought to monopolize the role of third party in the conflict. While suffocating any outside effort aimed at ending the conflict, it has miserably failed to be an honest broker. This time, Negroponte took his country to a new low, refusing to openly reject the forced deportation or even murder of an elected leader. Israel officially agreed to "remove" Arafat, a decision that meant, according to Israeli Deputy Prime Minister Ehud Olmert, killing, exile, or isolation.[43] Negroponte failed, and decidedly so, to mention that the U.S. veto had little to do with Israel's true intentions, the U.S. official stance on those intentions, or the language of the resolution itself, whether explicitly naming Hamas or not. The pro-Israel veto was a pre-calculated policy, which had been consistently employed for decades, but was only officially declared in August 2002. On August 2, Negroponte said that the U.S. would veto any Middle East resolution that fails to condemn Palestinian terrorism, explicitly listing all Palestinian groups that Israel singled out as terrorist.[44] The U.S. decision of 2002, hailed by Israel and pro-Israel groups in the U.S. as one that would "change the rules of the game", was a green light for Israel to do as it pleased without fearing any repercussions, except perhaps mere words of condemnation by the international body. A spokesman for the Israeli mission to the U.N., Ariel Milo, celebrated the decision, saying that now Arabs were in the spotlight, not Israel. "If they decide not to condemn Palestinian terrorism, then any resolution they come up with will be a nonstarter," Milo said. "The onus is on them to see if they're serious."[45]

If Israel went ahead and murdered Arafat, to ensure the passing of a resolution that would condemn the murder, the Security Council would have to condemn Palestinian resistance as terrorist with an "explicit" mention of every organization that Israel has singled out. This was indeed the logic that Negroponte used when he carried out his government's wish by raising his hand high on September 16. But what Negroponte and the U.S. government behind him seem to have ignored is that their latest veto didn't only cripple any attempt to move forward in resolving the Middle East crisis, it further contributed to the growing worldwide reputation of the United States as a dishonest broker and a biased party without any genuine interest in peace and stability in the Middle East.

STRIFE WITHIN THE P.A.

As the U.S.-brokered Road Map was turning into a deep quagmire, rumors circulated in the media of a "power struggle" between Arafat and his Prime Minister, Abbas. But these rumors were misleading to say the least. The issue at stake was not simply the drive for power. Yes, there was a kind of power struggle, but this was not your typical Third World quarrel between traditional and rebellious leaderships. Nor was it simply a scuffle between a leader representing the conventional chain of command and a vibrant new leader. Both Arafat and Abbas belonged to the "old guard." Moreover, Arafat was elected, and, despite his ups and downs, he was still highly regarded among Palestinians, while Abbas' popularity equaled 3 percent, equivalent to an opinion poll's margin of error. This is by no means an attempt to cheer for Arafat and taint Abbas. In fact, in a better, pressure-free environment, the appointment of Abbas would have been a step forward in the Palestinian nation's struggle for a healthy democratic reality. But wishful thinking aside, the pressure was on, if not because of the U.S. government's candid attempts to sideline Arafat, then because of the continued Israeli occupation of Palestinian cities—over which both Arafat and Abbas were supposedly presiding.

Maintaining respect as a leadership in an occupied land was hard enough for both leaders. Under these conditions, a power struggle over a land divided by settlements and ruled by a foreign army was utterly pathetic, to put it nicely. The real motives that fueled the so-called power struggle between Arafat and Abbas were manifested in the way the two leaders understood the current phase of the Palestinian–Israeli conflict, and their dissimilar visions for a solution to the conflict's impasse. Abbas could see no justification whatsoever for violent retaliation from Palestinian groups, no matter how much violence was perpetrated by Israel. Arafat on the other hand, while opposing suicide bombings or the targeting of civilians, believed that Israel's violence was doomed to suffer Palestinian retaliation. The best way to rein in "Palestinian militants," he argued, was to ensure an end to Israel's assassinations and the military occupation itself. Arafat cheered the U.S.-sponsored Road Map for the Middle East peace initiative. However, he maintained a strong belief that Israel aimed to write off the agreement through provocations that would result in Palestinian retaliation, and echoed that conviction during a televised interview from his bombed-out headquarters in Ramallah. He told C.N.N.: "The Road Map is dead, but only because of Israeli aggressions in recent weeks."[46] He also recounted another belief—that Washington's pro-Israel stance and passive involvement in implementing its own peace initiative were also to blame. Abbas, however, was gaining popularity in Washington and was received with respect by President Bush. Arafat never had the chance to confer with Bush, since Israel declared the Palestinian leader "irrelevant" to the peace process.

Abbas, unable to exert any kind of pressure on Israel, vowed to crack down on Palestinian groups who violently resisted the Israeli occupation and orchestrated suicide bombings in response. In his view, the success of such a campaign depended on the security apparatus being unified under his command. At that time, he controlled three of the barely standing security branches of the P.A. The rest, including the 35,000-strong national security force, was under Arafat's control. Arafat was experiencing an immense amount of outside pressure to concede some of his leadership privileges to Abbas. And he did just that. But Washington, Tel Aviv, and Abbas himself were seeking more concessions, to varying degrees. Arafat's fear was that leaving all of his leadership keys in the hands of Abbas, who in turn might attempt to implement Israel's demand for the dismantling of all opposition groups, could easily lead to civil war. Only Israel would benefit from the resulting chaos. Palestinians were not impressed with this leadership dispute. Most, although growing wary and resentful of the mounting outside pressure that fueled the conflict, seemed more disturbed by the timing of the political row, taking place when, more than ever, they needed unity and conformity.

No one expressed Israel's wishes more articulately than Israeli Defense Minister Shaul Mofaz, who told Israeli Army Radio that "Arafat needs to disappear from the stage of history."[47] Mofaz was not simply urging new Palestinian blood, he was actually offering to deport Arafat, as he had repeatedly suggested in the past. This latest remark, however, had a different spin, since it indicated Israel's growing interest in the internal Palestinian affair. Mofaz said that sending Arafat into exile was a matter of "finding the right moment" without damaging Abbas.

It's easy to rush to the conclusion that the so-called power struggle between Arafat and Abbas was rooted in the P.A. President's clinging to power and refusing to concede to the more moderate Prime Minister. But this was not a dispute of moderation vs. extremism, traditionalism vs. democratization. This was a struggle between competing visions amid mounting external and internal pressure, threats of assassinations, and a bewildered population who felt that the conflict was untimely—for it would serve Israel alone while seriously jeopardizing Palestinian national unity. In the midst of this quarrel between Arafat and Abbas, there probably could not have been a more untimely occasion for the Palestinians to lose one of their most beloved advocates.

EDWARD SAID DIES

"Edward Said passed away this morning," a troubling e-mail message stared me in the face. I knew that such a moment was inevitable. The man was stricken with leukemia and had suffered for years. His eyes sunk deeper into his handsome face with every lecture he gave. The last message I exchanged with the Columbia University professor was just a few short months before his passing. But after scheduling an interview several weeks in advance, Professor Said requested a delay for a period of one month, for he was about to undergo "very rigorous chemotherapy treatment" at a New York hospital. I imagined the courageous man absorbed in pain. The mere thought sickened me. We never did the interview.

Said stood for everything that is virtuous. His moral stance was even more powerful than the wealth of essays, books, and music he produced. It was manifested more evidently in his gentle, kind persona. He wrote whenever he managed to get hold of a pen. In his seemingly weakest moments of pain and struggle with the spreading cancer, he taught us strength and preached endurance. Said was an extraordinary intellectual. His intellectual capabilities, thoughtfulness, and genius were inimitable. And because of that, he was a target for those who wish to silence every voice that utters the tabooed words of truth. Said's words dug deep into our hearts, broke the boundaries of culture, religion, and politics. He tackled our humanity before reaching out to our minds. Palestinians are not the only ones who are mourning Said's death. Of this I am certain.

In his touching memoir, Said spoke of his life-long legacy of being "out of place." As a Palestinian denied the chance to live freely in his homeland, he circled the globe, from the Middle East to Europe to the United States, where he spent most of his life vividly and eloquently conveying the pain of his people in a way no other intellectual had done before him. Many tried to exploit the man's unscarred reputation, dishonestly building a name for themselves. An unknown Israeli writer rose to become a celebrated "intellectual" when he broke the news that Said was not a refugee.[48] Justus Reid Weiner's "revelations" made him a hero in the eyes of those who would never cease to demand Professor Said's expulsion from his position at Columbia University. "I have been moved to defend the refugees' plight precisely because I did not suffer, therefore I feel obliged to relieve the suffering of my people"—Said responded graciously to his accuser.[49] Weiner and his supporters were quickly brushed aside and the intellectual giant carried on with his mission, swimming against the current of the mainstream.

But those living and dying in isolation, so desperate in their attempts to let the world know of their atrocious destiny under a wicked Israeli occupation, those scattered in their refugee camps across Palestine and the Middle East, are the ones who will miss Said the most. Unlike many of us who chose to be so careful not to offend, Said was unrivalled in his honesty. He tackled issues that were too "politically incorrect" to confront. It is no wonder he was as much adored by the people as he was detested by the authorities. On more than one occasion his books were banned in the Middle East, even in the West Bank and Gaza. But being "bookless in Gaza" was hardly enough to dishearten Said. His lashing out at the Zionist ideology and his involvement in deconstructing America's foreign policy were deliberately and shrewdly misapprehended as "anti-Semitism." But the might of Said's logic always prevailed, and will continue to prevail, even after his death. Refugee or not, the tireless professor from Columbia University was gone. He died on September 25, 2003, on a New York morning, not like any other. He left us with a legacy that makes us proud that he was a Palestinian, with a heart that beat with endless humanity.

THE REAL WMD'S

Shortly thereafter, then top U.S. weapons inspector, David Kay, announced that Iraq had no weapons of mass destruction, and neither did it have the capability to produce such weapons.[50] The hype garnered by the story further underscored the double standards operative when dealing with nuclear powers, Israel being one of the world's strongest. A distinguished team of American scientists had just concluded a thorough and consequential mission in Iraq. The declared objective was to locate and dismantle Iraq's weapons of mass destruction. But hidden within this declaration was the hope of unearthing a belated pretext for a calamitous war on Iraq that cost billions of dollars and the lives of thousands. Shortly after Kay briefed the U.S. Senate and House of Representatives on his findings, or lack thereof, a declassified version of his report was released. Not only were no weapons found in Iraq, but the deposed Iraqi government, according to Kay, had no capacity to produce chemical warfare agents before the war.

So much for the British government's scare campaign, alleging Iraq's ability to launch a global attack within 45 minutes. As if the war party's lack of good judgment was not enough, the response to Kay's report displayed even greater shame. The Australian Prime Minister, John Howard, responded by saying he had no regrets: "You make judgments on the basis of the information available at the time you are required to make those judgments, and the judgment was valid," he said contemptuously, in startling defiance of the facts and with no remorse for the thousands of Iraqis killed by the allies' weapons.[51] President Bush, who was struck by the finding that most Americans—53 percent according to a new *CBS News–New York Times* poll—were now doubtful about his Iraq war, also continued to defy common sense.[52] "This administration will deal with gathering dangers where we find them," he said. Although the ambiguity of

Bush's mutterings was bewildering, they certainly raised an important question. If what truly concerned Bush was "gathering dangers," then why not go after those nations who unquestionably possess such weapons—such as Israel?

Of course, most people, whether opponents or proponents of U.S. foreign policy in the Middle East, understand the impossibility of such a demand. That is because U.S. foreign policy follows no moral code, but rather an amoral, imperial, and self-sustaining ideology, aimed only at rewarding its followers and punishing its antagonists. Those living outside this immoral dogma understand that well. One is South Africa's Nelson Mandela. In an interview with *Newsweek* magazine, Mandela stated that the war was motivated by Bush's desire to "please the arms and oil industries" in the U.S. Then he added: "But what we do know is that Israel has weapons of mass destruction. Nobody mentions that."[53] Israel's possession of such weapons was dubbed "the world's best-known secret." In a B.B.C. news documentary that was aired twice, first in March and then again in June 2003, the host of the show asked the following questions: "Which country in the Middle East has undeclared nuclear weaponry? Which country in the Middle East has no outside inspections? Which country jailed its nuclear whistle-blower for 18 years?" That dramatic introduction was followed by an enlarged title page with the words: "Israel's Secret Weapon."[54] Israel's refusal to ratify the Nuclear Non-Proliferation Treaty, in addition to strong speculation that it owns up to 300 nuclear warheads, and the Arab League's assertion to the International Atomic Energy Agency (I.A.E.A.) that Israel was capable of producing a hydrogen bomb, were not enough to convince the U.S. and its coalition partners that Iran and Iraq weren't the real, imminent danger.

The present hierarchy of power in the West seemed little concerned with logic and rationale. Bush, Blair, and Howard were chasing after the phantoms of Iraq's alleged armaments while Israel was amassing a wealth of illicit weapons. While the rational response to Israel's heedlessness would be a stern demand to allow unfettered access to weapons inspectors and the unconditional signing of the Nuclear Non-Proliferation Treaty, the opposite was true. The I.A.E.A. was ambushing Iran, a potential war target for the U.S., demanding "full disclosure" of its nuclear program. The agency set October 31, 2003 as the "decisive" and "non-negotiable" deadline. In the U.S., White House spokesman, Scott McClellan, pounded the war drums once more when he threatened to hold Syria "accountable" if it didn't stop harboring terrorists (in other words, providing safe haven to anti-Israeli Palestinian factions, who merely operate politically in Damascus). McClellan's threat "coincided" with a more blatant threat by John Bolton, the then U.S. under-secretary of state for arms control and international security, when he briefed a Congress committee regarding Syria, saying: "In short, if the language of persuasion fails, these states—starting with Syria—must see and feel the logic of adverse consequences."[55] Of course, Israel was not one of "these states." Israel, whose level of comfort with the U.S. and its war allies' unconditional patronage was at an all-time high, also had its own methods of responding to nitpicking media reports, like that of the B.B.C. Israel officially declared that it would boycott the B.B.C.[56]

The production or use of weapons of mass destruction should be vehemently rejected, regardless of any pretext. When a nuclear bomb is dropped, or when nerve gas is discharged, neither the identity of the attacker nor the victim should be of consequence. Equally, we should not be concerned with whether the pilot dropping the bomb is a citizen of a democratically elected government or assigned by a religious cleric. No one should be allowed to produce or attain such massive killing agents—not Iran, not India, and certainly not Israel. One can make the case that if one or more Middle Eastern countries are pondering the probabilities of attaining weapons of mass destruction, it is, in part, due to the fear that its lack of such weapons makes them vulnerable in the region. It is not easy to scold or kick around a country with a fully functioning nuclear weapons system. The Pakistani response to India's weaponry, and North Korea's admission that it possesses such weapons, are both cases in point. By granting Israel the right to produce weapons that can be used for one purpose only—mass killing—and then demanding that Iran stop expressing the mere desire to produce them is the epitome of hypocrisy. Pressure mounted like a ticking time bomb, the U.S. not only had its designs on Iraq, but on Iran and Syria too. Ironically, amidst the escalating animosity, the United Nations celebrated the anniversary of the Universal Declaration of Human Rights, on December 10, 2003, a declaration that is yet to be actualized in Palestine, five long decades after its drafting.

INK ON PAPER

A stimulating commentary by the United Nations Department of Public Information celebrated the triumphs and reflected on the

Photo 3.5   A 60-year-old olive tree is ripped from the ground by the Israeli army to make way for an extension of the illegal Jewish settlement of Zufim. Zufim is between the Separation Wall and the so-called Green Line (March 2005).

challenges still facing the Universal Declaration of Human Rights, decades after its inception. It stated proudly: "Since 1948, the Universal Declaration has been translated into more than 200 languages."[57] The striking number of translations may be inspiring, especially if one compares today's far-reaching awareness of those noble principles with the detrimental state of human rights affairs on the day of its signing. The United Nations, still a fresh organization, aspired to lead the world out of the quagmire manifested during World War II: "Whereas disregard and contempt for human rights have resulted in barbarous acts which have outraged the conscience of mankind,"[58] a brighter future awaited the post-war generation, it was hoped—a future enshrined in the "recognition of the inherent dignity and of the equal and inalienable rights of all members of the human family [as] the foundation of freedom, justice and peace in the world." Yet very few point out, that while the Declaration may have exemplified the end of a nightmare for some, for others it was, and remains, merely "ink on paper"—an overly used expression that is applied mostly by intellectuals of the so-called Third World, while pointing out systematically debased international laws and declarations.

Stripped of its political context, and from the palpable prospect of being circumvented altogether, the Declaration, nonetheless, delineated a future endorsed by the bulk of humanity, but most ardently by those who in fact were not "born free and equal in dignity and rights." While schools elsewhere might allude to the value of such a declaration, Palestinian school kids, born into military occupation, incarcerated within terribly poor and swarming refugee camps, and bounded (even branded) by their identity as Palestinians commemorated the anniversary of the Declaration by roving around the streets of the Occupied Territories, holding hands, carrying flags, and laboriously hauling a giant banner strewn with a poorly inscribed duplicate of Article 3 of the declaration: "Every one has the right to life, liberty and security of person." Those kids who roamed the streets of Gaza had no first-hand experience of what these resounding rights even meant in practice. The 2003 report by the Special Rapporteur of the U.N. Commission on Human Rights on the Right to Food, finally attached figures and numbers to the lamentable reality endured by Palestinians, but reflected most tragically on their children, over 22 percent of whom (under five years of age) suffered from either "acute" or "chronic" malnutrition. Most tragically, 9.3 percent suffered from irreversible brain damage, a direct result of starvation caused by Israeli military policies—collective punishment, closures, curfews, home demolishing, and the like.[59]

"No one shall be held in slavery or servitude," states Article 4 of the Declaration. Such an article may not be much use to the 6000 Palestinian prisoners held in Israeli military detention (mostly political prisoners, including 350 under the age of 18), except as an urgently needed moral validation that they too are an integral part of the "human family," as it was earnestly expressed by the Declaration. But Article 6, "Every one has the right to recognition everywhere before the law," remained for them a perplexing impasse; most of these prisoners were denied a trial, fair or otherwise, and if law was of relevance, then the "Landau Rules" of the Israeli Supreme Court which sanction "certain types" of torture would be implemented.[60] Nonetheless, no other article within the declaration came so close to home, so to speak, than that of Article 5: "No one shall be subjected to torture or to cruel, inhumane or degrading treatment or punishment."

Illustrations that so amply manifest the opposite of what Article 5 stands for are too many to chronicle. In the book entitled *Checkpoints-Twilight Zone*, written by a former Israeli Army Staff Sergeant, Liaran Ron Furer, the author stated that the Israeli army in Gaza behaved like "animals, criminals and thieves."[61] According to Furer, a common practice of the Israeli soldiers was to take photos of themselves with their Palestinian victims, wounded or beaten senseless—a stark reminder of the infamous snapshot of smiling Israeli troops locking shoulders behind a dead Palestinian man still soaked with his blood in the West Bank. "I remember how we humiliated a dwarf who came to the checkpoint every day on his wagon. They forced him to have his picture taken on the horse, hit and degraded him for a good half hour." "The most moral army in the world" found it fit to urinate on a Palestinian boy's head, according to Furer's account, for daring to smile at one of the soldiers. The seemingly brief Universal Declaration suddenly expanded. "No one shall be subjected to arbitrary attacks upon his honor," says one article; the innumerable Palestinians forced to strip naked at checkpoints and refugee camps throughout the territories might only comfort themselves with their precise knowledge of what such a law entails. Nothing more.

"No one shall be arbitrarily deprived of his property," declares another article. Yet under its shadow, millions of Palestinians have endured, without homes, without land, thousands of them once again dwelling in white tents, provided by the United Nations. As illegal Jewish settlements expand, thousands of Palestinians are ethnically cleansed. Not even an all-encompassing Declaration of Human Rights is of any tangible value then—mere "ink on paper" once again. But is it foolish for Palestinians to parade with hastily written statements celebrating rights they never attained? I think not. It matters little who drafted what and why. What endures is the "recognition of the inherit dignity and of the equal and inalienable rights of all members of the human family [as] the foundation of freedom, justice and peace." What's worth celebrating for those who acquire none of these values is the liberating hope, the vision, and the noble idea ingrained in the Declaration's lasting tenets, even if they only subsist as "ink on paper."

SPARING CIVILIANS

Throughout 2003 the Second Palestinian Uprising intensified, the increase in violence leading to many Israeli civilians being brutally killed. A resistance movement that for generations had been fairly non-violent was spinning out of control, with bombs blowing up almost routinely in civilian areas. And with this evolving change in tactic, Palestinians were, without a doubt risking losing moral ground. It can hardly be argued that the upper hand in this ongoing conflict belongs to Israel; that can be indicated clearly by the simple fact that Israel has an army, one of the strongest in the world for that matter, while the Palestinians have none. But the fact that the Palestinians have been the underdog for decades now does not in any way compromise the basic sanctity of human life, be it Israeli or Palestinian.

Palestinian resistance factions must desist from targeting Israeli civilians, with or without an officially negotiated ceasefire, and regardless of the course of action chosen by Israel and its reckless government in response. This decision is imperative if the Palestinian struggle is to safeguard its historic values and uphold its moral pre-eminence. For some, such reasoning may come into view as morally inconsistent, one-sided even; after all, the Israeli army continues to target civilians unhindered, so why deny Palestinians the right to retaliate? Palestinians have always possessed the legitimate right to self-defense, and the unequivocal right of ridding themselves of so lengthy and so vile an occupation. These rights have been recurrently highlighted in international law and require little debate or intellectual argument. But it is imprudent for the occupied—who surely possesses the moral edge—to utilize the unmerited methods of the occupier. International law makes a clear distinction, as should the Palestinian resistance, between occupying military forces and civilians. If Palestinians waver from this critical line of reasoning, their historically virtuous struggle risks being diluted with moral corruption.

The Palestinian revolution, with its formerly unrefined armed resistance, sprung from the orchards of the northern West Bank as early as the 1920s. It was and remains a freedom vow, a cry for justice that has been forcefully echoed in universally accepted and time-honored rights and principles. It was certainly not the unscrupulous ways of colonialists or the occupiers that guided the march for freedom. Typically, the methods used by the ongoing uprising in the Occupied Territories stand at odds with the ghastly practices of the Israeli government and army. In fact, since their early days of confronting occupation forces, Palestinians aspired to be inclusive, as they longed for equality and insisted on the universal applicability of human rights. These values must remain intact. But one must also agree that every nation, and Palestinians are no exception, has a breaking point. It is only human, following decades of disproportionately dispensed suffering, violence, and dispossession, that one's determination to attain freedom would partly concede to an overpowering sense of desperation and raw desire for vengeance. To those living in the Occupied Territories, the phenomenon of suicide bombings is not alien in the context of the reality into which Palestinians are born. Yet if Palestinians allow Israeli tactics to influence their resistance strategy, the authenticity of the entire struggle is compromised. But what would happen if Palestinian factions overcame their sense of dejection and unilaterally halted any attack on Israeli civilians, permanently and unreservedly?

Alas, even then, the perception of Palestinians and their struggle is unlikely to change, at least not in the United States, where political propaganda subdues reality and governs public opinion. It should come as no surprise then, that the Palestinian struggle—out of sheer ignorance, media distortion, or religious fervor—was equally and abrasively condemned in much of the Western hemisphere even prior to the first suicide bombing against Israeli civilians, a little more than ten years ago. This flawed perspective survives in complete defiance of logic. After all, the conquest of historic Palestine, with all the massacres it entailed, preceded any truly collective Palestinian struggle, whether violent or otherwise. The mainstream media, most markedly in the United States, has wholly omitted such a fact. As far as Israel (and thus pro-Israel media and governments) is concerned, the version of history that counts is the one that comprises Palestinian violence. Violence in the Middle East is largely defined by Palestinian attacks; in other words, Israeli violence may be rife in the Occupied Territories, and yet, if no Israeli casualties are reported, much of the world media perceives this period as one of "calm" or a "lull" in the violence.

The suicide bombing of October 4, 2003, and that of December 25 of the same year, are cases in point. Between these two incidents, Palestinian losses mounted. Reportedly, 117 Palestinians were killed, mostly civilians, including 23 children;[62] and several thousand Palestinians were made homeless as nearly 500 homes and apartments were brought tumbling down by Israeli army explosives or bulldozers, primarily in the already overcrowded and poverty-stricken Gaza Strip. But according to Palestinian-American media critic, Ali Abunimah, the corporate media in the U.S. (and in Britain, to a lesser extent) brimmed with regret over the squandered opportunity for peace that the December suicide bombing represented (keeping in mind that the latter targeted Israeli soldiers, not civilians). Newspapers and other media—such as the *Los Angeles Times*, the *Chicago Tribune*, and C.N.N.—dealt a blow to journalistic integrity when to mark the day of the Palestinian attack they chose such headlines as: "12-Week Lull in Mideast Ends," "Mideast Quiet Shattered," "Attacks broke a lull that had lasted more than two months and raised fears of a slide into violence," "There has been a relative calm since the Haifa bombing (last October)," and so on. Such manifest bias in reporting gives rise to the argument that the desire to condemn the Palestinian people's struggle is instinctive and utterly fails to consider the disproportionate hurt inflicted on the Palestinian people by Israel. This argument becomes even more plausible when pro-Israel pundits in the American media and government, and within the ranks of the noticeably influential lobby groups and think-tanks, find Israel's justifications for its senseless violence and occupation of Palestinian land substantiated, even compelling. After all, Israel will always maintain a level of "moral superiority" over the Arabs, as declared by U.S. under-secretary of defense for policy, Douglas Feith.[63]

Nevertheless, even with this troubling state of affairs in mind, injustice must not be an invitation to respond with morally degrading acts equivalent to those advocated by the Israeli government of Ariel Sharon and its apologists everywhere. Sharon and his henchmen, of all people, should not be allowed to in any way manipulate the nature and magnitude of Palestinian resistance. To maintain its moral edge, the Palestinian revolution should not depart from its all-encompassing, tolerant, and inclusive path, it should not be tainted by the fallacies of the occupier, it should not fall into the trap of fury, racial and religious exclusivity, and revengeful acts against civilians. True, the U.S. media will hardly acknowledge such a realization. But should we remain confined by media partiality and overly concerned with the validating words of some government spokesman? Were these the values that inspired and sparked the current uprising and the uprisings of the past? Countering Israeli crimes against Palestinian civilians by lashing out at Israeli civilians, no matter how outwardly gratifying revenge might seem, should be removed from the everlasting principles of the Palestinian struggle for freedom. These values must remain untainted, wholesome even, so that the will of the people might some day prevail over tyranny and oppression. And it will, of this I am certain.

4
Profound Changes,
Insurmountable Challenges (2004)

The year 2004 brings incomparable suffering as Israel's Separation Wall cuts off Palestinian towns, villages and cities. Acre after acre of land is confiscated to make way for the towering monolith. This year also witnesses an alarming trend of mysterious and often graphic killings of Palestinian journalists, as well as attacks on newspaper offices in the Occupied Territories. Problems of corruption and nepotism, which for long had tainted the reputation of Arafat and the P.A., continue to plague the political scene, and as always the ultimate victims are ordinary Palestinians. Key members of the ongoing resistance fall victim to Sharon's brutality as Israel kills Hamas spiritual leader, Sheikh Ahmed Yassin, and then less than a month later top Hamas leader Dr. Abdelaziz Rantisi. Yet hope is also rekindled as the International Court of Justice finally rules that the Israeli Separation Wall is illegal and must come down. The demands go unheeded by Sharon and his government. The year also witnesses a profound transformation in

Photo 4.1 Palestinian boys in Qalqilya play near the Israeli Separation Wall engulfing their town (September 2004).

the Palestinian struggle and political landscape, as Palestinian Authority President, Yasser Arafat, the icon of the struggle and the popular leader of the Palestinians for more than 40 years, dies, having been besieged in his Ramallah office by the Israelis since the early months of the Intifada.

DEFENDING THE WALL

The violence of 2004, like the previous year, claimed the lives of hundreds and the hopes of an entire generation, Palestinian and Israeli. Sharon's dream of a Separation Wall became a reality, as construction wreaked havoc throughout scores of Palestinian villages and towns. Human rights groups screamed in vain, and world governments did all they could to divert attention on to the "militants" and "terrorists" in the Occupied Territories. One can hardly overlook the reverberation of triumph in the words of Ariel Sharon's own chief spokesman, Ranaan Gissin, on January 29, 2004. When commenting on a suicide bombing that had killed ten Israelis and wounded others in Occupied Jerusalem, Gissin exhorted: "This

Photo 4.2   A Palestinian student climbs over a section of the Israeli Separation Wall to reach his school.

terrorist attack is the best argument that we can use to defend the sacred right of Israel to exercise legitimate self-defense."[1] The Israeli Prime Minister's somewhat eloquent spokesman used the bloodshed in Occupied Jerusalem to kick off a major propaganda campaign, aspiring to persuade Europe and the United States. The campaign was aimed at defending Israel's unilateral action of building a Separation Wall that would thrust deep into the Occupied Territories, annexing much of what many Palestinians hoped to be part of their future state. Fearing a potentially embarrassing ruling by the International Court of Justice, which was due on February 28, 2004, regarding the legality of the Israeli wall, the Israeli cabinet vowed to challenge the court's own legal "competence" to rule on the contentious subject. It was followed by a pledge to carry out a "ramified information campaign [to be] conducted parallel to the legal proceedings." And shortly thereafter, it was affirmed: "bus bombing vindicates [the] West Bank barrier," wrote A.F.P., citing Gissin.[2]

Needless to say, the suicide bombings played well into the hands of Israel, thanks in part to the unbalanced and out-of-context media coverage throughout the United States and, to a lesser extent, Europe. Only Palestinians seemed to target civilians "in the hearts of their cities." Israel's much higher rate of killing Palestinians in the heart of their overpopulated refugee camps was always justified under the banner of "self-defense." Just one day prior to the Occupied Jerusalem bombing, Israeli occupation forces killed eight Palestinians, the majority of which were unarmed. Most of those killed in the assault on Gaza, were shot at close range, according to hospital reports.[3] Among the wounded was an 11-year-old child, whose left eye had been penetrated by a sniper's bullet. The Palestinian casualties, unlike in the case of Israelis, were immediately divided into categories by the media, a stunt that is often used to dilute the magnitude of the action. Some of the Palestinian victims were "militants" belonging to "Islamic Jihad," a "radical Palestinian group," dedicated to the "destruction of Israel," and so on. The Israeli aggression was therefore downplayed, to become simply an immanent necessity, not a choice. Palestinian bombings in Israel were hardly ever rationalized by the fact that they often occurred as a reaction to much more calculated aggressions carried out by Israel, such as the raid on Gaza. And when the tide was not turning Israel's way, then a quick cabinet meeting, a press conference, and a decision to launch an "information campaign" in the West, were often all Israel needed to maintain its "moral superiority" over the Palestinians.

But what else did Israel fail to put forth while defending its wall? Of course, the wall was not erected along the 1967 borders, nor was it designed to shield Israel's border. Its deceiving and all-encompassing line swallowed a significant percentage of the West Bank, scores of its towns and villages and thousands of its people. If the idea was to shield Israel, then why rob Palestinians of their land in the process? If the goal was to protect Israelis, then why relocate them into the heart of the West Bank and Gaza, "settling" on stolen Palestinian land? An honest look at the situation truly validates the viewpoint that Israel was only using Palestinian counter-violence as an excuse to further its territorial interests in the Occupied Territories, slowly annexing much of the West Bank, Gaza, and Occupied Jerusalem, under the pretext of security and legitimate self-defense. Meanwhile, the Palestinian National Authority's helplessness lingered on. The P.A. condemned the incursion and killings in Gaza, while simultaneously expressing willingness to speed up a proposed meeting between Prime Minister Ahmed Qorei (who had replaced former Prime Minister Abbas after the latter's long-foreseen resignation and the collapse of his government in September 2003) and Sharon. With the reality on the ground not changing, the future looked quite bleak; tit for tat was undoubtedly the name of the game. The future was captive to the incompetent, and frankly irrelevant, Palestinian Authority, manipulative Israeli

Photo 4.3 The Israeli Separation Wall encircles the Qalandia refugee camp near Ramallah, completely isolating its residents from the rest of the West Bank.

politics, and a biased American government whose only role seemed to be that of further marginalizing the Palestinians and embracing the policies of Sharon. The suicide bombing in Occupied Jerusalem was yet another tragedy, provoked by equally tragic carnage in Gaza. The greater tragedy however, was the exploiting of bloodshed for political gain, in place of a clear realization that violence will always beget violence.

ANARCHY IN GAZA?

The early part of 2004 also witnessed an alarming trend of assaults on and killings of journalists, particularly those reporting from the Occupied Territories. Khalil al-Zabin, a 59-year-old Palestinian journalist, was ambushed outside his office in Gaza on March 2, 2004. His body was riddled with bullets. All that was known about his executioners is that they were masked. No faction claimed responsibility for his murder and the P.A. had no suspects. This disturbing episode would likely have been filed away in the ever-expanding cabinet containing the details of Gaza's victims of anarchy and disorder, where Israel was ultimately held responsible. This time however, the stakes were much higher, and blaming Israel alone simply would not suffice. Reporters Without Borders (R.S.F.) condemned the murder and called on Arafat to "act." R.S.F., among other groups, weighed the crime in terms of its relation to a trend of assaults targeting Palestinian journalists by unknown assailants.[4] Several other incidents were cited to further highlight the alarming trend: the ransacking of a newspaper's office, the torching of a journalist's car, and others. Al-Zabin's murder was certainly the bloodiest.

Although one ought to appreciate the significance of the fact that al-Zabin was a journalist, it must be equally clear that the issue was much more urgent than the need of some to suppress free speech and hush up, to say the least, those who advocate it. Indeed, the issue was much more perilous and far-reaching. Al-Zabin was a close advisor to Arafat; he ran a newspaper which was funded by the P.A. and was entrusted with the complex and controversial subject of human rights. Considering the P.A.'s own record, his task must have been grueling. Al-Zabin, a member of the popular Palestinian faction, Fatah, was killed just a few days after the movement's top members concluded intense talks in Arafat's Ramallah headquarters. Although Fatah's senior members appeared to have patched up their differences by the final day of talks, the rift was not truly mended.

Since the mass desertion of hundreds of its members in December 2003, and the substantial disparity among Fatah's various offshoots on the mandate of the movement's military wing, Fatah was facing one of its toughest challenges in recent years. The turmoil within, however, if not contained, was likely to cause subsequent tremors throughout the Occupied Territories, especially in the highly volatile Gaza Strip.

The recent and unexpected announcement by Sharon, revealing his intention to evacuate and relocate to the West Bank most of the Gaza Strip's illegal Jewish settlements, ignited an array of unpleasant predictions of power struggle among Palestinian factions, each wishing to dominate the "liberated" Gaza. "Palestinian power struggle worsens," wrote the *Age* newspaper of Australia, commenting on the "dirty assassination"—as described by Arafat—of al-Zabin. The U.S. *Christian Science Monitor* went further in decoding the hidden indications of the assassination. "Hamas seeks primacy in Gaza," it alleged, although the article failed to fully explore such a claim.[5] But the touting of the media was not the only indicator of the feared power struggle. P.A. officials themselves were hardly discreet in their anxiety over the prospect of the "alternative authority" allegedly posed by Hamas in Gaza, as stated by Mohamed Dahlan, former P.A. interior minister. Many in the Israeli press were up in arms as well. Commentators employed the anarchy-in-Gaza scenario to express resentment over Sharon's Gaza evacuation proposal, and, once again, to underscore the claim that Palestinians were simply incapable of ruling themselves, thereby justifying the military occupation of Palestinian land. Moreover, by playing up the projection of power struggle in Gaza, Israel managed to shift attention from its rapid land grab in the West Bank under the ruse of building a "security fence" to keep suicide bombers at bay. Israel's Gaza "concession" once again posed a challenge to the P.A., still unable or unwilling to unite with Palestinian resistance movements who were equally engaged in achieving the long-sought national unity. Yet while Israel was hoping to get Egypt involved in the Gaza scheme, bypassing the Palestinian people's representatives, the P.A. and various factions displayed few indications of their ability to face Israel's maneuvers.

Even though Egyptian President Hosni Mubarak made it clear that his country had no interest in getting involved in Gaza again, it was unlikely that Israel would carry out a partial withdrawal from Gaza, if any, without "guarantees" of security, an ambiguous demand that often meant the opposite to Palestinians. Certainly, the media might have overstated the political consequences of the killing of Arafat's trusted advisor. This was in part a result of the timing of the assassination; as tension within the Fatah party increased, and as rumors of a Gaza takeover by Hamas flourished. But, although Palestinian society was still functional despite years of systematic attempts by Israel to force it into total chaos, one must admit that: anarchy is not an alien concept in Gaza and other parts of the Occupied Territories. Although one can fathom the direct relationship between anarchy and military occupation, this should not excuse actions that could possibly have brought a tragic ending of the Palestinian uprising. If the killing of al-Zabin had been a first step on the path to political mayhem and power struggle, then Israel would have been able to prove its historic allegations that Palestinians are unfit to rule themselves. Israel played a primary role in the Gaza mess, but this time it was not Israel alone that deserved the blame. Palestinians themselves were falling into a trap, already bickering over the Gaza prize before it was even offered to them. By failing to take charge of their own destiny in a unified fashion, Palestinians, regardless of their political and ideological affiliations, were taking the risk of being marginalized and victimized by mandates and caretakers. "If it's not possible [for Palestinians to take charge of Gaza] under the present circumstances, why should an interim Egyptian role not be considered?" wrote Hasan Abu Nimah in the *Jordan Times*.[6] Those Palestinians who lived under a cruel and self-serving Egyptian mandate in the 1950s and 60s knew the answer to that question only too well. True, the death of al-Zabin was not the first politically motivated assassination and, sadly, it would not be the last. But for Palestinians the stakes this time were much higher, and an internal dispute coupled with muscle-flexing would deeply harm all that the Palestinians had fought long and hard to achieve. The media was, as ever, willing to condemn and lambaste Palestinians, their incompetence and failures, retrospectively validating Israel's policy and persistent allegations of Palestinian ineptitude. Taking this one step further, Israel pressed ahead with its assassination policy, continuing to claim that Palestinian governance was a ruse, and that in their attempts to rule themselves they appointed terrorists to lead the way.

THE KILLING CAMPAIGNS

On March 22, 2004, Sheikh Ahmed Yassin, the spiritual leader of the Hamas movement, was brutally murdered by the Israeli army, while on his way home from early morning prayer in a Gaza mosque. The old and paralyzed man, whose wheelchair was left twisted and beyond recognition, was struck by an Israeli missile, which also claimed the lives of nine bystanders. Sharon personally supervised the assassination, according to Israeli radio. Living side by side with the residents of Gaza's camps, Yassin was respected and cherished by many, even by those who hold no ideological or political affiliations to Hamas. His death sparked sorrow and rage not only throughout the Occupied Territories, but also throughout the Arab and Muslim world. In Israel, then Finance Minister Benjamin Netanyahu hailed the killing of Yassin, saying: "Even if in the short term there will be a harsh response from Hamas, in the long term the effect will be to rein in Hamas and the rest of the terror organizations because their leaders will know that they will be destroyed."[7]

Less than one month later, on April 17, 2004, Israel assassinated top Hamas leader, Dr. Abdelaziz Rantisi. The motivations behind the two assassinations had clearly contrasting goals. While Yassin was a spiritual leader, whose military sense was not of significance, Rantisi was involved hands-on in all Hamas decisions and actions. The killing of Yassin was an attempt to break the spirit of Hamas' supporters, whereas Rantisi's assassination was part of the ongoing attempt to destroy the actual infrastructure of the Hamas movement altogether. These killings would continue, extended to target even moderate leaders within the various Palestinian movements. But this ruthless policy would prove a costly move for the Sharon government. In addition to the fact that the policy of political assassinations represented a flagrant violation of international law, the killing of resistance leaders constituted a counter-productive military strategy as well.

A quick look at Gaza during the 1970s is helpful here. Following the military defeat of several Arab countries in 1967 at the hands of Israel, Palestinians sought alternative strategies. One was taking charge of their own fate by organizing popular resistance in refugee camps across the Occupied Territories. The new tactic demanded reliance on a form of organized struggle that was constructed by local militants who were the product of the Palestinian experience of oppression and defiance. This was when the talk of a self-sufficient resistance movement was at its peak. However, unlike popular rebellions in the past, those of the 1970s witnessed a surge in armed struggle, so resilient and robust that it baffled the still fresh Israeli occupation. For a range of reasons, Gaza was the hub of the growing movement. One obvious reason was Gaza's extreme poverty and overcrowdedness;

another was the Strip's close proximity to Egypt, which served as an ideological backdrop, especially for Islamic groups. The armed struggle of the 1970s introduced yet a new image into Gaza's already symbol-laden reality: the refugee standing in a long line seeking a small ration of food provided by some U.N. facility was now armed and eagerly waiting to battle Israeli armored vehicles raiding his camp. Palestinians were determined to become the defenders of their own plight and, despite their unrelenting calls for Arab unity in the face of Israel, they continued to embrace this resolve. Israel, on the other hand, wanted to ensure full and complete control over the new conquests by eliminating any influence, however minimal, of the "troublemakers" and "terrorists." It took Israel several years to win the disproportionate war of the 1970s even though they certainly had the upper hand. This is not to suggest that the Palestinian resistance was not fierce enough, quite the contrary. But the Palestinian factions commanding the armed struggle in Gaza were new; they received little training and possessed limited resources. These groups offered almost nothing to the refugees living in so dire a situation, aside from the chance for recruitment. Their relationship was further hampered by the ideological blurriness that marked some of these factions.

Israel's swift and ruthless military strikes left the local infrastructure of these groups, if any even existed, in a shambles. Almost every member of the resistance was either killed, imprisoned, or fled Gaza to Egypt or through Israel to Jordan. Stories of fighters executed in public were all too common. The armed struggle experiment inside the Occupied Territories was forced into an early hibernation period, forced to yield to the better-prepared and equipped resistance movements outside. But the Israeli invasion of Lebanon in 1982 and the dispersal of the P.L.O.'s various factions away from its strongholds compelled the return of the idea, and then the reality, of "homegrown resistance." Although the Palestinian Uprising of 1987 was a popular revolt, stemming from the Palestinian people's outright rejection of the occupation and its incessant colonial designs, there were ceaseless calls for the Intifada to be better organized and armed. Exactly 80 days after the outbreak of the Intifada, Hamas was born. What many rightly note is that Hamas used the ideological framework of Egypt's Muslim Brotherhood to structure its own. But many fail to observe that what allowed Hamas to thrust so deep into Palestinian society, and to blossom at such an astonishing speed, is that its existence was essential for Palestinian society (particularly in Gaza) to avoid complete institutional breakdown. Unlike the local militias of the 1970s, Hamas was an integral part of the Gaza Strip; it was introduced to Gaza years before it became a full-fledged political and military force under the banner of "The Islamic Resistance Movement Hamas," through its vast charity networks, clinics, universities, and even daycare centers. While there was a total lack of any municipal governance in Gaza, Islamic movements stepped in, providing what the regional political leadership usually supplies. It was only natural in a highly politicized society that a movement with social and religious dimensions would become involved in politics and all that politics in an occupied land entails.

Palestinian resistance movements fundamentally altered their approach during the late 1980s and early 1990s, by fostering a strong sense of solidarity among the population. Unlike in the 1970s, the tragedy of the killing of one resistance fighter created the opportunity of having ten others join the struggle. But while these groups seemed fully capable of modifying their course, the Israeli government reverted to its iron-fist policies of the past. The result, as far as Israel was concerned, was disastrous. Following the elimination of leading members of the resistance, using the all-purpose justification that these individuals were "terrorist masterminds," new and equally effective leaders would rise up and prove just as fierce and crafty as all previous other "terrorist masterminds." Israel nonetheless continued with its "hit list" military mentality. From the beginning of the Intifada, hundreds of activists were assassinated, but to no avail. In particular neighborhoods and refugee camps in the West Bank, like in Jenin, almost every resistance fighter was either killed or captured. Yet, a few months later, resistance resumed as defiant and fierce as ever. Whether or not the killing of Sheikh Yassin and Dr. Rantisi was just another round of Israeli military muscle-flexing prior to a promised Gaza withdrawal, the fact remains that Israel persisted with a grievous military policy that only invited further bloodshed on both sides.

LIFE AND DEATH IN RAFAH

On May 14, Israel carried out an overwhelming assault on the Gaza Strip town of Rafah which claimed the lives of scores of Palestinians, many of them children. It was reported that the Israeli onslaught was in retaliation to the killing of at least five Israeli soldiers when their convoy was detonated by homemade landmines, planted by Palestinian fighters. The number of casualties was compounded by the large amount of explosives being hauled by the Israeli armored vehicles.

The Rafah refugee camp, a small strip of land at the southern edge of Gaza, became the target for Israel's most ruthless attack in years. Between May 14–20, nearly 40 Palestinians were killed in Rafah, mostly civilians, and scores more elsewhere in the Gaza Strip. Among the Rafah deaths were nine children, most of them struck by missiles while protesting in non-violent demonstrations.[8] The attack sparked fury and outrage throughout the Occupied Territories. But even before the Rafah atrocities subsided, President Bush assured the lobbyists of the American Israeli Public Affairs Committee (A.I.P.A.C) that Israel had the right to defend itself.[9] Israel could assassinate any Palestinian at the time of its choosing with a ready-to-serve verdict. It killed and wounded hundreds of civilians in its "targeted killing" sprees. Yet, Palestinians were condemned if they showed the mere desire to respond. Even the targeting of occupation soldiers was taboo. So what were the Palestinians permitted to do in self-defense, in accordance with the twisted pro-Israeli Bush doctrine? How about marching in a peaceful demonstration? In Rafah, that too was anathema and could not be tolerated. It was handled with resolute vigor, the same way any "terrorist" threat deserved to be handled: A missile fired from a U.S.-supplied Apache helicopter was all that it took to eliminate that option of resistance.[10]

"Photos below are too graphic," read a warning posted on a Palestinian website, referring to images of dead civilians in the stricken refugee camp. The photos were of the dozen bodies piled up in a local farmer's cooler, since the hospital's morgue was overfilled with victims. One picture was of an olive-skinned child with slightly opened eyes, killed in one of the many missile strikes. An unknown hand holds the child's wholly disjoined arm closer to the body, as if he is telling the camera: "This arm belonged here." The boy, like the rest of the innocent victims, was nameless.

In the case of Israeli victims of suicide bombings, reality can be equally gruesome. But Bush dared not use the same logic when Palestinians fell victim: "Palestinians too have the right to defend themselves." Never once had he uttered these words. So what other methods of resistance, self-expression even, could Palestinians employ, now that even peaceful protests were deemed to be crossing the line?

Peter Hansen, the chief of the United Nations agency for refugees in the region, confirmed that in the Rafah refugee camp, homes were toppled on their dwellers. Even as Hansen himself walked through the camp assessing the damage, Israeli soldiers were still shooting. "We have now confirmation from the hospital that a girl was shot and killed in one of the two gun bursts we heard," he said.[11] She was three-year-old Rawan Abu Zeid. Her peers said that she was making her way to a local shop. Two bullets struck her, one in the head and the other in the neck. Was she taken to the same makeshift morgue, or did they find room for her tiny body in the local hospital?

What must Palestinians do to stand up to the Israeli occupation without being blamed for their own misery, now that suicide bombings, resisting occupation soldiers, even protesting peacefully, warrant so violent an Israeli response? Of course we are expected to pay little attention to the Palestinian victims, to ask who they are and who will be called to account for their death. In fact, few of us bother to find out what can be done to help those fortunate enough to evade the bullets and the bulldozers. But we indulge enthusiastically in analyzing Sharon's motives, as if such senseless murder might possibly adhere to some kind of logic. Was it blatant revenge that compelled the killings? Was it another campaign of ethnic cleansing of areas adjacent to the border with Egypt to establish yet another Israeli "security zone"? Was it a round of muscle-flexing, such as that following the defeat in South Lebanon, prior to a partial pull-out from Gaza? Whatever the reasons, the fact is Sharon would not cease in his murdering of Palestinians with impunity. His actions, however twisted, would continue as long as the United States government continued to supply him with all the weapons, money, and political clout needed to defy international law. His victims would maintain their status among the "unimportant people," and would be reprimanded whether they dared to respond violently or peacefully.

It wouldn't be long before the name of Rafah gave way to make room for more important headlines, or before another foreign-sounding Palestinian name associated with tragedy and death was introduced—and with it a long list of Israeli pretences, coupled by a quote or two from President Bush claiming that Israel has the right to defend itself. It was likely that the Rafah morgues would be emptied and dusty yellow bulldozers would remove the debris of over 230 destroyed homes. As for the refugees of the devastated camp, left alone atop the rubble of their homes, scores of death certificates, and hundreds of wounded to care for, they, astonishingly, had a way to cope. For one, they insisted that there were millions of people around the world who cared about them. Anyone chanting for their rights and freedom anywhere in the world fed them with urgently needed hope for one more day. Speaking to Gaza's Voice of Freedom Radio, a physician in Gaza City told the station that by the time the 40 Palestinians had been killed in Rafah, 39 others had been born. "I am so happy because the births were some compensation for the human loss," he said.

I.C.J. RULES

It was just two short weeks after the carnage in Rafah that Palestinians finally received some international recognition in the historic ruling of the International Court of Justice (I.C.J.) on July 9, 2004. The wait was over. The I.C.J. at The Hague finally ruled on Israel's Separation Wall, kicking the ball out of its court, and into that of all major players in the Arab–Israeli conflict. But the question remained: Would the historic decision of July 9 become yet another memento of United Nations incompetence, U.S. and Israeli arrogance, and Arab political worthlessness? "The construction of the wall and its associated regimes are contrary to international law," read the document of the ruling, leaving little room for misinterpretation.[12] The ruling was convincing, not only because of the clarity and meticulousness of the language used, but also because there was a near consensus on all the provisions it entailed. Only the American judge, Thomas Buerghenthal, opposed the ruling, in an obvious, albeit disheartening loyalty to political considerations rather than to the legal substance of the matter.[13]

The I.C.J. ruling went even further than expected: "All states are under obligations not to recognize the illegal situation resulting from the construction of the wall." The court had successfully contextualized the wall within the framework of the overall conflict, in which the wall was only one disturbing product. Thus it reminded Israel that it was "bound to comply with its obligations to respect the right of the Palestinian people to self-determination and its obligations under international humanitarian law and international human rights law." The ruling of the world's most respected and presumably influential legal body illuminated the legal perception of the now formally illegal Israeli wall. But it doubtlessly achieved more than that. First, it re-shifted attention back to international law as the only viable frame of reference for solving world conflicts, rendering irrelevant all that had resulted from political coercion imposed on Palestinians through the U.S. and Israel, and that resulting from the

Photo 4.4   The Israeli Separation Wall snakes its way through a neighborhood near Ramallah, on the way to Jerusalem (March 2005).

imprudence of the Palestinian Authority itself. Second, it restated the historic and political relevance of past United Nations resolutions, particularly 242, which demands an Israeli withdrawal from the Occupied Territories. Third, it reminded the international community and major signatories of the Fourth Geneva Convention of 1949 of their obligations under international law, holding them accountable to any transgression upon Palestinian rights or the direct or indirect support of those who violate those rights. Finally, it deprived the Arab and Muslim countries, as well as the Palestinian leadership, of any reliance on the incompetence or indecisiveness of international law to justify their own shortcomings.

For years, the Palestinian leadership supported peace initiatives, from Oslo to Wye River to the Road Map, and with each agreement more Palestinian rights, which for decades had been clearly reaffirmed by international edicts, were slowly sidelined and eroded by the deliberate ambiguity of the initiatives. For example, while international law unequivocally endorses the right of return and repatriation of Palestinian refugees, the so-called peace process willingly determined that this thorny issue must be cast aside for final-status negotiations that seemed to be more of an Israeli pretense than a realistic negotiations timetable. The I.C.J.'s pronouncement breathed life into the long-deserted, albeit still relevant, U.N. resolutions, conveniently interpreted to fit Israel's timeline and expectations. Nonetheless, the I.C.J. had done all that a legal body of its capacity could do. It could do no more, nor should it be expected to carry out the provisions of the advisory ruling. This was a job for U.N. member states and for those who claimed to champion the rule of law. Israel's response to the ruling held no surprises: Various Israeli government officials declared their country's intention to move forward with the construction of the 640 kilometer-long Separation Wall, now officially declared illegal by international law. Israel's conceit was most evident in comments made by then Israeli Finance Minister, Benjamin Netanyahu. When asked by a C.N.N. anchorwoman: Why not build the wall on Israeli land (since the wall would eventually swallow large swaths of the West Bank), Netanyahu answered: the West Bank is not Palestinian land, it's "disputed land."[14]

If Israel insisted on living in a world free from the constraints of international law, world courts, and U.N. resolutions, shouldn't the U.S. government have adhered to the I.C.J. ruling? Not, it would seem, in a context where Israel was the antagonist. This was the resounding reality that put Israel above the law, thanks to coercive U.S. politics and generous Security Council vetoes. U.S. officials greeted the ruling with the same tired argument: that the I.C.J. had no place in a political dispute, that the ruling would complicate matters not solve them, and that such a decision would make difficult the implementation of the U.S.-advocated Road Map peace initiative. If a transgression as deep and ingrained as that of the Arab–Israeli conflict, with its tremendous human cost on both sides and constant threat to an entire region, topped with an illegal Separation Wall, is not a matter for the I.C.J. to decide, then perhaps the courts are better off filing for an early retirement.

As far as the Palestinians were concerned, the I.C.J. ruling helped reinstate, in so decisive a text, the legitimacy of their struggle. However, while it absolved the Palestinian people from the incoherent political line adopted by their leadership, through the re-establishment of the role of international law, it further exposed the P.A.'s bankrupt approach. The P.A.'s political reasoning had for long contributed to the localization of the Palestinian struggle, stripping it of its regional and international contexts, reducing it to a platform of corruption and nepotism. In fact, the I.C.J.'s decision coincided with an historic scandal involving several Palestinian companies, tied to prominent individuals affiliated with the P.A., which were taking part in the construction of illegal Jewish settlements in the Occupied

Photo 4.5   The Israeli Separation Wall makes its way through the neighborhood of Abu Dis adjacent to Jerusalem (April 2005).

Territories.[15] But what is even more pertinent to the I.C.J. ruling was a report prepared by the Palestinian Legislative Council committee. The report, which took months in the making, concluded that major Palestinian companies had been smuggling and selling cement to Israel at a cheaper rate to speed up its construction of the Separation Wall. These companies were said to be directly affiliated with some P.A. ministers, who had been accused repeatedly of helping construct illegal Jewish settlements. Not only were many top P.A. officials accused of playing a role in completing the transaction (involving 420,000 tons of Egyptian cement), but the P.A.'s highest leadership seemed inclined to sweep the accusations under the rug, as it had done so often in past scandals.

It became almost nonsensical to demand that the international community fulfill its obligations to implement international law, including the latest I.C.J. ruling, while rich Palestinian fat cats were helping build the cage that would imprison their own people for years to come. The International Court of Justice did an honorable job in granting this moral victory, not only to the Palestinian people, but to politically weak and unprotected nations worldwide. But the ruling will remain in the realm of the intangible until those involved in the conflict recognize their legal and political duty toward international law. Without such an awakening, the Sharon and Bush doctrines will likely prevail, above the law, above the I.C.J. and its judges, and above our world's moral decency, or whatever remains of it.

DISORDER

Meanwhile, political crises continued to mar inter-Palestinian affairs, as Arafat and his Prime Minister, Ahmed Qorei, quarreled publicly and privately. Arafat wanted to maintain the status quo, giving himself a disproportionate share of power, while Qorei, under intense American and Israeli pressure, labored to undermine Arafat's influence. The latest dispute was more or less a repeat of that between the Palestinian leader and the former Prime Minister, Abbas. This time however, the pressure was mounting and Arafat's concession was anticipated. On July 27, both Qorei and Arafat emerged from the P.A.'s battered headquarters in Ramallah to address a group of anxious journalists. They shook hands and embraced in an attempt to show that the crisis had once again been averted. Not too far away, Israeli army Special Forces monitored the situation with the help of hi-tech binoculars, as Arafat enthusiastically announced that Qorei would remain atop the

P.A.'s cabinet. The journalists eventually dispersed as Arafat returned to his office, where he had been confined for many long months since Israel had declared him irrelevant and threatened his "removal."

Concurrently, Israeli forces increased external pressure on Arafat, wreaking havoc in the Occupied Territories. The Israeli government, on the other hand, continued incessantly with its attempts to re-mold the Palestinian political structure in a way that would undercut uncooperative figures and give rise to "moderate" ones. Inter-political disputes amongst the Palestinians, coupled with rising internal violence in the Gaza Strip and the West Bank produced among Israeli officials and media reverberations of delight. Finally, Israel had a powerful argument that would demonstrate through the Western media that Israel's early calls for Palestinian reforms—which were unquestioningly parroted by President Bush's administration—were well reasoned, and that under the current Palestinian leadership a "viable" Palestinian statehood could not possibly be attained. In short, Palestinians were not capable of ruling themselves.

To Israel however, there was more to this argument—now central to Israeli political discourse in light of the internal crisis in Gaza and the West Bank—that Palestinians were incapable of directing their own fate. Such a contention was often the prelude to a much more dangerous and elaborate political scheme, the latest of which was the most iniquitous. "It can well be said that never has the very existence of the Palestinians—both as a nation and as individuals—been in greater danger than now," Uri Avnery, an Israeli journalist and long-time peace activist rightfully noted.[16] The source of danger was not only the obviously aggressive policies of Sharon, but the almost complete lack of any consequential opposition to these policies anywhere. Additionally, the fact that American foreign policy in the Middle East continued to serve the interests of only one party, Israel, had granted Sharon free rein to pursue his ruthless policy with unilateral moves. But what Avnery really meant to emphasize, through his solemn warning, was the dispiriting strife within the ranks of the P.A.'s leading faction, Fatah. The Fatah power struggle had tragically manifested itself at an extremely critical time.

Bleak is too optimistic a word to describe the reality on the ground during those days: a series of giant walls, trenches, and fences were effectively breaking down the West Bank into miniature entities with little hope of any political or economic continuity; a huge investment in further illegal Jewish settlements in the West Bank took place; as did an extension of the inhumane policies Israel had pursued for years—assassinations, house demolitions, night raids, and roadblocks, to name just a few. The ongoing strife in the Occupied Territories, including both political dispute and militant disorder, helped distract attention from Israel's land grab and settlement expansion project. However, while Israel's role in inviting and exploiting the crises must be fully recognized, one should not completely discount the ominous role played by Palestinians themselves.

Palestinian factions who took it upon themselves to cleanse the P.A. of corruption in Gaza and elsewhere couldn't have possibly picked a worse time, since the world's attention was supposed to remain fixed on Israel's Separation Wall, deemed officially illegal by the I.C.J. verdict. Chances are these factions—some understandably fed up with the unmistakable corruption among Arafat's Fatah party—bought into the ruse that Sharon did in fact intend to "disengage" completely from Gaza. In reality, Sharon was determined to merely reconfigure the impoverished Gaza Strip to serve Israel's "security" interests while allowing for limited Palestinian control over the territories, inhabited by over a million people living a hapless life of utter poverty. While methods used by disfranchised Palestinians to bring attention to the problems of corruption and nepotism among the political elite reflected the level of urgency of the situation, an incident involving the kidnapping of foreign nationals (which took place in Gaza and lasted for several hours) was an unforgivable mistake—scapegoating those who dared to stand alone in the face of world apathy in support of Palestinians and their cause will taint the legacy of the Palestinian struggle for years to come. However, such desperate measures were both indicative and reflective of the grim situation on the ground. Palestinians were clearly thoroughly disillusioned and their historic level of tolerance would no longer suffice. Complaints of overriding militancy among pro-Arafat factions, accused of deviating from their supposed role as defenders of Palestinians against Israeli occupation, were now surfacing. The grievances of the past, of a judicial system that lacked both independence and integrity, of an authority that had grown to imitate a family business, not a responsible government were all forcing Palestinians to temporarily disregard Israel's ominous threat and demand major change and reform. As the situation in Gaza was engulfed with uncertainty, Arafat ordered yet another cosmetic touch, replacing Gaza's corrupt police chief with Mousa Arafat, the Palestinian leader's cousin, also accused of corruption and cruelty.[17] However, as the future would reveal, Arafat and the P.A.'s quandary was too profound and too entrenched for superficial repairs.

140 FUNERALS

As 2004 progressed, and as prospects for the future grew yet grimmer, Israel launched a devastating attack on Gaza that left 140 people—the vast majority civilians and many children—dead. Those who understand the depth of the tragedy—unhampered by the desensitizing Arabic media and its dehumanizing Western counterpart—may often wonder why such blatant state terrorism compels no serious response, especially from those who endlessly decry poor human rights records of countries far superior to Israel in their respect for international law and human rights treaties. "I understand the politics of it all," a friend wrote, as Israel announced its "redeployment" in northern Gaza, "but what really bothers me is the benign response of average people everywhere. How callous have we become?" As I see it, however, the casual callousness of humanity at large is not what is to blame here—after all, few can claim that they were not horror-stricken by the awesome terrorist strikes in New York and Washington D.C. on September 11, 2001, or the more recent school massacre in Beslan, Russia. What made these tragedies much more appalling than others was the media's eagerness

Photo 4.6   The mother of a Palestinian victim from the Balata refugee camp. Her son was shot and killed at the camp's cemetery while reading verses from the Qur'an by the grave of his friend, also killed by the Israelis, a year earlier. The mother said her son was first shot in the leg and as he tried to crawl away was killed by a bullet to the head.

to embrace the "official narratives," with their one-sided framing of any conflict, omitting the needed overall context, deeming it an undesired nuisance. The Arab–Israeli conflict is a case in point.

Let's briefly examine the period immediately preceding the current Palestinian uprising, which had now marked its fourth year. The Israeli narrative was, until recently, consistently adamant and it goes something like this: President Arafat orchestrated the Intifada all along; he had no intentions of reaching a final and comprehensive peace agreement with Israel, turning down a very generous offer presented by then Israeli Prime Minister, Ehud Barak, at Camp David in July 2000; Arafat was no partner of peace; no such partner among Palestinians exists. (This idea has been thoroughly addressed in chapter 1.) Palestinians too had their own narrative, but for them, it was too little, too late—the American government and media had already championed the Israeli narrative, with much more enthusiasm even than the Israelis themselves. Any Palestinian daring enough to show up for an interview with an American mainstream news program, to offer an alternative viewpoint, was bombarded with all kinds of accusatory questions: "Why did you waste such a golden chance for peace, why do you insist on violence? Why turn down Barak's generous offer?" and so forth. Despite my attempts to always stay calm and collected, I often reacted angrily to the endless finger-pointing myself.

But there is another dimension that should be equally considered: Sharon's unilateral Disengagement Plan, which was the outcome of the same "erroneous" premise. It reads: "Israel has come to the conclusion that, at present, there is no Palestinian partner with whom it is possible to make progress on a bilateral peace process."[18] Regrettably, the Middle East "Quartet"—the U.N., the E.U., Russia, and the U.S.—recognized the plan, and appreciatively. The U.S. was especially grateful to Israel for her painful concessions. But that too was a scam. Dov Weisglass, Israel's former chief of staff, and Sharon's closest personal advisor (according to the *Washington Post*), effectively diminished the entire discourse that accompanied Sharon's phony concessions. Weisglass told *Haaretz* that the Disengagement Plan was intended to "freeze" the Israeli–Palestinian peace process, to guarantee that 80 percent of the West Bank's illegal Jewish settlements would remain in place, and to eradicate any possibility of establishing an independent Palestinian state—all this with the knowledge and "blessing" of the United States government. "What I affectively agreed to with the Americans was that part of the settlements would not be dealt with at all, and the rest will not be dealt with until Palestinians turn into Finns," Weisglass revealed. The Disengagement Plan "supplied the amount of formaldehyde that is necessary so there will not be a political process with the Palestinians." He continued, in an unmistakably self-congratulating tone, "[as a result] you prevent the establishment of a Palestinian state, and you prevent a discussion on the refugees, the borders and Jerusalem."[19]

There were two immediate consequences: First, the Palestinian narrative—even if it was closest to the truth—held little weight in much of the Western, especially U.S., mainstream media. Only Israel's narrative—despite its repeated untruths—counted. Secondly, when Israeli officials themselves dismissed their own forgeries and wished to come clean, the U.S. media failed to see a need for a change of course, leaving fraud to write history, while being fully aware that some historic revision was needed. Meanwhile, in northern Gaza, 140 funerals were underway, hundreds of people were left disfigured or paralyzed, orchards of ancient olive trees were destroyed, and an entire nation was left in mourning including an unsurpassed mass of youth who would now take up arms. Israel said that it did what any civilized country would do to protect its citizens. President Bush strongly agreed. Palestinians say that what happened in northern Gaza was a "massacre" intended as a form of "collective punishment," and that Sharon never intended to completely leave Gaza, as he claimed, nor was he ever a "man of peace" as the U.S. held him to be. Two narratives, one truth, 140 funerals, and the rest is history.

ANATOMY OF OUTRAGE

One can only imagine the outrage of world leaders and media if a series of Palestinian bombings were to rock an Israeli town, and in less than four days kill 60 people and wound hundreds, mostly innocent civilians. Indeed with every passing and horrifying suicide bombing, we have seen this mobilization in full force. Not even the most open-minded of media pundits could dare justify the crime; not even the most lucid of government officials could rationalize the orgy of flesh and blood made of mangled bodies, some so beyond repair that you wish them death for their own sake. How repulsive and insensitive, if Fox News decided to inundate its helpless viewers with self-congratulating "terrorism experts" describing the "surgical procedure" followed by the Palestinian bombers whose intent was merely to target a few unidentified Israeli army officers accused of

Photo 4.7   Residents of Jurit al-Dahab neighborhood in Jenin emerge from the rubble of their homes after a deadly two-week Israeli assault that left scores dead and hundreds wounded. Several neighborhoods in the refugee camp were completely destroyed in April 2002.

threatening the life of Palestinian civilians. Picture the horror on the dusty faces of firefighters amassing in a small Tel Aviv street to quell an inferno of homes, shops, and roofless buses, while medics, too busy to tend to the blown up bodies, are frantically attempting to revive the surviving few. Who would dare step up in a moment like this and attempt to contextualize the massacre: "Palestinians were retaliating to Israel's use of air strikes that killed two Hamas militants a day earlier." And while Israelis are fighting their tears and mounting fury, fixing their eyes on a very bloody spectacle on their TV screens, they learn that the White House has refused to condemn the atrocity. Equally outrageous, isn't it? In turn, a State Department spokesperson agrees with the Hamas fighters' basic premise, but urges them to "take every measure to ensure that only proportional force is used to counter the threat that it faces."

To offset the inhumanity and callousness of America's officials, Israeli viewers switch to another channel, where U.N. Secretary General Kofi Annan's statement on the massacre is read. Yet Annan merely asks the bombers, who remain determined to blow up more Israelis, to do all they can to avoid civilian casualties, reminding them of the risks their acts may have on the "peace process." Even Israel's traditional friends in the West seem not to care. Instead, their media sounds overly sympathetic to Hamas' reasoning, lending airtime to its officials as they spread propaganda and disseminate further warning messages to hapless Israelis: "If you don't repent, there is more where this came from." In fact, Hamas inconsiderately chooses to name its Tel Aviv massacre, "Days of Penitence." Western media parrots the codename of Hamas' "operation" with unmistakable approval. And when two Israelis infiltrate the border into Gaza, in a shabby operation to distract Hamas' attention from the unfolding massacre, it ends up being a golden opportunity for media allies in the United States to justify Hamas' carnage in retrospect: "This is exactly the kind of Israeli threat that Hamas is trying to counter," some "state-terrorism expert" barks in a self-vindicating tone. To ensure that the average American does not question their moral standing on why they are blowing up Israelis, Palestinians deploy their apologists and lobbyists throughout Washington D.C., heaping yet more pressure on U.S. government officials who are eagerly complying. In fact, they compel the U.S. President himself to acknowledge "Hamas' right to defend itself." Rumors immediately circulate that the President defies his conscience often these days for fear of losing "Hamas money" in the coming election. Instead of immediately seeking to halt the Hamas aggression, the P.A. in fact decides to take advantage of the mayhem, approving a plan during one of its cabinet meetings to push Gaza's border nine miles deep into Israel to create a buffer zone. And what if the Hamas bombers and hundreds like them are never tried for war crimes and simply carry on with their lives and jobs without being held accountable, without being reprimanded, even if verbally? Indeed, what if they are now more qualified than ever to receive medals of honor for their "heroic" conduct in Tel Aviv?

None of this, of course, has occurred. But its exact antithesis has. In early October 2004, in a small refugee camp called Jabaliya, the mighty Israeli army perpetrated one of its worst war crimes during the Palestinian Uprising.[20] But just imagine if the picture was reversed. Would our humanity permit us to be equally outraged, to demand and expect justice? Yet, that is for you to worry about. As for me, I am a Palestinian; I grew up in the Gaza ghetto and need not reverse the picture to understand. Outrage is now part of my anatomy.

LOSING ARAFAT

As the Gazan refugees buried their dead and struggled to resume normalcy after their most recent loss in Jabaliya, Palestinians would be shocked and overcome with grief as they mourned the loss of one of their greatest icons of the decades-long struggle. If Yasser Arafat's illness, unexpected departure to France, and subsequent death on November 11, 2004, represented the end of an era, as some rashly suggested, it was because the absence of Arafat, even as a living symbol, was indeed a matter of great consequence. But that said, we must not indulge in misrepresenting the Palestinian struggle by reducing it to the legacy of one man. It is still too early to assess Arafat's contribution to the Palestinian march for freedom. It might take years before an accurate assessment is possible. To some, he was just another autocratic Arab ruler clinging to his position, refusing to share power or allocate responsibility to anyone but his cronies, and with nothing new to offer save the worn out rhetoric about a "light at the end of the tunnel" and the "mountain [that] cannot be shaken by the wind." But those who see only this side of Arafat ignore the heady political, cultural, and intellectual mix represented in his person, his ability to mean many different things to many different people. Arafat—whether deliberately or not—managed to associate himself with every hardship faced by Palestinians over the decades. From his early years as a student activist in Cairo, in 1949, to the momentous formation of the Fatah movement in 1965, Arafat was always present. For Arab leaders, despite his fall-outs with some on occasion, Arafat was a godsend. His presence justified their absence. It was Arafat who insisted on referring to the P.L.O. as the "legitimate and only" representative of the Palestinian people, and Arab regimes passionately embraced the slogan. This was an exoneration of their utter failure to defend the cause of Palestine and its people.

Palestinians, of course—even those who opposed his political line and unconditional peace offerings—saw Arafat in a different light. When a military helicopter hauled him out of his headquarters in Ramallah to a Paris hospital, ending a three-year-long Israeli siege, Palestinians silently observed Arafat's departure and connected it to the history of dispossession of which they had all been part. Palestinian commentators wrote about distant, yet unforgotten, history, relating Amman to Beirut to Tunis to Gaza to Ramallah, and finally to Paris. Arafat's legacy was one of undiluted symbolism—a symbolism at once substantial and meaningful. Throughout the years, he was the only Palestinian leader who truly succeeded in unifying the Palestinians in their struggle. Even if he acted as though his journey to France was like any other, Palestinians knew that this time was different. In 1982, under intense U.S. pressure and mediation, P.L.O. leaders and fighters were forced out of Lebanon, the then headquarters of the P.L.O. in exile. As Arafat left Beirut, the historic leader stood defiant and told his comrades that the path to Jerusalem was coming closer and that Lebanon was just another stop on their long journey back to the homeland. They believed him, and kept on fighting. The distance from Beirut to Tunis, their next interim destination, seemed to matter little. Arafat's presence lingered, not only among Lebanon's refugees but in the camps of Gaza.

As a child I often witnessed Israeli soldiers forcing young Palestinians to their knees in my refugee camp in Gaza, threatening to beat them if they did not spit upon a photo of Yasser Arafat. "Say Arafat is a jackass," the soldiers would scream. But no one would exchange his safety for insulting an image of Arafat. They would endure pain and injury, but would say nothing. It was not the character of Arafat that induced such resilience but what the man represented. This explains why Gazans stood enthralled as the legendary leader returned following the signing of Oslo. Retrospectively, it also explains the level of betrayal that many Palestinians felt when their icon, who in some ways had been deified in his exile, failed to live up to their expectations upon his return to the homeland. It felt as if Arafat's era was coming to a close following his return to Gaza in the mid 1990s. Such feelings were motivated neither by his old age or faltering health, nor by Israel's irrelevant designation of the man as a peace partner or otherwise. It was just that the man who promised the moon failed to save even a desolate refugee camp. The man who promised Jerusalem was in unending negotiations over the small neighborhood of Abu Deis. The astute leader who spoke of the peace of the brave had little to say as the Israeli military machine once more overran the West Bank. It was never easy for Arafat to maintain the image of warrior and bureaucrat. Israel wanted him to crack down on those who fought by him and for him. The United States wanted him to "condemn terrorism, not by words but by deeds." But it was armed resistance that had sustained Arafat's struggle for decades. Arab leaders pressured him, conveying the Israeli and American messages, completely sidelining themselves in what for decades had been the Arab cause. His cronies exploited him. His balancing act slipped and his aura slowly faded.

When Israel bombed Arafat's headquarters in Ramallah and imprisoned him—with the blessing of the U.S. government—it hardly intended to provide the aged leader with a platform to claim a heroic last stand. Israel's occupation of the West Bank and physical confinement of Arafat absolved him of political accountability before his people while reinvigorating his image as the warrior who never surrenders, even in defeat. Even as Fatah descended into power struggles and charges of corruption flared, Arafat remained immune. The head of Al-Aqsa Martyrs Brigades told me during a telephone interview just a few months before Arafat's passing: "[He] is our symbol and our leader and nothing will change that." When the Brigades burned down a P.A. building in Jenin protesting the P.A.'s corruption, its fighters salvaged a photo of Arafat from the ruins and protectively carried it away. Very few leaders can claim a legacy like Arafat's, or his ability to cater to such competing interests.

In the days that followed, Israel, the U.S., and Arab regimes would be scrambling to ensure that the post-Arafat era served them best. In the case of Arab governments, this period would have to absolve them from any meaningful responsibility toward Palestine and its people. But Palestinians are resilient. They would learn how to deal with life without Arafat and his mystique. Their national unity remains and it would strengthen their fight, even in grief. Warriors, sages, and leaders would come and go, some would stay for longer than others, but the march to freedom would certainly carry on.

MERCI

When the day of Arafat's passing finally came, Palestinians were overcome with two emotions—grief for their loss, and profound gratefulness for the dignified and regal way his life and passing was honored by his host country, France. By honoring President Yasser Arafat, France honored every Palestinian man, woman, and child. Even the French President, Jacques Chirac, may not have realized how deeply esteemed were his gestures toward President Arafat and his just cause. His endearing utterances strengthened the bond of friendship between France and Palestinians for years to come. Just before Arafat's body was transported to the airport for its final journey to Cairo then to Ramallah, Chirac insisted that political correctness should not stand in the way of moral uprightness: "I came to bow before President Yasser Arafat and pay him a final homage."[21] Draped in the Palestinian flag, President Arafat's body departed France in the presence of the country's Prime Minister, Jean-Pierre Raffarin. The solemn scene is reminiscent of Arafat's first official trip to the West— also to France, after the P.L.O. opened its offices in Paris in 1975.

Former French President, Valery Giscard d'Estaing, was one out of many who spoke with kindness about Arafat's legacy: "His complete life was mixed wholly with the Palestinian cause. My feelings are of sadness at the departure of someone who presented an idea, an inspiration." Indeed, it was Arafat-the-idea that most of us have and still mourn. He proved that it was still possible to speak of a "peace of the brave" when his nation was only expected to cave in to a humiliating defeat. He and his people defied the odds and proved that neither Diaspora nor slow genocide could render them "irrelevant" as Bush has repeatedly suggested. Thanks to the courage of France and its leadership, Arafat remained relevant to the end. This was neither the first nor the last bold stand to be taken by the French in support of the just cause of Palestine and just causes elsewhere. They clashed with the world's only superpower repeatedly, most memorably over the unwarranted invasion of Iraq in March 2003. Now, only a fool would argue that France's position on Iraq was not right all along. Yet what was overwhelmingly touching in France's token of friendship to the Palestinian people is that it came when much of the international community was absolving itself from its legal and moral responsibility. Even among Arab governments, there is a prevailing sense that the conflict is a political liability, thus

Photo 4.8 A helicopter carrying the body of Palestinian leader, Yasser Arafat, attempts to land in his Ramallah headquarters as thousands of Palestinians rush to receive his body before burial.

the Arab–Israeli struggle has quietly evolved into a struggle solely between the Palestinians and the Israelis.

As far as the Bush Administration was concerned, neither morality nor international legality was a factor in this conflict. Thanks to the political extremism of President Bush during his first term, a peace opportunity was squandered. The man who had the legitimacy and clout to reach an historic agreement with Israel on the basis of international law was to be confined to a battered office in Ramallah, surrounded by Israeli tanks amid Israeli threats to murder him. Bush lacked the courage to challenge the rogue act of the pariah state. In fact, he supported it, compromising thereby, the reputation of his country whose image would be tainted like never before. Even then, French officials refused to be intimidated or coerced. Arafat was the elected leader of his nation and they treated him as such, with the dignity and respect he deserved. Knowing all of that, Chirac's words were of little surprise: "France will continue to tirelessly act for peace and security in the Middle East and will do so with respect for the rights of the Palestinian and Israeli people." At that moment, every Palestinian, especially refugees longing to return, felt the warm embrace of France and its people. It proved that, after all, the spirit of revolution that France helped define many generations ago has prevailed over the rhetoric of hate and mindless wars. Beside his resting place in Ramallah, Palestinians raised the French flag, a simple and profound expression of their gratitude.

ANOTHER YEAR

The passing of Arafat also marked the passing of the fourth year of the Second Palestinian Uprising. It has always been an old habit of mine to sign off messages in the days preceding the New Year by expressing: "I pray that the coming year will bring peace and justice to our troubled world." Despite disappointing experiences, I persist in this, because hope is essential. It is like air and water. At first glance, the events in Palestine seemed to signify only hopelessness and despair. An Israeli wall continued to swallow the remains of the state Palestinians hoped to embrace. The livelihood of Palestinian farmers was squandered with every new and mammoth section of the wall, which Israel was erecting on their land. The numbers of Palestinian casualties, especially children, were breaking new records every day. Yet one would read in the American media that it was all the fault of the victim and that Israel longed for peace. The problem, we were told, lay in Palestinian political culture; thus only democracy and transparent semi-presidential elections would bring peace and an end to the conflict. To fulfill this vision, Palestinians were expected to elect a semi-president or a shadowy political body that had neither the legitimacy nor the territorial sovereignty to carry out the will of the people. Although it defied all logic, we were expected to believe that democracy under military occupation was possible. What is more, this was to be a splendid opportunity for peace. But with every uprooted tree, there was a farmer holding tightly to its roots; with every inch of confiscated land, there was an old man kneeling to the ground, sticking his fingers deep into the soil and refusing to part; with every fallen child, there was another child coloring a flag. Just when Sharon hoped that his policies had forever silenced every call for peace and reconciliation, Arabs, Jews, and volunteers from all over the globe—like Rachel Corrie, Tom Hurndall, and Caoimhe Butterly—flocked to Palestine, shielding school children with their bare chests, defying curfews, and chanting for peace and justice. Some lived to tell the story, while others didn't.

Because of this and more, I am hopeful. I am hopeful because the rules of the game are changing. Onslaughts that were designed to ravish and destroy a land and its people were in fact creating unity and igniting an awakening among the forces of good all over the world. The corporate media's attempt to dictate the discourse was increasingly challenged by our desire to confront the lies of the spin-doctors, the warmongers, and the like. With the violations of women's rights, children's rights, and labor rights, there was an equally robust desire to restore them. Is it not enough that when Venezuelans restored their elected popular President, Hugo Chávez, to power, after the failed attempt to sabotage the country's democracy, many raised Palestinian flags when celebrating his return? Is it not enough that during the funeral of President Yasser Arafat, flags representing countries all over the world waver in solidarity beside the hundreds of Palestinian flags? True, there was an abundance of reasons that would justify our sense of anguish and fear as we cast our eyes toward 2005, but there was certainly ample hope to carry us through the turmoil and trial of another year.

5
End of the Intifada? (2005)

There has been no official announcement of the end of the second Intifada. However, following the death of Arafat, presidential and municipal elections are held with partial or full participation of Palestinian factions that have long opposed the political structures and processes introduced by Oslo. The level and intensity of both popular resistance and armed struggle declines and there are increasing talks of a third Intifada. Hamas and other Palestinian factions agree to a one-sided ceasefire with Mahmoud Abbas in Cairo, in anticipation of several new rounds of Palestinian elections and of the promised Israeli "Disengagement." However, in spite of concessions made and measures taken by Palestinians, Israeli and U.S. officials are resolute in their accusations that Palestinians are solely responsible for the unrest and that they are no partners in peace. Internal Palestinian politics take on a new intensity following speculation of a face-off between opposing Palestinian factions over the post-Disengagement status of Gaza, once Israeli forces deploy out of the Gaza Strip while maintaining control over border crossings, airspace, and water. The Gaza airport and seaport stand in ruins, and safe-passage routes between Gaza and the West Bank, as promised in the Oslo agreements, are yet to become a lasting reality. Palestinians are left debating the benefits of five years of costly struggle, and how much closer they are to attaining their national aspirations—which

Photo 5.1 The separation wall encircles the Qalandia refugee camp, thus further cutting off Occupied East Jerusalem from the rest of the West Bank.

can only be secured with a complete and unequivocal end to the Israeli occupation. The Intifada faces a painful impasse, leaving wide-open many possibilities for a multi-dimensional political row, and perhaps another violent showdown.

POLITICAL ALTERNATIVES

Talks about national unity among various Palestinian factions, and about the "opportunity" that might emerge following the sudden death of Yasser Arafat, all faded into uncertainty. What remained was the most predictable, albeit consequential, outcome of the upcoming presidential elections scheduled for January. Islamic movements Hamas and the Islamic Jihad, along with the socialist Popular Front for the Liberation of Palestine (P.F.L.P.), were undoubtedly interested in reconciling their differences with the mainstream Fatah movement that dominated the Palestinian Authority, and thus, the Palestinian political scene. They remained firm on finding a formula that would allow them to translate their popular support into political influence. Under the circumstances, compromise was nothing short of necessity.

But for these factions, the dilemma was very intricate. Nominating a candidate to run for "office"—so to speak—would have suggested that Hamas, among others in the Palestinian opposition, had finally come to terms with the premise upon which the political process was founded. A casual rejection of the Oslo Accords would no longer suffice if a candidate representing Hamas ran for an office that would have not existed if it weren't for Oslo. This, in part, explains why Hamas was more inclined to concentrate on the parliamentary and municipal elections, which were scheduled for a later date. By winning a substantial vote, Hamas would achieve its goal of demonstrating its popular influence in the Occupied Territories, without setting itself up as a politically, rather than morally or religiously, motivated party. Winning the presidency without a parliamentary majority would certainly result in an internal and external political deadlock between a lone Hamas President and a disgruntled Fatah Parliament, not to mention an international community that would not dare go near the ill-reputed Hamas leadership.

Hamas was out of the picture for a while, joined by less influential Palestinian factions. Moreover, Marwan Barghouti, who had twice nominated himself for the contested position, once again withdrew his nomination, after giving a double scare to the traditional Fatah leadership who knew too well that the charismatic young man could have easily won the presidency from his prison cell. Remaining was Mahmoud Abbas, the P.L.O.'s new boss and the favored candidate of the status quo party at the P.A., who also received unreserved support from both Israel and the United States. Even before his almost certain victory, Abbas insisted on providing a model of the P.A.'s political line under his leadership. His categorical condemnation of armed resistance against the Israeli military occupation was by no means an indication of his leaning toward non-violent struggle. The man was neither a visionary nor did he have any meaningful alternative to armed resistance. Moreover, Abbas made unqualified apologies "to Kuwait and the Kuwaiti people for what we did," referring to the P.L.O.'s siding with Iraq during the 1991 Iraq war.[1] While the P.L.O.'s position was clear before and during the war—that no foreign troops should be allowed to get involved in an affair that must be resolved internally—the P.L.O. should have kept its distance considering the fact that ordinary Palestinians have often been the scapegoat in such conflicts. The liberation of Kuwait brought a great deal of misery to tens of thousands of Palestinians whose human rights seemed the least of Abbas' concerns.

The Bush Administration, despite its refusal to conform to the foreign policy doctrines of past administrations, understood the psychological importance of the rhetoric of democracy, and insisted on associating itself with democracy charades around the world: in Afghanistan, in Iraq, and now in the Occupied Territories. It urged Israel to do all it could to help the newborn Palestinian democratic experience. Israel obliged, vowing to evacuate its troops from major Palestinian population centers for 72 hours during the elections, with a subtle promise to return to occupation as usual. Although this scenario was closer to travesty than democracy, the show must go on—so long as the mainstream media in the United States could report with unending gratitude that Israel had performed a great deed in aiding the first genuine democratic experience in the Arab world. Meanwhile, in order to guarantee a sweeping win for Abbas, Israel resorted to its usual tactic of intimidating other candidates who dared to challenge the man who seemed more interested in Israel's security than the security and rights of his own people.

Dr. Mustafa Barghouthi, the main candidate running against Abbas in the presidential elections, was one who dared to challenge the status quo. An eloquent and dedicated physician and activist, Dr. Barghouthi was beaten by Israeli soldiers at a checkpoint during a campaign trip. He was "choked with his own necktie, and left with wounds on his hands, foot and nose."[2] It was neither the first, and it would not be the last time that this courageous activist would be bruised by Israeli occupation troops. Dr. Barghouthi was categorized as neither old guard nor a compromiser. He was never part of a corruption scandal. The free medical services provided by an organization that he established reached tens of thousands of the poorest Palestinians, in villages that Abbas hardly knew existed. Not only did Dr. Barghouthi believe in democracy and national unity, but also he was also one of the most influential founders and leaders in the democratic opposition movement, Al-Mubadara, jointly established with the late Professor Edward Said and the respected Dr. Haider Abdul Shafi. The clarity in this man's political vision, respect for human rights, and insistence on national unity was certainly a prerequisite to any successful Palestinian struggle. Unfortunately, these were not the qualities that seemed to be of essence when it came to Election Day.

KEYS TO PEACE

In the early part of 2005, preparations for the Palestinian presidential elections were underway. But the atmosphere created by the elections was nothing but a charade, and, sadly, this was nothing new. Throughout the years, any hope for peace between Palestinians and Israelis had been based on a faulty premise: That Palestinians must show serious interest in peace before Israel could be expected to reciprocate. Even the Road Map, which many Palestinian officials lauded, was no exception. The Road Map was the handiwork of pro-Israeli elements in the U.S. Administration. It failed to rebuke Israel, even slightly, for its disproportionate violence against the Palestinian people. The underlying premise was always the same: that only by reining in Palestinian terrorism could Israel and the P.A. achieve common ground for a lasting peace. The problem began and ended with the Palestinians. Israel could only be urged to display patience, restraint and symbolic gestures of good will. Predictably, the P.A. responded with a big unconditional "yes," so that Palestinians would not be viewed once again as the obstacle on the road to peace. Israel hesitated, deliberated, and finally agreed on conditions that disfigured the face of the already unsightly agreement. But the Israeli "response" was at once celebrated as a victory for peace and symptomatic of Israel's ever-compromising nature.

Photo 5.2   Children in Bethlehem hold a large key in the midst of a protest. The key symbolizes the Right of Return for all Palestinian refugees.

Of course, the Road Map was neither the first nor the last of these historical dramas. The path to peace in the Middle East was swamped with staged shows totally divorced from reality. The overstated value of Palestinian elections fully conformed to these past experiences. According to the implied rhetoric of various Western commentators, only by altering their backward political culture and fully committing to the everlasting principles of democracy could Palestinians achieve peace with Israel; only by being at peace with themselves could Palestinians be at peace with Israel; only by shunning the anti-democratic elements in their midst could Palestinians be a worthy peace partner with the "only democracy" in the Middle East. And once again, Israel was asked to do nothing in return, save take some mythical steps of reciprocity and "confidence-building" measures devoid of any real political value.

Israel carried on with its abrasive and bloody policies even during the election campaign. It repeatedly arrested Palestinian candidates, beating them on camera. One candidate was shown on TV being jerked by his necktie, and having his arm twisted in a painful way by some thuggish-looking Israeli soldiers. Dr. Barghouthi was arrested on more than one occasion during the brief campaign; he was beaten and harassed repeatedly. But we were supposed to treat all of this as irrelevant to the moment, and simply reflect on the golden opportunity facing Palestinians who had finally seen the light of democracy, even if it was under the chains of a tank or a soldier's boot. And, as was to be expected, the candidate who was hailed by the U.S. and Israel, Abbas, was victorious. This was, of course, the furthest possible scenario from genuine democracy. What was happening in Palestine was nothing but a construct, an illusion, which only indicated that Palestinians and their deficient political culture were in need of serious revamping, while Israel could only be expected to exercise restraint. But restraint never meant a freeze on settlements, or an end to land-confiscation, house demolitions, tree-toppling, or a mini-massacre every now and then. There was nothing new about this routine. It was old as the conflict itself.

WESTERN DEMOCRACY

What was touted as an American-supported Palestinian democratic experience only highlighted—outside the realm of mainstream media interpretation—a level of mistrust and resentment that most Arabs have harbored toward the United States and its policies, not only in Palestine, but throughout the Middle East. Just a few weeks later, a poll was carried out by the Arabic website of Al-Jazeera satellite television, which found that more than 80 percent of respondents distrusted "Western democracy." The results simply restated the obvious. The survey, of course, hardly meant to question "Western democracy" in its own right, but rather its imposition on the Arab world. Needless to say, one needs no poll, scientific or otherwise, to conclude that the majority of Arabs were in desperate need of democratic measures. But they needed democracy for their own sake, not for the sake of one who wished to legitimize an occupation and to tout the virtues of a superpower. If Al-Jazeera tested its readers' views on democracy itself, as a political model without the word "Western" accompanying it, the overwhelming votes would probably have been cast in favor of democracy—that honorable value first coined by the ancient Greeks as "citizen-rule."

Iraq experienced an admittedly impressive turnout in elections in the end of January 2005. The Western spin suggested that the high turnout was a vote of satisfaction for the post-Saddam Hussein era. The prevailing discourse dominating the Arab media however, continued to suggest that the Iraq experiment was a make-believe democracy that still had little to do with rule of the citizenry. Arab peoples covet democracy because they are disenfranchised and have very little control over their individual or collective destiny. But most Arabs find it difficult to make a choice between the governance of theocratic and totalitarian regimes on the one hand, and a spurious, foreign-imposed democracy which they perceive as a U.S. invention on the other. The choice would be difficult for anyone, and it is anything but fair. Despite President Bush's constant exhortations that he too wished to set the Arab masses free, his words resonated nowhere in the Middle East, save perhaps Israel. For ordinary Arab peoples, Bush was simply a hypocrite; for the politically savvy, his mission of "freedom" was a disguise for his corporate drive for power. Most Arabs saw the paradox of Western democracy in practice, in the West and in their own region. In fact, they lived the paradox. If you find yourself engaged in a conversation with an Arab you'd be surprised to learn of a deep admiration for Western democracy—in the West. You'll hear fantastic, often exaggerated stories, of the freedom enjoyed by Western societies, freedoms that not many Arab countries can match—not by a long shot. But the wheel of Western democracy either grinds to a halt or completely changes course once it reaches the Middle East; the values, style, and goals become different, even though much of the rhetoric remains the same. So Arabs are very suspicious of "Western democracy" vis-à-vis their own region.

Democracy is "a form of government under which the power to alter the structure of government and laws lies, ultimately, with the citizenry," one definition reads.[3] It is "a government by the people in which the supreme power is vested in the people and exercised directly by them or by their elected agents under a free electoral system," states another, quoted on the U.S. Department of State website.[4] Abraham Lincoln's famous phrase that democracy is a government "of the people, by the people, and for the people" further stresses the point. As U.S. actions in the past half-century have demonstrated, the "people" of the Middle East have hardly been the ultimate recipients of "Western democracy," as understood by most Arabs. The differences between Arafat and his successor Abbas, as mentioned earlier, offer an illustration. Arafat was elected by a decisive majority in the P.A. elections in 1996. Though he lived and died popular among his people, he was undercut and deemed "irrelevant" for embracing a political line incongruous with the American and Israeli agenda. Abbas, on the other hand, held a fraction of Arafat's popular support and won a less impressive victory in the P.A. elections. But he championed a political line that was acceptable to both Israel and the U.S. Thus, his victory became the standard that defined what was right and proper, and what was not.

This is hardly the first case of such double standards. There was the C.I.A.'s toppling of one of the first genuine democracies in the Middle East in 1953—the overthrow of Iranian Prime Minister, Mohammed Mossadegh, and the installation of the pro-U.S. dictatorship of Shah Mohammed Reza Pahlavi.[5] Since then, the U.S. has lent support to the most oppressive regimes as loyal guards of American interests in the region. The high turnout in Iraq's elections would now be spun to mean approval of continued U.S. presence there. That was a spin on a kind of democracy that Arabs opposed. It was not democracy itself that they distrusted. It was the cynical exploitation of the term for imperial or geo-strategic purposes that they refused. And it is this refusal that the citizens of the U.S. must understand. But if one depends on the U.S. media to convey the message, it's going to be a long wait.

PROBLEM OF THE MEDIA

Thus, Western media misrepresentation obviously presents another major dilemma that deserves to be duly noted. Considering the almost insurmountable problem with the presentation of the Arab world in the Western media in general, and in the U.S. media in particular, what can be done to combat the inherent bias? Despite the perpetual need to address the issue, nothing of value has been realized on this front, particularly after the terrorist attacks of September 11, with the awesome intellectual, social, and cultural backlash unleashed thereafter on the Arab world. Many of the attempts to bridge the gap between East and West have been crude at best. These endeavors have facilitated the emergence of two classes of Arab intellectuals and media voices. One group has been "uncompromising." It has refused to acknowledge that a Western audience has an entirely different frame of reference and thus cannot understand an Arab or Muslim argument that simply conforms to what is accepted and what is not in an Arab society. The other group has simply endeavored to blend in or assimilate to the existing surroundings. Intellectuals of this type have conveyed to the media exactly what they wanted to hear. They preferred to draw the audience's applause, rather than endure its taunts and heckling. Needless to say, both groups have failed miserably. This is not to suggest that a common ground is far-fetched or that an eloquent as well as courageous third voice lies outside the realm of possibility. For decades, Israeli and pro-Israeli officials, academics and the like have been swarming American news networks, talk-radio programs, and the opinion pages of American newspapers, large and small. But if one is to scrutinize their approach, one will find an almost complete deviation from the issue at hand, scarcely revealing that their ultimate allegiance is to Israel. They come across as very much American. Thus, they justify the killing of Palestinians in Rafah by comparing this with America's need to uproot terrorism in Afghanistan, and explain the suffocating closure of the Occupied Territories by referring to the U.S. army's occasional move to seal Iraqi borders in the face of "infiltrators." Listening to an Israeli media expert talking to Fox News about democracy, liberty, freedom, and so on, it might slip your mind that the real goal of this expert-impostor is to justify the denial of democracy, liberty, and freedom to someone else.

I cannot think of more superior conmen than these Israeli and pro-Israeli "experts" in the field of media packaging. Of course, Israel invests substantial sums of money in media training, and in the construction and operation of media centers in Israel, the United States, and elsewhere. In short, Israel understands the impact of the media in the world, and takes the business very seriously. Arabs don't. Most Arab countries are nowhere close to Israel's impressive media triumphs. Part of the obstacle is the incessant corruption that plagues most Arab institutions. In any given Arab country, chances are that the authorities in the fields of media and international relations are chosen for reasons based on anything but experience, wisdom, and competence. Family affiliations play an important part, as well as allegiance to the ruling party or close ties to men in charge. Thus, it is typical that Arab media experts lack fluency, persuasiveness, and are "just too important" to submit to the notion of instruction or training of any sort.

One must not mistake this critique as a justification for the Western media's deliberate bias. The reproachful tone used on C.N.N. or Fox News to interrogate an Arab guest can hardly be discounted. It is this approach—accusatory and indicting—that drove the late Professor Edward Said to distance himself from mainstream media altogether. But acknowledging this bias should not be a justification for the ineptitude and ineffectiveness of the Arab voice in Western media. The issue of bias must be raised continually as a part of the ongoing debate on media ethics and fairness, not as a justification for shying away from the media challenge. It should be of no surprise that

Arab governments employ American P.R. firms, with a total lack of knowledge regarding Arab affairs, to revamp their image before Western audiences. The dilemma is that most Arab countries lack the resources to engage in this important undertaking. Real potential resides in collective action. Countries such as Qatar, U.A.E., and Saudi Arabia possess the financial and material resources to sponsor serious media initiatives, making use of the remarkable wealth of brilliant Arab minds brimming all over the world. This is not a matter of policy, far from it. It is a cultural imperative, a response to the media pundits who justify the hard-line foreign policy of the Bush Administration and sell the idea of wars and Abu Ghraib-like torture chambers being essential for American freedom, security, and democracy.

OSLO REINCARNATE

In the early part of 2005, and shortly after Abbas' election victory, the media went to work again, backing up the U.S. Administration's plan as it worked on another front to facilitate a Palestinian surrender to the Israelis, this time under the disguise of peace talks on the lovely Egyptian coast. While the Sharm el-Sheikh summit in Egypt on February 8, 2005, was supposedly a great success according to Western media, it was anything but a triumph as far as Palestinians, the occupied party, and genuine peace-seeking Israelis were concerned. Leave out the spectacular view of the Red Sea resort, the impressively meticulous Egyptian hospitality, the heart-rending speeches, and the touting of the media thereafter, and you'll have an off-putting view of the upcoming weeks and months: relative calm followed by the typically disproportionate violence the region has known for years. But before we cast judgment on the summit's initial outcome—as either laying the ground for a lasting peace or as merely introducing an interval of calm before the resumption of war—we are obliged to examine further the historic context of the present Palestinian uprising. Only then can one begin to offer an informed and critical analysis.

Israeli governments have mastered the technique of pushing Palestinians to the brink, through collective punishment, brutal military policies, house-destruction, and so on. However, the implicit objective of Israeli policy has not been exclusively aimed at subduing Palestinians. Its ultimate aim has been the expropriation of Palestinian land in the Occupied Territories of the 1967 borders. Being pushed to the brink, Palestinians resisted, violently and otherwise. Their resistance occasionally produced a campaign of collective action, mostly spontaneous, though often galvanized by local political movements to articulate a well-defined program. Both Palestinian uprisings in 1987 and 2000 articulated a message that largely reflected the political aspirations of most Palestinians toward the creation of a truly sovereign Palestinian state in all territories illegally occupied by Israel in 1967, including Occupied East Jerusalem. One must also remember that even in the most radicalized and revolutionary phases of their modern history, Palestinians demanded barely 22 percent of the total size of historic Palestine as it was defined prior to the creation of Israel.

These demands frustrated Israel, who continued to make false and outlandish claims throughout the Western media to the effect that the lightly armed Palestinian uprisings (the 1987 Intifada's most common weapon was a slingshot used to hurl rocks at Israeli attack-helicopters) posed a threat to the very existence of the state of Israel. One can hardly claim that Israel's position remained static over the years. But it would be harder to argue that Israel's changes of position were anything but cosmetic, symbolic, and rhetorical. Without a doubt, we've come a long way since the days when the overriding consensus in Israel was that the Palestinians as a nation should be eradicated by any means necessary. Also long gone are the days when top Israeli officials labored to omit the historical truth that a people called the Palestinians even existed. Nonetheless, the reality on the ground still reflected the same beliefs as were held by past Israeli governments and realized in their policies. For example, despite the frequent utilization of the term "peace" by Israeli officials—on both sides of the political spectrum, and especially after the signing of the Oslo Accords in 1993—there was an intensive Israeli campaign to drive Palestinians out of their land, to expand the settlements, to expropriate large chunks of the West Bank as "security zones," and to further alienate and completely fence off Occupied East Jerusalem. According to the records of Israel's Peace Now movement, the number of illegal settlers in the Occupied West Bank has doubled since the signing of the "historic" Oslo agreement in 1993.[6] Israel never changed its ultimate objective. We know this because Israel's illegal practices on the ground continued unabated. Granting Palestinians long-denied rights and cohesive territorial sovereignty, and honoring international law, were never on the Israeli agenda. Most likely these issues will continue to be disregarded until the political imbalances (read, the U.S. government's dishonest role in the conflict) are rectified. Then, why bother talking peace to begin with?

Israel had long reverted from its past policies of mass expulsion. Such stunts simply generated too much bad publicity. They embarrassed devoted benefactors in Washington and helped Palestinians garner international attention, significantly slowing down Israel's expansionist designs in the region. The 1993 Oslo Accords were thus intended to serve the particular purpose of removing the Palestinian–Israeli file from the critical list of international conflicts, while buffing up Israel's tainted reputation—and giving rise to a corrupt and self-consumed Palestinian leadership—under the banner of "fighting terror." And while Palestinian negotiators were pitifully lost in an awesome edifice of detailed proposals—containing thousands of pages of legal rhetoric describing in unfathomable language every trivial "deployment" Israeli tanks were to carry out—Israeli bulldozers were digging out the West Bank to erect new Jewish settlements. In 2000, the first year of the Second Palestinian Uprising, two major factors once again hampered the Israeli blueprint. First, Yasser Arafat departed from the role with which he had been entrusted and unexpectedly, yet decidedly, refused to sign off all Palestinian rights. Second, the Palestinian masses—the dual victim of Israeli occupation and of the utterly corrupt P.A. elite—rose in rebellion. Israel's Prime Minister, Ariel Sharon, proved merciless in his response to both.

Arafat's death on November 11, 2004, had indeed "revived hope," so the media parroted. The "hope" extracted from the death of frail Arafat, however, was the hope of returning to the Oslo legacy and returning to the status quo that had defined the Palestinian–Israeli conflict for years. This yielded nothing—save a few symbolic gestures—for the Palestinians. On the other hand, it won extra time for Israel's unilateral expansionist project. Thus, welcome to Sharm el-Sheikh—another Oslo but with an Arabian scent and flavor. The Palestinian political elite would rule once more, reclaiming their rightful position in society, while the vulgar Philistines would be pushed back to the gutter where they would forever remain. Israeli bulldozers would carry on with the construction of the mammoth, illegal wall, and illegal settlements would "naturally expand." Israeli troops would "re-deploy," but snipers would maintain their positions at tall buildings adjacent to every Palestinian town, village, and refugee camp. Diplomatic life would be restored between Israel and its immediate neighbors—and maybe a few others—and Sharon would be King of Israel, for only he triumphed in war and in peace.

The Sharm el-Sheikh summit was a "success" because it kowtowed to the expectations of Israel and its American benefactor. It fell short of making any serious effort to bring a peace settlement in accordance with the principles of justice, as entrenched in international law and a long list of relevant United Nations resolutions. It demanded that Palestinians, who have no army of their own, overcome their violent tendencies, and expected this long-victimized nation to provide Israel, a nuclear power with an army ranked among the world's most powerful, with the security it "rightfully needs and deserves." Not once was the term "occupation" mentioned throughout the whole conference, noted the *Independent*'s Robert Fisk.[7] Not once. Sharm el-Sheikh failed to address the major grievances that have defined the Palestinian national struggle for generations: an end to occupation, the right of return, and the removal of the settlements, among others. The summit was almost exclusively reserved for talks about Israel's security: since when was it acceptable for an occupying power to demand security from its captives? The summit was a failure, rife with all the symptoms of Oslo, with which, no doubt, it will share the same fate. But by the time such a failure could be recognized, Israel's imperial project—the wall and the settlements, and the calculated annexation of most of the West Bank—would become accepted as "facts on the ground." Perhaps by now, P.A. President Abbas, the co-author of Oslo, would understand the consequences of his self-defeating pragmatism. But by now, would it even matter?

UNEQUIVOCAL POLICY

Some months after the botched summit, President Bush declared that the removal of illegal Jewish settlements from the Occupied West Bank was "unrealistic."[8] There were no conspiracies to dissect, no hidden agendas to sort through, and no oblique idioms to decode: the Bush Administration's position on illegal Jewish settlements in the Occupied Territories was crystal clear. Bush did all of us a great favor when he once more articulated his stance on the settlements during a joint press conference with Sharon on April 11, 2005. Bush's talk of the "new realities on the ground" referred to none other than the already existing settlements in the West Bank that were erected following the 1967 war and the subsequent Israeli occupation. The settlements violate international law as dictated in numerous U.N. resolutions, and their dismantlement is demanded. It was no secret that the billions of dollars spent to build and sustain them had been provided in large part by successive U.S. governments, Republican as well as Democrat. The huge sum of money given by the United States to aid this systematic violation of international and human rights law continued unabated.

However, those who struggled to fathom the American role in Israel's grand project of populating the biblical land of Judea and Samaria could no longer claim confusion regarding this topic. The U.S. President found it "unrealistic," to dismantle the large Jewish-only population centers in the West Bank and Occupied East Jerusalem. This acknowledgment rendered much of the anticipated peace talks irrelevant, for it sidelined international law, invalidated the U.S. claim to being an honest broker in the so-called peace process, and unequivocally declared support for the Israeli position on the matter. The Israeli position was also clear and required no ingenious inter-pretations. "It is the Israeli position that the major Israeli population centers [illegal Jewish settlements] will remain in Israel's hands under any future status agreement, with all related consequences," Sharon helped clarify further.[9] Both Bush and Sharon simply restated their positions, which were one and the same, save a few minor details. One of these concerned the expansion of existing settlements.

Israel had been busy connecting the numerous Jewish settlements by Jewish-only bypass roads, which compelled the creation of new

Photo 5.3   The Israeli Separation Wall completely surrounds Occupied East Jerusalem, regarded as the capital of the future Palestinian state.

security zones in the West Bank that were quickly incorporated into the ever-growing original colonial infrastructure. The location of the settlements was selected on strategic grounds. They were mostly built within reasonable proximity of the 1967 border, to ensure territorial contiguity with Israel while contributing to further territorial disintegration in the Palestinian territories. They seized the most fertile of Palestinian land and water reserves. And with the introduction of the encroaching Separation Wall, the plan was near completion. The wall was a de facto annexation of Palestinian land. It cut off entire communities from their farms and livelihood outside their ever-shrinking population centers. It locked in whole towns and villages like Qalqilya, and it presented tens of thousands of Palestinians with two most difficult options—either indefinite imprisonment or "voluntary" transfer.

Another trial that Palestinian farmers faced was obtaining permits from the Israelis to farm their own lands. If no permit was granted, no access was granted, and if the land was not harvested for a period of three years, it could become the property of the state of Israel.[10] But the project would never complete without the absorption of the entire city of Jerusalem, including Occupied East Jerusalem; hence the expansion of the largest illegal Jewish settlement of Maale Adumim. Once an additional 3500 units were completed, Occupied East Jerusalem would be entirely disengaged from the rest of the West Bank, rendering Palestinian demands for a capital in Occupied East Jerusalem equally "unrealistic," according to Bush's logic.

Those who would occasionally play up the rift between Israeli and American positions on the settlements need not look beyond the outcome of the vote at the Geneva-based U.N. Commission on Human Rights (U.N.C.H.R.). On April 14, 2005, the world's foremost human rights body passed a resolution, condemning Israel's illegal expansion of its settlements in the Occupied Territories. The resolution was widely approved, with the exception of two countries, one of which was the United States. U.S. Ambassador, Rudy Boschwitz, argued that the resolution was both "imbalanced and unjust."[11] While again there was nothing shocking about the U.S. position in the U.N.C.H.R. or any other international body critical of Israel, it confirmed that no meaningful change had occurred or could have been expected to occur in the Bush Administration regarding the issue of settlements. Furthermore, the U.S. Administration's clarity on other primary issues could hardly be doubted. Bush reiterated time and again that demanding a right of return for the Palestinian refugees was equally "unrealistic."[12] While this clarity by no means exonerated the U.S. Administration's reprehensible, imbalanced, and self-defeating stance regarding the perpetual Middle East conflict, it demanded a complete reversal in the P.A.'s unconditional surrender to and trust in Washington's pro-Israel policies. President Abbas and his circle of supposedly pragmatic and moderate officials seemed to completely ignore Bush's anti-Palestinian rights position, reducing the Palestinian struggle to a mere quest for foreign aid. It would only be a matter of time before the temporarily fatigued Palestinians rebelled once more against Israeli oppression, American complacency, and the P.A.'s subservient response to both. As long as the above equation carried on with its values unaltered, the region would remain hostage to instability, violence, and extremism.

RECORD NOT REASSURING

But for the moment, though only briefly, Palestinians were pacified— the precise intention of the pseudo-summits and peace talks that had taken place over the past twelve years. The main fallacy of these so-called Israeli–Palestinian peace talks was the complete omission or the indefinite postponement of fundamental Palestinian demands— demands sustained and cemented by international law, and most recently by the July 2004 ruling of the International Court of Justice. The problem lay in the Israeli occupation of Arab lands, Palestinian and others. It invited a legacy of violence and counter-violence that claimed the lives of thousands of Palestinians and Israelis. It systematically and intentionally destroyed any chance for peace. It insisted on punishing the victim for the sins of the aggressor. Undoubtedly, throughout this ordeal Palestinians were victims, and their rights, security, and welfare should have been the priority of the international community. Israel had no right to demand security from its victims; it lost that right the moment it breached international law when its tanks rolled onto Palestinian land.

Unfortunately, however, it was as if the opposite were true. This dreadful habit of blaming the victim also defined U.S. foreign policy and media discourse for years: If Palestinians would only unify their security forces, clamp down on terrorism, reform their political institutions, cease incitement, put down their weapons, and become more democratic—only then could they become worthy peace partners. But even then, Israel was under no obligation to do much, since, democratic or otherwise, the mere existence of

Palestinians was problematic. This is not an exaggeration. The fact that the birth rate among Palestinians was higher than that of Israelis was termed a "demographic bomb," a problem in the eyes of Israel to be countered by any means necessary, including the fencing off and the caging of Palestinian towns and villages to keep the unwanted multitudes of people out of Israel's domain, while retaining Palestinian land. Israel's real motives behind the impetus in the peace process were anything but a secret, and thus must not be seen as a Palestinian construct. While Israel was commended for its courage and "painful compromises" in deciding to "disengage" from Gaza, Israeli officials spoke openly of Israel's dishonest objectives of wanting to partially withdraw from Gaza to simply strengthen its grip on the West Bank.[13]

Strangely enough, this repugnant Israeli ruse was translated (thanks to Israel's friends in the media and in the U.S. Administration) into an Israeli gesture of good will. As revolting as the Israeli government's intentions were, they supposedly placed the ball in the Palestinian court. Palestinians were now expected to reciprocate, having been offered only an illusion deprived of any substance or value. A just peace was indeed possible, but not according to the current standards, which the P.A. sadly accepted. If the two-state solution was to work, Israel was under obligation to dismantle all of its settlements in East Jerusalem, the West Bank, and Gaza and to withdraw to the June 1967 borders in accordance with U.N. resolutions 242 and 338. Palestinian refugees would have to be given the choice to return to their land in accordance with U.N. Resolution 194. The Israeli wall would have to come down in accordance with the ruling of the International Court of Justice of July 2004. Israel would also have to accept its responsibility for Palestinian dispossession and suffering over the last five decades. The international community would be obliged to do all it could to ensure the implementation of the laws that it drafted. Palestinians, on the other hand, would have to continue to create alliances among peace forces around the world, including Israel itself, and under no circumstance could they forfeit their right to defend themselves. Shortly before his untimely death, Professor Edward Said wrote in Egypt's *Al-Ahram Weekly*: "So far all we hear is that Palestinians must give up violence and condemn terror. Is nothing substantive ever demanded of Israel? Can it go on doing what it has without a thought for the consequences? That is the real question of its existence: Whether it can exist as a state like all others, or must always be above the constraints and duties of all other states in the world today. The record is not reassuring."[14]

HORNS OF A DILEMMA

Palestinians were pressed to single-handedly deliver peace and security to the Israelis, while Israel was hardly encouraged to reciprocate; and the newly elected Abbas was not doing much to address these challenges. Among the Palestinian masses, many were questioning his legitimacy as well as his ability to lead the Palestinian people effectively. To the uncritical eye, Abbas looked like an ordinary statesman presiding over an equally ordinary political reality. Nothing could be further from the truth.

As I disinterestedly watched Abbas accompany Russian President Vladimir Putin during the latter's "historic" visit to the West Bank on April 29, 2005, I was struck by a disconcerting notion: no matter what path of politics Abbas would choose, his efforts were doomed. Unlike Arafat, Abbas lacked legitimacy. Legitimacy here is defined according to the prevailing definition employed by successive Palestinian generations throughout their revolt: a leader whose past record proves beyond a shadow of a doubt his adherence to the constants of the Palestinian struggle. Abbas hardly met this standard. Worse, since the eruption of the second Palestinian Uprising in September 2000, Abbas and a small clique of individuals within the ranks of the P.A. have been utterly forthright in their objection to it. Their doubts created disunity and threatened to transform the theoretical clash into a physical one. That possibility cannot be dismissed even today. Left to fight and die alone for nearly five years, the Palestinian people were browbeaten and fatigued. While this realization can hardly be interpreted as the end of the Palestinian struggle as we know it, it does serve as the context that delineates the relationship between Abbas and his Palestinian constituency. Palestinians were not fond of Abbas; they simply saw him as the last resort and, frankly, as a dignified way out, even if temporarily.

According to a study conducted by U.S.-based writer Jennifer Loewenstein, by the end of 2004, in Gaza alone, 28,483 Palestinians had been made homeless as a result of Israel's wholesale destruction of Palestinian dwellings throughout the Gaza Strip.[15] Considering the extreme poverty residing in this tiny stretch of land already, and coupled with all the other oppressive Israeli military practices which wrought untold death and devastation, one can begin to understand why the arrival of Abbas, as unpromising and compromising as he may seem, constituted an ironic opportunity of some sort. But without overriding legitimacy, Abbas' mandate as far as the Palestinians were concerned was quite limited. The man had the reputation of being too flexible on issues that should not be subject to bargaining; the right of return of Palestinian refugees being one. His dilemma hardly ended there. On the contrary, it barely begins. The urgent yet difficult question to answer is: how could Abbas adhere to Palestinian expectations of, among others, full sovereignty over the West Bank, Gaza, and East Jerusalem, the right of return for Palestinian refugees, and the removal of Israeli settlements down to the last one, at a time when the peace scenario envisaged by the U.S. and Israel eradicated these demands altogether? In fact, the Palestinian prerequisite for a just and lasting peace seemed to be the complete antithesis of the Israeli—and thus the U.S.— interpretation. Sharon and the Bush Administration were insistent in their disregard for the principal cause of the conflict—as defined by international law; namely, the illegal Israeli occupation and confiscation of Palestinian land. For Sharon, the occupation was a non-issue, for according to his perverse reasoning, Palestinians were in fact the intruders on the biblically promised land of Israel. If he wished to evacuate a few settlements from Gaza, the motivations would be decidedly strategic, and have more to do with demographics than moral imperatives. For Bush, on the other hand, it was all about Israel's security, and how his continuous support for Israel would ensure the patronage of the Israeli lobby, Congress, and the mainstream media.

Abbas understood that his days as a statesman would last as long as Sharon had no convincing reason to render him "irrelevant"— as he did with Arafat—or take him out of the political equation altogether—as he did to hundreds of assassinated Palestinian activists and leaders. And as long as Abbas agreed with Washington's view on the disarming and dismantling of resistance as a top priority, he would remain a welcomed friend on the White House lawn. Otherwise, Arafat's bombed-out basement office in Ramallah would have to suffice. Abbas also understood that regional alliances were of no great value, at least as far as breaking Washington and Israel's dominance over the entire political equation was concerned. Arab neighbors were either completely helpless or eagerly awaiting to normalize relations with Israel with or without a just end to the conflict. The Arab failure was of course symptomatic and consistent. Abbas was clearly aware of his dilemmas; thus his overly enthusiastic response to Putin's Ramallah visit. The Russian President was hoping to break away from the blunders in Ukraine and Kyrgyzstan by reviving his country's once influential role in the Middle East. The *Globe and Mail* was already predicting a "rebirth of the Cold War," as a result of the Russian venture, a war that the U.S. would do its utmost to avert, but one that Russia lacked both the means and the will to fight.

The coming months would only exacerbate Abbas' problems. Israel had allowed him no victory, however merely symbolic, to lay claim to, and was not expected to do so. Poverty in Gaza and elsewhere in the West Bank would grow due to increasing unemployment, as any progress in the Palestinian economy remained exclusively an Israeli decision. The popularity of the Islamic movements, such as Hamas and Islamic Jihad, would continue to rise and translate into electoral successes, parallel to the incessant demands from Israel and the U.S. to crush those same parties. It would only be a matter of time before Abbas would decide to end his balancing act and confront his problems head on. But would he choose to lock horns with fellow Palestinians to prolong his illusionary reign in power, or would he decide to face up to Israel's disregard for justified Palestinian demands and the blind U.S. support of Sharon's anti-peace policies? Abbas' dilemma was most arduous. And to make his task even more challenging, municipal elections, which later followed, proved Hamas to be an ever-growing force among ordinary Palestinians.

HAMAS' RISE

Hamas' electoral success since the first round of local elections in Gaza in December 2004 signaled a dramatic shift in the way the movement was perceived both nationally and internationally. The defining moment was not Hamas' direct participation in the three rounds of local elections, but the passing of Arafat in November of the same year. Arafat's death convincingly shifted the political pendulum in favor of Hamas. Arafat's unanticipated absence brought to the surface an array of conflicts within his own party, Fatah. This internal strife manifested itself in open power struggles between the movement's traditional, elitist leadership—labeled the old guard—and the younger generation. Fatah, in the past a force for unity among Palestinians, had become a focus for political and social volatility, rendering reforms within the party not just desirable but imperative. One cannot overstress the importance Fatah's structural and organizational mayhem had in fortifying Hamas' repute among ordinary Palestinians, who voted in large numbers in favor of Hamas candidates in successive municipal elections. Hamas was now in control of over one-third of the Occupied Territories' municipal seats, including most of the major cities. Since its formal inception in the late 1980s, and even earlier, Hamas had garnered support among Palestinians through its active involvement in relief work and educational projects, but also, most notably, through its violent and often deadly responses to Israeli military policies.

All of this made the Israeli government's demands that Abbas "dismantle" Hamas closer to wishful thinking. Hamas was no longer a few fiery young men circulating a badly inscribed flier, but a united and growing political force whose consent in any future political settlement would be a necessity. Abbas made the right choice when he decided to "engage" Hamas. The P.A. President succeeded in deferring a further Hamas response to Israeli military provocations in the Occupied Territories, in the hope that Israel would not falter on its commitment to "disengage" from Gaza. Hamas' commitment to the ceasefire contributed to the movement's reputation as a credible political player that enjoyed unequaled discipline. As always, the strong showing of Islamic factions at polling stations ignited dilemmas for democracy advocates, mostly in the West. European Union member-states were the first to wrangle with the quandary of dealing with formally blacklisted elected officials, after having proscribed the military and political wings of Hamas in 2003.

Although the E.U. had yet to declare an official turnaround on Hamas, British Foreign Secretary, Jack Straw, admitted to journalists that British diplomats had met with officials representing Hamas' political wing on two separate occasions.[16] In fact, a meeting between Hamas officials and E.U. diplomats, in the Occupied Territories and abroad, took place "every 10 days to two weeks," according to a senior member of the Islamic movement, Mohammed Ghazal.[17] The timing of these meetings indeed surpassed the realm of mere technicality. The fact that the U.S. government had not harshly repudiated Europe's intent to engage Hamas could be understood either as tacit support of these contacts, or as an incapacity to provide an alternative to Europe's diplomacy, aimed as it was at accommodating and eventually pacifying Hamas' rising political power. Israeli officials were reported to have been "fuming" over these contacts. "We believe Europeans should be strengthening moderate Palestinians and not appeasing the extremists," Israeli Foreign Ministry spokesman, Mark

Roger, said. "Anything that demonstrates acceptance of Hamas as a legitimate player is a problem."[18]

This Israeli response was to be expected if Israel was to maintain the belief that it could ignore Hamas' rising political importance. However, the Israeli position looks less clear when one considers announcements made by the Israeli army's "Civil Administration" in the West Bank that "it has no problem with contacts between its own officials and Hamas members elected as mayors and other ranking local officials," according to the *Independent* and, later, the Israeli *Jerusalem Post*.[19] It must also be said that the growing recognition of Hamas as a political force that must be engaged with rather than boycotted posed a dilemma for the Hamas movement itself. Fully aware of the double standards according to which the West had long perceived the Palestinian–Israeli conflict, Hamas had to realize that advocating and executing suicide bombings—even as a response to Israeli targeting of Palestinian civilians—was likely to stamp out any possibility of political legitimization. The contacts between Hamas and European diplomats would likely continue and perhaps evolve into higher-level exchanges as long as all the parties concerned—including Israel and the P.A.—would benefit from such "engagement." Both Israel's proposed "disengagement" from Gaza, scheduled for August 2005, and the Palestinian parliamentary elections, were two important factors that would likely influence the direction and magnitude of the exchanges. Yet the central factor that would likely decide the character and attitude of Hamas was Israel's own political attitude and military policy in the post-Gaza phase. Continued Israeli domination of the West Bank, expansion of illegal settlements, and insistence on completing the Israeli Separation Wall built illegally on Palestinian land, were good enough reasons for Hamas to preserve its militant posture toward Israel.

NUCLEAR PUZZLE

Several months after the revelation of regular meetings with Hamas and European officials, the spotlight was taken off the controversial movement and was once again focused on Israel—as a result of an exposé broadcast on the B.B.C. The B.B.C. program, *Newsnight*, broadcast on August 3, confirmed that Britain was in fact the original source of heavy water, the crucial ingredient that allowed Israel to transform its generic nuclear reactor in Dimona in the Negev Desert, initially developed with French help, into a proficient nuclear manufacturing plant.[20] It was always assumed, following the dramatic disclosures made by former Dimona technician, Mordechai Vanunu, to the *Sunday Times* in 1986, that the 20 tonnes of heavy water had originated from Norway. Norway opted for complete silence on the nature of the deal. But according to the B.B.C., the well-guarded deal made with Israel had been concealed as a resale to Norway of a heavy-water consignment that was of no use to Britain. The shipment was dispatched in 1958 to Israel, who within three years had apparently exhausted most of the 20 tonnes of heavy water. In 1961, according to the report, Israel asked for more, but the uncovering of Israel's nuclear ambitions by the *Daily Express* seemed to have made any additional sales a more complicated matter.

Many years later, thanks to the audacity of Vanunu, the world was able to grasp the extent of Israel's perilous experimentations with deadly agents—they now possessed hundreds of nuclear warheads (by modest estimates), which, according to Western experts, made Israel one of the world's leading nuclear powers (number six to be exact). But Israel persisted in neither confirming nor denying the increasingly well-documented charges of its nuclear program. Thus, Israeli Vice Prime Minister, Shimon Peres—who was the director general of Israel's defense ministry from 1953–58 and was seen as the leading architect of the country's nuclear program—refused to comment on the B.B.C. report, according to the Associated Press a day later.[21]

The acknowledged involvement of France and Norway, and Britain's recently exposed role in making Israel's nuclear aspirations possible, clearly demonstrated a European intent on ensuring Israel's unique military superiority over its Arab neighbors—which, incidentally, was a key phrase reiterated by top American officials when describing the U.S. commitment to Israel. While at the time, the U.S. Administrations of Eisenhower and Kennedy tried "to stop Israel from going on to build nuclear weapons," as reported in the *Guardian*,[22] the right-wing Bush Administration completely disregarded the Israeli nuclear build-up while considering "all options," including military intervention, to crack down on Iran for allegedly endeavoring to develop a nuclear bomb. Iran, a signatory of the Nuclear Non-Proliferation Treaty, insisted that its nuclear ambitions were peaceful and worked on several diplomatic fronts to resolve its problems with the U.N.'s International Atomic Energy Agency. Meanwhile, Israel had yet to join the N.P.T. community, and was under no pressure to do so. Israel's superior stance continued despite the call made by the I.A.E.A. chief, Mohamed ElBaradei, to surrender its nuclear weapons and to sign the non-proliferation treaty. Israel's attitude was reinforced by unconditional military and political support from Washington. The mockery became almost unbearable when U.S. officials tied their Middle East crusade to Israel's security. In a January 2005 interview with M.S.N.B.C.'s *Imus in the Morning*, Vice President Dick Cheney warned that Iran has a "fairly robust" nuclear program and charging that the Islamic Republic's prime objective is the destruction of Israel. He then appeared to be giving a green light to Israel (with an estimated 200 nuclear heads) to take on Iran, whose nuclear ambitions, according to the I.A.E.A. itself, are yet to raise serious suspicions. "If, in fact, the Israelis became convinced the Iranians had significant capabilities, the Israelis might well decide to act first, and let the rest of the world worry about cleaning up the diplomatic mess afterwards," Cheney claimed, in response to *Imus's* heedless inquiry: "Why don't we make Israel do it?"[23]

Only the naive would argue that perhaps Cheney was not aware of the magnitude of Israel's destructive nuclear capabilities when he made such remarks. Yet, despite the near complete fraudulence of the many pretexts used to invade Iraq, victimizing millions of people while further destabilizing an already unstable region, the U.S. government carried on unhindered with the same logic. Now the menacing wolf was Iran and the harmless sheep was unsurprisingly the state of Israel. However, the last piece of the puzzle had been recovered, now that the international community knew where Israel's heavy water, used for enriching nuclear fuel, originated from and—thanks to Vanunu—what became of it. Even the often weak-willed ElBaradei had the nerve to tell *Haaretz* that his agency was operating under the assumption that Israel possessed nuclear weapons.[24] The concern, and indeed the fear, was that neither the B.B.C.'s report nor the outcry of many states in the Middle East and beyond would jeopardize or halt for a second the grinding wheel of death and destruction nurtured in Israel, with European help, American blessings and protection. It was in fact this duplicity and these double standards under which the West continued to operate that made peace in the Middle East an illusion, as the furnace of weapons of mass destruction continued to burn in the Negev Desert.

DISENGAGEMENT

Concurrently, in the Occupied Territories there was little argument that the Second Palestinian Uprising had reached an impasse, despite the fact that the causes which led to it remained in place. This is not to deny the looming prospect of an awakening in the revolt, nor does it undermine the unbroken will of the Palestinian people to carry on with their resistance by any channel available. However, unfolding events in the Occupied Territories, headed by Ariel Sharon's declared intentions of "disengaging" from the Gaza Strip, with a first phase scheduled for August, shifted internal Palestinian focus, if only temporarily, from confronting the Israeli occupation to taming the looming chaos in Gaza and to settling factional and political grievances. As far as the Israeli Disengagement was concerned, Sharon's real motives were starkly clear. In a noteworthy policy speech delivered on June 30, 2005, Sharon, while taking on settlers opposing the Disengagement from Gaza, clarified once again that the conditional move was motivated purely by demographics. This was certainly a clear insinuation that Sharon's actions were hardly motivated by the recommendations of the U.S.-led quartet on Middle East peace, the provisions of the U.S. forged Road Map, or relevant international law regarding unconditional withdrawal from the Occupied Territories. "We concluded that we are going to leave Gaza, where there is no chance of establishing a Jewish majority," he said in Cesaria, Israel. "It is clear to everyone that Gaza will never be part of Israel in any final agreement. At the same time, we are turning our resources to the most important areas, which we need to safeguard for our existence: the Galilee, the Negev, Greater Jerusalem, the settlement blocs, and security areas."[25]

Sharon once more demonstrated that he was anything but a changed man. His words and actions were the single required testimony. In fact, one might argue that his commitment to the illegal settlement project, which had been so dedicatedly pursed over the years, was approaching its apex: caging in Palestinians in the whole Occupied Territories, effectively annexing 58 percent of the total size of the West Bank, expanding the borders of "Greater Jerusalem" to include major "settlements blocs"—Maale Adumim, Betar, Ariel, Gush Etzion, and others, working diligently to offset Palestinian population growth by dispatching thousands of Jewish settlers to the West Bank, expropriating a large percentage of Palestinian land by extending the illegal Separation Wall which already snaked its way around scores of Palestinian towns and villages, incarcerating tens of thousands of Palestinians behind walls, fences, trenches, and locked gates. This was what the Israeli Prime Minister had to offer Palestinians in response to their unilateral ceasefire begun in February

Photo 5.4 As the world's media covered the evacuation of Jewish settlers from the Gaza Strip, little was said about the expanding settlements in the West Bank. The illegal Jewish settlement of Maale Adumim is the home of tens of thousands of Jews living on confiscated Palestinian lands. Most of the settlement's houses are vacant, yet giant cranes can be seen at all times constructing new homes.

2005, and to Abbas, whose foremost priority seemed to be proving to Washington and Tel Aviv, that he, unlike Arafat, was a worthy and "relevant" peace partner. Meanwhile, audiences worldwide watched with shock and amazement Israel's overpublicized clashes between Jewish settlers and soldiers. "Israeli vs. Israeli in Gaza," read a *Christian Science Monitor* headline.[26] Media all around the world did their best to diminish the ingrained conception that Sharon's commitment to the illegal settlements was total. If the man who earned the title "Bulldozer" for destroying so many homes in Gaza during the 1970s was willing to take on his extremist and most loyal constituency for the sake of peace, then, so many must have concluded, he must have been genuinely earnest in his efforts to bring the conflict to a halt. But there is more to "Arik's horror show" in Gaza, wrote veteran Israeli journalist and peace activist, Uri Avnery, following a noisy clash between settler youth and Israeli troops on June 29, 2005. He asked: "why were the riots not put down everywhere," as was the case in the Gaza sideshow, which was well attended and covered by the media? "There is no escaping the simple conclusion. It is in [Sharon's] interests that TV screens in Israel and all over the world show the scenes of the terrible riots. That's how he sows in the heads of the viewers the natural question, 'If the evacuation of a few small settlements causes such a huge uproar—how can one even dream of removing the big settlements in the West Bank?'"[27] Moreover, if the transfer of Gaza's settlers to the West Bank (estimated at 1700 families) would needlessly cost the Israeli government hundreds of thousands of dollars per family, then how would the Israeli public ever back the removal of hundreds of thousands of illegal settlers infesting the Occupied West Bank? Sharon indeed calculated well, creating enough political, ideological, technical, and financial hindrances that placed a serious Israeli settler evacuation from the West Bank in the realm of impossibility. And of course, if the settlers remained, then the army would have to stay put in order to provide protection, more walls would be erected, more Jewish-only bypass roads would be carved throughout the West Bank, thus more land would be confiscated and many more Palestinians would be forced to leave to make way for new residents.

On the political front, the Disengagement served a great purpose and compels one to recall remarks made by Sharon's lawyer and most trusted advisor, Dov Weisglass, not long ago, when he told *Haaretz* of Sharon's political motivation for the Disengagement policy. He revealed that "The 'disengagement' would actually supply the amount of formaldehyde necessary so there would not be a political process with the Palestinians."[28] And indeed, there was no political process and none should have been expected. Highly touted meetings like that between Sharon and Abbas in Jerusalem on June 21 were simply used by the Israeli premier as a way to pacify any censure for neglecting the peace process in favor of his unilateral moves across the Occupied Territories. The meeting was just another opportunity for Palestinians to be duly reprimanded for not doing enough to curb violence and uproot the "terrorist infrastructure" and so on. And while Sharon's plan was being realized to the last point, Palestinians were haunted by a long legacy of corruption and nepotism, which was as old as the P.A. itself. Left alone to battle Israeli tanks and army helicopters, the Palestinian masses were also undeniably weary and in need of a ray of hope, however faint it might be. And sadly, it was highly unlikely that such a ray would arrive from neighboring Arab countries, some being very eager to embrace political and economic normalization with Israel, and unreservedly at that. Egypt, for one, agreed to supply Israel with cheap gas in a lucrative deal signed on June 30, estimated at $2.5 billion. It was still unclear why Israel should be rewarded with cheap Arab gas while it continued to subjugate millions of Palestinian Arabs to untold misery.

Only Palestinian resistance was capable of defusing Sharon's dangerous plan, whose blueprint was repugnantly highlighted in his infamous speech on March 5, 2002.

It won't be possible to reach an agreement with them before the Palestinians are hit hard. If they aren't badly beaten, there won't be any negotiations. Only after they are beaten will we be able to conduct talks. I want an agreement, but first they have to be beaten so they get the thought out of their minds that they can impose an agreement on Israel that Israel does not want.[29]

If history was of any use at all, Sharon might have realized how horribly mistaken he was following every act of carnage against Palestinians. After all, it was a Palestinian who once wrote, "like the trees we die standing," a phrase that has been ingrained in the Palestinian psyche for generations and was demonstrated in heroic resilience throughout the Occupied Territories, echoing from Jenin to Hebron to Rafah to Gaza, on every street and in every corner. But neither Sharon nor most of Israel's decision makers seemed to be proficient students of history. They would be damned to repeat the same mistake again, and with every unlearned lesson squander an untold number of lives and countless opportunities for a genuine, just, and lasting peace.

Alas, it was rather peculiar how the P.A. opted to support the Disengagement process that was aimed solely at excluding it, and peculiar how the debate completely shifted from Israel's real motives to internal Palestinian quarrels over post-withdrawal details and definitions. When Sharon announced his plans to "disengage" from Gaza and a tiny West Bank enclave, he pressed the notion that his unilateral move was principally compelled by the fact that Palestinians were no partners in peace. They never were, his right-wing officials parroted—a reality, they claimed, that most likely will not change in the near future. Thus "Disengagement," for the sake of Israel's security, boils down to demographic supremacy, not Palestinian rights. The Israeli narrative was always clear, albeit iniquitous. "Israel was leaving Gaza in order to retain large chunks of the West Bank," as the *Jerusalem Post* summarized the declared positions of Israel's top officials. This idea was originally initiated by the ever-blunt Weisglass last year, then by Israel's top military strategist, Defense Minister, Shaul Mofaz, and, according to the *Post*, by Sharon himself.[30]

Those unfamiliar with the situation on the ground held their breath for the supposedly ground-shaking Disengagement. Those familiar with Israel's military and political maneuvers however, must have understood. Sharon was once again toying with land, politics, and demographics, yet the same sorry ending awaited Palestinians: the lock, the key, the prison guard and the ever familiar scene of Palestinians being held captive at checkpoints. True, the settlements were more or less the core issue. Removing 21 settlements from Gaza, four from the West Bank and evacuating over 8000 Jewish settlers was a good thing, it was assumed. But blindly accepting that conclusion risked forfeiting a very valuable lesson that should have been taken from the botched Oslo experiment: Israel is very keen on details. The odd part is that the Israeli government labored little to give false impressions regarding the real meaning of its deployment of its army and settlers. Israel did not wish to hide the fact that it would retain control over the borders of Gaza, its land, its air, and its water. Equally there were no real efforts made to hide the fact that Israel maintained the right to strike the impoverished and utterly crowded Gaza Strip at the time of its choosing or that it wished to have total control over anything or anybody that entered or exited the area. Gaza's "open-air prison" status, in place since the Israeli occupation in 1967, would hardly be affected. Nonetheless, much would be gained. For one, Israel could comfortably subtract Gaza's 1.5 million inhabitants from its demographic nightmare, maintaining, for a while longer perhaps, the Jewish majority. The move would also end Israel's futile military quest to subdue a strategically inconsequential enclave, thereby escaping the unfavorable international attention given to its occupation of Gaza, reducing the demoralization of its armed forces, and avoiding further loss of life as a result of Palestinian attacks on its fortified yet still unsecured settlements in Gaza. So while journalists and commentators debated the fate of the rubble of the Jewish settlements following the limited Israeli withdrawal, and whether extremist organizations would claim control over Gaza or if Abbas had what it takes to "rein in the militants," a more relevant debate was almost completely cast aside: Would Israel become less of an occupier after a few thousand settlers were relocated to a less vulnerable spot with their pockets full of cash?

It is critical to recall that Sharon's Disengagement was Israel's response to Bush's Road Map, which was hypothetically approved by both Israel and the P.A. in June 2003. As "painful" as the Disengagement was, it was perhaps Sharon's only way out of being bogged down by any kind of mutual commitment (although trivial considering the pitiable Road Map text), by deadlines, by reciprocity, and ultimately by a dynamic political peace process. "Never again," was what the disengagement from Gaza really meant. Never again would Israel be scolded for not carrying out its part, for not fulfilling a scheduled deployment; never again would Israel's actions be pondered, and judged by a U.N. official, by an E.U. diplomat, or even by the Americans themselves. Israel would do as Israel saw fit. That was the bottom line. Israel's accountability was waived and replaced by the Hamas bogyman, ready to strike and strangle Palestinian secularists—the men for not wearing beards and the women for not covering their hair. The fact that Israel intended to maintain "security control" over Gaza and the evacuated parts of the West Bank would change nothing, apparently. Meanwhile, the Israeli Separation Wall carried on consuming West Bank land, snaking in to include the illegal settlements, disfiguring the topography, the demographics, everything. As far as Occupied East Jerusalem was concerned, effectively it was no longer a part of any Palestinian territorial continuity.

It is unfortunate that Palestinians dignified the Israeli move by willingly "cooperating" over the post-Disengagement fate of Gaza, rather than drawing international attention to the foreseeable reality in the Occupied Territories. It's troubling, to say the least, that the fear of a Hamas takeover has in some ironic way unified Israeli and P.A. concerns. Palestinian official, Saeb Erekat, told foreign journalists in Jerusalem of a visit he paid to Sharon upon the latter's announcement of the proposed "Road Map," according to U.P.I. correspondent Joshua Brilliant on August 11: "I want to be your partner in this," Erekat appealed to Sharon. "Please. Weigh the consequences of what you call unilateral steps. We don't want Palestinian extremists to stand up in Gaza and say this [withdrawal from Gaza] is the result of suicide bombers and Qassam [rocket attacks]."[31]

What Erekat had seemingly forgotten is that the legacy of blood espoused by successive Israeli governments in Gaza should have been a greater, more urgent concern than the fear of an inflated Palestinian interpretation regarding driving the Israeli military out of the wretched enclave. What has also been conveniently omitted by the official Palestinian account is that had it not been for the Palestinian people's steadfastness and acts of resistance and sacrifice since the first hours of the Israeli occupation some 38 years ago, Israel would have never for a moment have pondered leaving the cheap, yet scenic and marvelous Gaza settlement resorts. Who cared if Palestinians marched in victory and inscribed the names of fallen fighters on the decaying walls of Gaza, celebrating their sacrifices and courage? Was it the fear that the popularity of Hamas might win it a few extra seats in the upcoming elections? Was it because the P.A. could claim no credit, not for its persistence nor for its political achievements?

In the final analysis, regardless of what Israel aimed to achieve by disengaging from Gaza, a process that started at the end of August 2005, and regardless of how Palestinians wished to interpret such a move, the Gaza Strip was still an occupied land, constituting a very small fraction of the overall size of the Occupied Territories of 1967. Gaza's fight for freedom was still intrinsically linked to the Palestinians' suffering and struggle in the West Bank and in Jerusalem, and in the fight of millions of Palestinian refugees demanding recognition of their right to return. So, while the Disengagement successfully drew the attention of international media and created quite a stir within internal Israeli and Palestinian politics, it was posed to change very little on the ground. Only within the framework of a complete military withdrawal from Gaza and the rest of the Occupied Territories, in accordance with international law and based on mutual agreements by both parties, would a real solution evolve. Other than that, it was politics as usual.

BREAKING AWAY

Ongoing talks in the post-Disengagement period were centered on the issue of control over border crossings, the airport, and the seaport. Both Egypt and Jordan were actively involved in facilitating those talks. While Palestinians wished to break away from Israel's control over their economy, as has been the case for decades, Israel was adamant in maintaining this skewed relationship. It is not an overstatement to suggest that this issue lay at the heart of Palestinian national aspirations and of the surge of hope that followed the Israeli withdrawal. In fact, the issue of freedom of movement, access, and an end to the long-imposed Israeli dominion over the Palestinian economy, goes back to the very early stages of the peace process.

Among the many contentious issues that had consumed Palestinian–Israeli talks since the ceremonial signing of the Declaration of Principles between Israeli and P.L.O. leaders on September 13, 1993, was the issue of freedom of movement for Palestinians, within and outside the Occupied Territories. Predictably, this matter was critical as far as Palestinians—who have continually been confined by Israeli military restrictions, checkpoints, and complete control over border crossings—were concerned. The physical confinement of the Palestinian population goes back decades, most markedly to June 1967. While the catastrophic outcome of the 1967 war brought about the least desirable situation for Palestinians generally, Israeli restrictions on freedom of movement were most visible at border crossings in Gaza and the West Bank, chiefly those bordering Egypt and Jordan respectively. The economic and social impacts of this new arrangement were devastating to say the least. For one, a substantial portion of the underdeveloped Palestinian economy was wholly reliant on neighboring entities. Both Egypt and Jordan were used as starting points for Palestinian professionals seeking jobs in many oil-rich Arab Gulf states. Much of the income generated by tens of thousands of Palestinians abroad found its way back to the economically stagnant Occupied Territories, thus helping struggling families cope with poverty and the near total absence of a meaningful economic infrastructure.

The Israeli takeover of Palestinian borders, thus restricting freedom of movement, resulted in the serious interruption of the flow of labor abroad and for long changed the legal status of those professionals who had departed the Occupied Territories prior to June 1967—from being residents of the Occupied Territories to being permanently exiled. Palestinians confined to the Occupied Territories, and subjected to the subsequent suffocating economic reality therein, found themselves turning to Israel for financial relief. The relatively vibrant Israeli economy with its constant need for manual labor was the only respite Palestinians could find, as tens of thousands of them were quickly transferred to become Israel's cheap-labor force. Lacking any other viable option, Palestinian laborers working under harsh and often inhuman conditions were meagerly compensated and were denied any sort of benefits, such as insurance, whether for injury, death, a pension, or anything else. Predictably, the arrangement was of most benefit to Israeli companies, for their business costs drastically decreased and profits rose sharply. For Palestinians, this relationship signaled the commencement of an historic period of severe economic dependency, which for decades made Palestinian economic growth subject to Israeli decisions. The Israeli army's recurrent closures of the Occupied Territories, which were justified as a "security measure" and often extended for weeks to months on end, rendered great swaths of Palestinian laborers unemployed. In the poorest areas in the Gaza Strip, such closures often amounted to humanitarian crises and were often employed by the Israeli military as a form of collective punishment and as a tool of political pressure.

It is against this backdrop that ordinary Palestinians welcomed the signing of the Oslo Accords in 1993. While the Oslo agreement was most ambiguous on the Palestinian national aspiration to complete sovereignty and statehood, it was still perceived as an opportunity to shake off the choking economic reliance on Israel, to establish freedom of movement within and without the Occupied Territories, and to free up the economy. It was also assumed that Palestinians would soon take control over their own border crossings, those between the West Bank and Jordan and between Gaza and Egypt. Moreover, Palestinian officials spoke at length of a Palestinian-manned seaport, an airport, and a safe passage to link the West Bank and Gaza, promised under the provisions of Oslo to be implemented at later stages. The fate, scope, and implementation of the Gaza seaport, airport, and safe passage projects were all directly linked, and were symptomatic of the peace process itself, with all its fallouts and shortcomings. The Wye River Memorandum, signed on October 23, 1998 under American auspices, was an attempt to reinvigorate and implement outstanding commitments made under past treaties—particularly that of 1995, known as Oslo II. The Wye River Memorandum promised the opening of the Gaza airport and safe passage.[32]

The then American President, Bill Clinton, and P.A. President, Yasser Arafat, finally opened the Palestinian airport on November 27, 1998. At a cost of $75 million, most Palestinians celebrated their airport as a symbol of sovereignty and nationhood. However, they hoped that the airport would surpass its mere symbolic status and become a first step toward the attainment of their long-sought economic independence. Though the active airport bore Palestinian signs and symbols, it operated under strict Israeli control, with Israeli personnel, less visible to the Palestinian public, making the final determination of who should be granted or barred entry. Palestinians quickly discovered that their emblem of sovereignty was yet another false start. Less than two years later, following the eruption of the Second Palestinian Uprising of September 2000, the Gaza airport was shut down by the Israeli army who at gunpoint ordered the airport's nearly 450 staff to evacuate. In the early months of 2001, in another strong message to the P.A., Israeli tanks and bulldozers completely destroyed the airport's runway and control tower. Following the Israeli unilateral "Disengagement" from Gaza, in August and September 2005, the P.A., under the presidency of Abbas, sought to rebuild the airport (at an estimated cost of $26 million). Israel, while in principle agreeing to the Palestinian demand, expected to retain control over the facility due to "security concerns," expecting to revert to the old arrangement instituted during the airport's short-lived operational phase.[33]

In September 1999, the Sharm el-Sheikh Agreement (also referred to as Wye Plus Agreement) had stipulated the need to open a Gaza seaport for exclusive Palestinian use. "The Israeli side agrees that the Palestinian side shall commence construction works in and related to the Gaza seaport on October 1, 1999," the agreement in part read.[34] The construction of the port did not begin until July 2000, only to be halted by Israel in October of the same year. Frequent Israeli raids on Gaza, and Israel's refusal to facilitate construction, sent the project back to its starting point. The terms according to which the Knesset voted in favor of "disengaging" from Gaza required Israel to retain control over Palestinian territorial water. If such conditions remained in place, even the construction of a Palestinian port would be of little use as a consequential step toward ending Israel's command over the Palestinian economy.

The issue of safe passage aimed at facilitating movement within the Occupied Territories involved more than economic or even symbolic consequence. It touched the core of Palestinian national identity, disjointed as a result of the territorial fragmentation that marred the Occupied Territories. Safe passage was a constant topic of discussion in the early rounds of negotiations. Under the Oslo, Wye River, and Sharm el-Sheikh agreements, Israel agreed to the institution of two routes of safe passage that would enable Palestinians to move freely between the Gaza Strip and the West Bank. Sharm el-Sheikh provided October 1, 1999 as the date for the operation of the southern route, while the northern route was deferred to a later date. According to the agreement, Palestinians wishing to travel between the West Bank and Gaza, or to transport their goods, would be required to apply to the P.A., who would then have to acquire an Israeli agreement to a selected number of applications within two weeks. Those who passed the Israeli security check would be allowed to use the routes during fixed hours and for specific periods before having to apply again. The southern route of the safe passage was eventually opened on October 25, 1999, and was shut down a year later. The northern route, scheduled for February 5, 2000, was delayed indefinitely. As expected, Israel's "disengagement" from Gaza, which officially ended on September 12, 2005, had little impact on freedom of movement between the supposedly liberated Gaza Strip and the West Bank.[35]

The Gaza airport, seaport, and safe passages were all indicative of the stumbling, unrewarding, and outright hurtful peace process, as far as Palestinians were concerned. The airport, now named Yasser Arafat International Airport, was half destroyed and abandoned. The seaport was also in ruins. Meanwhile, thousands of Palestinians from Gaza, mostly students, were trapped in the West Bank, unable to be reunited with their families since the so-called safe passage had been sealed off by Israel years before. Thus the Palestinian economy and people remained captive to the same lasting elements—Israeli political advantage and continuing military dominion—as the peace process was once again reduced to empty rhetoric, handshakes, and broken promises.

POST-DISENGAGEMENT

Sharon and his right-wing government could not possibly have envisioned a more gratifying scenario for the post-Disengagement period than the one that was advancing in the Gaza Strip. Events on the ground all pointed to the disquieting conclusion that internal Palestinian strife in Gaza was imminent and that Israel would continue to determine the future of the Occupied Territories unabated, and aided by the U.S. government, alongside the total marginalization of the rest of the international community. Subsequent to the Israeli government's official announcement regarding its intent to evacuate illegal Jewish settlements and their adjacent military posts from Gaza, Sharon's government intensified its forceful rhetoric, warning that Israel would ruthlessly respond to any supposed Palestinian provocation during and after the pull-out. It was obvious that Israel's military strategists were very concerned that the Israeli move could be interpreted as an indication of military failure, following the same line of thinking that accompanied the Israeli withdrawal from South Lebanon in May 2000. Back then, Lebanese and Palestinians had celebrated the Israeli retreat as a military defeat for the once invincible Israeli army; it was perhaps the first genuine and unblemished victory claimed by an Arab force in an extensive history of military conflicts with the Jewish state. Israel was determined to closely monitor and control the narrative surrounding its pull-out from Gaza. On one hand, it wanted to convey to its right-wing constituency that the move was merely tactical and aimed at strengthening Israel's control over the more strategic settlements of Occupied East Jerusalem and the West Bank. On the other hand, it promoted the pull-out internationally as a painful concession for the sake of peace with its ever-ungrateful Palestinian neighbors. TV images of weeping settlers being "uprooted" from their homes in the Gaza settlements evoked untold emotions, yet failed to honestly address the unspeakable injustices done to Palestinians through the illegal presence of those same settlers: the uncompensated financial loss, the virtual and perpetual imprisonment within Gaza, the daily murders committed in the name of protecting the settlements, and so forth. The Israeli narrative successfully obliterated much of this relevant context, under which the whole Palestinian population in the Occupied Territories was still subjugated. Palestinians, who ultimately conceded to the much-resisted unilateral Israeli action, attempted to fathom the Israeli move in a way that could prove politically and strategically beneficial. According to a media plan drafted by the P.A.'s Interior Ministry, the withdrawal was "a political victory" for "the peace and moderation camp." The P.A. was obliged, understandably so, to construct its own reading of the Israeli move, within which the P.A. was, in fact, the least relevant factor.[36] Hamas on the other hand, joined to a lesser extent by other factions, celebrated the withdrawal as a victory for armed resistance, one that was comparable in meaning and magnitude to that of Hizbollah in Lebanon. Among the poor and destitute refugees throughout the Occupied Territories and in Diaspora, the Hamas narrative was the most compelling.

Almost immediately after the Gaza pull-out, a violent Israeli assault took place. Frequent deadly raids and bombardments, with Israeli airforce jets breaking sound barriers over the Gaza sky several times a day triggering sonic booms, were meant as a cruel reminder of Israel's sheer military advantage over the incarcerated population of the Gaza Strip. Concurrently, Israel's illegal settlement project in the West Bank and Occupied East Jerusalem received an historic boost, with the allocation of more funds toward settlement expansion, coupled with American assurances by the outgoing U.S. ambassador to Israel, Daniel Kurtzer, that the "United States will support the retention by Israel of areas with a high concentration of Israelis."[37] Kurtzer, speaking to Israeli radio on September 18—less than a week after the pull-out from Gaza—read an excerpt to listeners from a letter by the U.S. President sent to Sharon in April 2004, where Bush declared that it was "unrealistic to expect that the outcome of the final status negotiations [would] be a full and complete return to the armistice lines of 1949," and where he also bluntly rejected the Palestinian refugees' right to return in accordance with U.N. Resolution 194. Former head of Israel's National Security Council, Uzi Dayan (who, in 2002, recommended a one-sided withdrawal from Gaza), offered further insight and a more candid translation of Kurtzer's comments. In a press conference in Tel Aviv on September 20, Dayan proposed an Israeli withdrawal from minor settlements in the West Bank and the creation of a de facto border that would claim vast Palestinian lands as Israeli territory.[38] This new territory would envelop the lands hosting the illegal Jewish settlements of Maale Adumim, Ariel, Kiryat Arba, and Bet El, among others, and along with them nearly 200,000 Jewish settlers. According to Dayan's computation, 28 Palestinian towns would become part of "Israel proper." Considering the atrocious effects created by the Israeli Separation Wall and the integrated land theft, Israel's future plans for the West Bank and Jerusalem constituted new and horrendous crimes which would have painfully lasting consequences.

While Israel was actively and openly pursuing its own designs, altering the geopolitical nature of its conflict with the Palestinians for years to come, there was no political process of which to speak. Abbas' announcement on September 13, regarding his readiness to "immediately engage" in peace talks with Israel, was purposely undermined by Sharon's terror campaign in the Occupied Territories. Israel's predetermined role for the P.A. was no different than the one envisaged by past Israeli governments following the signing of the Oslo Accords in 1993: that of the prison guard, not the peace partner. Little had changed, despite five arduous years of Palestinian revolt. The P.A.'s adherence to its assigned role would once again determine the nature of the relationship between the Israeli government and the P.A., and naturally thereafter between the latter and the U.S. administration. The Abbas government's failure to disarm Palestinian factions and to crack down on "this and that" would eventually be understood as a faltering on its commitment to Israel's security, which would invite, as it already had, more Israeli wrath, murder, and mayhem.

Israel's conduct following its pull-out from Gaza confirmed that its ultimate objective was to maintain a high level of chaos among Palestinians. Such insecurity would confirm the claim that the Palestinians were innately lawless and irresponsible, rationalizing Israel's unwarranted attacks on Gaza and continued occupation elsewhere. The U.S. mainstream media had already established that Gaza was a "test" for Palestinians and their ability to govern themselves, and, since Israel was claiming that Palestinian factions continued to threaten Israeli borders, Palestinians were evidently failing the test. Israel's ongoing attempts to provoke Palestinian clashes, coupled with a lack of responsibility on the part of various elements within the P.A., were certain to deliver. This was demonstrated in the six-hour-long fight between Hamas members and Palestinian police near the Shati refugee camp in Gaza on October 3, which resulted in the deaths of three Palestinians. The Shati clash was the deadliest confrontation since the 1996 revolt staged by Palestinians against P.A. police. It once again reintroduced the term "civil war" as a dreaded yet viable possibility. And as Hamas and the P.A. traded accusations over responsibility for the fight, Israeli officials seemed at ease that Palestinian weapons were finally being pointed in their intended direction. This quarrel marks "the beginning of the beginning," Israeli army chief, Dan Halutz, told Israeli radio.[39] One can only imagine the full scenario Halutz and other Israeli officials had in mind. Nothing less than civil war would meet Israel's expectations, and nothing else could better serve Israel's future designs. The Palestinian uprising marked its fifth anniversary on September 29, a time when the future of the struggle was facing one of its most consequential challenges yet.

Epilogue

REALITY VERSUS RHETORIC

In spite of dashed hopes and failed summits, peace and justice movements around the world, representing an array of struggles, continue to look to the Palestinian people as an icon of resistance. Regardless of its many flaws and imperfections, no other national struggle in the world has come to symbolize so many things to so many different people. And yet, despite the intricate layers of explanation and understanding that have sought to encapsulate the Palestinian struggle, Palestine itself lingers in the world's consciousness merely as a symbol. Palestine is the ultimate for those seeking deliverance, and the last resting-place next to heaven for those in quest of salvation. There, so it has been written, the tireless hunt for spiritual truth shall come to an end; the armies shall meet there once more; they shall fight in the name of God, unleashing an Armageddon unlike any other, in which victory has already been promised to the righteous. Palestine has also been a rallying point for the dispossessed and for the aspiring underdog. Its letters have been inscribed in blood on prison walls throughout Israel and the Arab world as a promise of victory or as a lamentation of defeat. When anti-globalization

A Palestinian woman from the West Bank village of Jayyous returns with a sack of olives after twelve hours in the olive fields (October 2004)

activists take on neo-imperialist institutions, they raise a Palestinian flag; and when Venezuela's poor brought Hugo Chávez back to power in April 2002, a Palestinian flag also fluttered in the wind.

Palestine has also had its fair share of political exploitation. Former Iraqi President, Saddam Hussein, fought his Iranian foes, through cruel and costly wars, in the name of Palestine, and in the name of Palestine Iran fought back. Arab nations have long hidden behind liberation-of-Palestine slogans to excuse their ineptitude and to rationalize their oppression. And in the United States, Palestine takes on a plethora of unique and often deadly meanings. It is seen as the site of a prophecy waiting to be fulfilled and a market for politicians prepared to sell their will to the highest bidder. It remains a major and ever-present news headline that, despite its ominous significance, seems to produce nothing except the intentional misrepresentation of the facts. As for Palestine the reality—the suffering, the loss, the hopelessness and hurt, the refugee camps, the checkpoints, the expanding settlements, the encroaching Israeli wall, the ruined lives, the packed prisons, the anger and prevailing sense of betrayal, the desperation and the human bombs, the shattered economy, the bulldozed orchards, the more than 50-year-old fear of the future—all this seems to be the least relevance.

Symbolic Palestine—Palestine the dream—has for long hijacked Palestine the reality. Thus when Palestine is discussed, examined, and scrutinized, the frame of reference is hardly ever the one invoked when any other similar conflict is discussed. Its resolution is rarely seen as being pertinent to international law or human rights edicts and is barely understood, as it should be, in terms of power and strategy. Rather it is a subject inviting fearful imaginings, religious fantasies, and fictitious constructs. One cannot and must not undermine the efforts of the inspiring activists whose awareness of the Palestinian reality on the ground is unmatched, and whose sincere efforts to achieve peace with justice in Palestine translate into more than a few heart-rending words and phrases—rather into resolute action and an unequaled readiness to labor and even sacrifice themselves for their beliefs. However, it is this struggle between the real as opposed to the figurative and abstract awareness of Palestine that will define the course of action that is likely to follow. If Palestine continues to be understood—or misunderstood—outside its proper frame as a national struggle for rights within the appropriately corresponding international context, then little can be expected from any attempts to remedy its ailments. It is time to distance Palestine from further misinterpretations and to understand it as it is. Otherwise, Palestine, its people and its conflict, will be subject to ever-increasing displays of rhetoric with no connection to the real aspirations of a real people with real demands, awaiting justice and a moment of peace.

LIONIZING SHARON

On December 26, 2005, just months after the historic end of the Second Palestinian Uprising, Ariel Sharon suffered a stroke, which left him in a coma for weeks. The unprecedented media frenzy regarding the demise of Sharon reflected a worldwide collective case of severe amnesia. The outpouring of love and sorrow expressed by individuals and world leaders alike seemed to out-do even the praise bestowed on great and authentic peacemakers, from Gandhi to Martin Luther King to Mother Theresa. A few U.S. newspapers admitted, although reluctantly, that Palestinians "perceived" Sharon as a war criminal who had wrought untold hurt and misery.

Wary of being viewed as hate-mongers, most Arab media and spokespersons desperately attempted to balance the sense of vindication felt in the streets of their own countries, now that the "Butcher of Beirut" was too ill to order any more "targeted killings" or military onslaughts. A former Egyptian diplomat told B.B.C. World that Sharon was capable of delivering peace. He used the opportunity to wish Sharon's most prominent political ally, Shimon Peres a "long and happy life." Other intellectuals explained the Arab street's sense of vindication as something only to be expected from over-emotional "ordinary people," rather than the middle and upper classes. Arab elitism is always barefaced.

Meanwhile, the U.S. media's pandering continued: "Replacing the Irreplaceable," read the headline of one *St. Petersburg Times* article, quoting an ill-advised conclusion that most people, including Palestinians, "are probably not feeling good [about Sharon's illness] because even those who didn't like him at all are now sure he's the only person who can lead Israel to peace and security." One may never know who is responsible for disseminating such utter falsehoods, recycled by hundreds of newspapers all around the world. Even the man's gruesome violations of human rights were celebrated as milestones in the life of a great statesman. But when all is said and done, Sharon the person will matter little. His age and faltering health were doomed to sideline him sooner or later. What will have a greater bearing is his wicked legacy, one which he has already passed on, one that glorified unhindered violence and extremism to achieve political ends. Those who would wish to fill Sharon's shoes will likely strive to prove as violent and cruel as he was. Sharon once said that Palestinians "must be hit hard" and "must be beaten" before they could be permitted to talk peace with Israel—peace according to Israeli terms, not international law. Most of Sharon's possible successors were also strong believers in such a philosophy; a philosophy unlikely to fade away with the fading of individuals, Sharon or any other.

THE HAMAS VICTORY

In the midst of this political vacuum in Israel, and just weeks after Sharon's political demise, on January 25, 2006, Palestinians carried out elections for the Palestinian Legislative Council. The vote was historic by every definition, not just because it marked another milestone of democracy for Palestinians and the region at large, but most significantly because of its striking outcome. This was the P.L.C.'s second election ever, and in one of the most significant moments in Palestinian history, Hamas experienced a landslide victory, claiming 74 of the 132 seats in Parliament. The news gripped the media and governments around the world, for it had without question given rise to a new era of politics in Palestine, the Middle East, and in the Arab and Muslim world as a whole. The implications of Hamas' historic win in Jerusalem, the West Bank, and Gaza cannot be limited to the geopolitical boundaries of the Occupied Territories. Indeed, they will surpass such borders to include a region trapped in an outdated political process, which is neither meaningful nor equitable.

As the prospect of Hamas' strong showing or even victory loomed, the Bush Administration seemed to show little interest in ensuring that the rules of a genuine democracy be preserved. Double-dealing, intimidation, and outright threats quickly replaced the rosy promises once passionately delivered. News reports spoke of last-minute U.S. funding geared toward boosting the ratings of Hamas' formidable contender, Fatah. But the Palestinian voters were obviously fed up with the Israeli occupation, the U.S.'s dishonest role as a "peacemaker" and the indefensible corruption of the Palestinian Authority. They made their choice, decidedly opting for Hamas, whose commitment to social services and corruption-free history ensured its performance at the polls went beyond all expectations.

All eyes were on Washington as the election results came out. European Union members were careful not to validate the victory of a "terrorist" group, and the Arab front was suspiciously hush. Concerned not to fundamentally expose her government's farcical position, Secretary of State, Condoleezza Rice, among other U.S. officials, attempted to articulate a response that would approve of Palestinian democracy, yet object to its outcome. An international campaign—led by Washington, and Rice in particular—was promptly devised to counterbalance the results of one of the most democratic elections ever experienced in the Arab world, resorting to arm-twisting over aid and out-and-out political blackmail. One has only to consider recurrent U.N. reports of the extreme poverty and the alarming number of malnourished children in the Occupied Territories to appreciate how appalling the Bush Administration and its Western allies' threats were regarding their future funding of the P.A. The tirelessly repeated argument from Washington and almost every European capital was that no donor money should flow to a government led by a group that doesn't acknowledge Israel's existence and is "dedicated to Israel's destruction." But how could a nation unconditionally recognize its own occupier—one who adamantly refuses to honor scores of United Nations resolutions and deems international law neither binding nor relevant? Wouldn't it be odd for a Hamas-led government to declare its commitment to peace on the same day that top Israeli officials declare that elected Palestinian ministers are not immune to assassination?

Of course, any reasonable American or European assessment of Hamas as a maturing political and social movement would recognize a pragmatic trend that has hardly been matched by Israel itself. Hamas' commitment to the ceasefire throughout most of 2005, for instance, was exemplary by any definition, especially if compared with Israel's daily violations. Even while Palestinian ballots were being counted, Israeli troops shot dead a nine-year-old girl, Eya al-Astal, in Gaza, for no apparent reason. But from Washington's point of view, the burden was still on the Palestinians—to legitimize the same entity that had illegitimately expropriated their land—despite the remarkable strides they had made throughout the years under the most extreme circumstances.

While many Palestinians still opposed some of Hamas' past methods—such as the reprehensible targeting of Israeli civilians— many saw the movement as an antithesis to the ills of the Oslo Accords, with its dreadful stagnation and countless failures. It is rather remarkable that the long years of collective punishment, and the persistent threats and intimidation simultaneously pouring from Tel Aviv and Washington, were of no avail as Palestinians voted for reforms and for a political platform that is based on national unity, not exclusion. Moreover, though the Hamas victory may possibly mark the end of the U.S.'s Middle East democracy-project charade, it may also strongly enhance the chances of regionally fostered democratic initiatives—initiatives that reflect the peoples' own needs and interests, not those of the beleaguered Bush Administration.

Despite the uncertainty that the future still carries, despite the many coercive tricks that Israel and the U.S. will likely pull, and despite the hypocritical E.U. stance and the terrible political inertness of the Arabs, one can only hope that true democracy will deliver what empty rhetoric has not—not only in Palestine, but throughout the region.

FORCE TO BE RECKONED WITH

Five years have passed since the Palestinian people transformed their hunger for long-denied rights into a commanding display of will and valor: the Al-Aqsa Intifada.

First, the uprising was not a local experience by any standards. Not only did it impose itself in the arena of regional and international politics, it also grew in value and meaning to become a central icon in the emerging global consciousness of a new generation in the West as well as other parts of the world, from Latin America to Africa and Southeast Asia. Thus, and despite the uniqueness of the Intifada for those who have lived through it, one simply cannot ignore its iconic status nor diminish its international significance, which have been, even before the official manufacturing of the State of Israel in 1948 at the expense of Palestinian lives, utterly crucial. The State of Israel, as the late Professor Edward Said and others have long argued, existed in Zionist consciousness, where it was deliberately transformed to become an essentially Western priority, before the actual physical construction of the State on the ruins of hundreds of Palestinian towns and villages. Therefore, a deconstruction process was, and still is of the essence, if Palestine is to become not just a Western but an international priority. How to go about making it an international priority is an entirely different topic.

In closing, I wish to register here four points: First, that despite the Palestinian uprising's initial success in breaking away from the over-internalized and self-defeating political discourse characteristic of the dominant sector of the P.L.O., and later of the Palestinian Authority, the same failed approach has been adopted again, and thus the legacy of the Intifada is being discredited, if not silenced altogether.

Second, the Palestinian struggle has been woven together, in all of its failures and triumph by successive generations of Palestinians inside and outside the Occupied Territories. Therefore, any mandate over an historic settlement with Israel would have to take into account the millions of Palestinians in neighboring Arab countries and those scattered the world over. (It must be noted that the overwhelming support for Hamas in the January 2006 Legislative Council elections was to a large degree due to Hamas' insistence on this crucial issue.) A P.A. president, whether elected by a decisive or a modest majority, has no exclusive mandate over critical matters that touch all Palestinians in Diaspora, especially the matter of the right of return for Palestinian refugees. That right—enshrined in international law, notably in U.N. Resolution 194 of December 11, 1948, and reconfirmed numerous times since then—is the cornerstone of the Palestinian struggle, and discarding it is tantamount to an historic validation of the very racially prejudiced principle that created and recreated Palestinian catastrophes throughout the years.

Third, there is the issue of those factors that ought to remain non-negotiable constants in the Palestinian struggle. Various historic periods of the struggle, and the different stages of the Arab–Israeli conflict, have greatly shaped the prevailing priorities of the time. In the early stages of the conflict, due to the absence of a major Palestinian political voice, the problem was confined to that of the refugees and the immediate humanitarian calamity created by their displacement. There was no Palestinian nation to speak of, no shattered prospects of a statehood to urgently restore, and no unified Arab front with a decided agenda to bring about such a state. That said, one can hardly overlook the existence of a Palestine in the minds of Palestinians since the earliest generations of the twentieth century. The existence of that Palestine can be argued on more than a material basis—a nation that called itself Palestinian is one. Palestinians knew what Palestine was and what it meant to them, they recognized its boundaries, geographical uniqueness, and political reality and prospects. They revolted as a nation and celebrated as one. Not even the uprooting of nearly a million Palestinians in 1948 has changed that identity or disfigured that relationship. In fact, it could be argued that the rapport between Palestine and the Palestinians evolved to a higher level of consciousness following their forced departure in the middle and latter parts of the past century. One of the many challenges posed by the Oslo process however, was the molding of a considerable political culture that no longer adheres to fixed constants: Anything can be negotiated, bargained, and "resolved," depending on the degree of Israel's cruelty in dealing with Palestinian political tenacity—or "inflexibility" by a different definition—and the American pressure to make a one-sided "compromise" possible. The likely growth of this "pragmatic" political culture may prove devastating and paralyzing in the quest for a politically sovereign and territorially meaningful Palestinian state. If this culture is not confronted and overpowered, another self-destructive political "compromise" is likely to be imposed on those truly representative of the Palestinian struggle.

Finally, it must be stated that Palestinian resistance, which has for the most part taken the form of a non-violent and popular movement, will continue as long as the circumstances that contributed to its commencement remain in place. In fact, Israeli oppression is now going beyond the traditional outrages of daily murders and small-scale land confiscation. Under the smokescreen of "Disengagement" from Gaza, West Bank lands are being vigorously expropriated, while Israel's Separation Wall, illegal according to the International Court of Justice decision of July 2004, is swallowing up whole towns and villages. This reality, as history has taught us, will likely only be a prelude to another popular Palestinian response, which is already echoing in the angry chants of destitute farmers whose lands are being effectively annexed by the encroaching Israeli wall. Regardless of how historians choose to chronicle the Second Palestinian Uprising, it will always be remembered by most Palestinians, as well as by people of conscience everywhere, as a fight for freedom, human rights, and justice. It will remain a powerful reminder that popular resistance is still an option—and one to be reckoned with at that.

Appendix I

Total Deaths and Other Losses During the Second Palestinian Uprising
September 29, 2000–September 29, 2005

Total Number of Palestinian Deaths: 4166	
Children:	886
Women:	271
Men:	3009
Palestinians killed by Jewish settlers:	72
Palestinians killed as a result of Israeli shelling:	834
Deaths as a result of medical prevention at Israeli checkpoints:	117
Of them stillbirths (born dead at checkpoints):	31
Number of Palestinians Extra-judicially Assassinated:	554
Of them bystanders killed during extra-judicial operations:	253
Total Number of Israeli Deaths:	1113
Children:	113
Women:	305
Men:	603
Settlers:	213
Soldiers:	322
Area Distribution of Palestinian Deaths:	
West Bank (including East Jerusalem):	1973
Gaza Strip:	2193
Palestinians Injured by Israeli Forces and Settlers:	36,585
Live ammunition:	8153
Rubber/plastic bullets:	6356
Tear gas:	6336
Miscellaneous:	8250
Number of Palestinians Disabled or Maimed by Injuries:	3530
Number of Palestinian Detainees in Israeli Prisons:	8600
Of them children:	288
Of them females:	115
Educational Statistics (Palestinians):	
School students killed:	576
University students killed:	199
Teachers killed:	32
Number of students injured:	4713
Number of students detained:	1389
Destruction of Palestinian Property	
(1 dunum = 1000 m²):	
Confiscated land:	2,329,659 dunums
Razed land:	73,613 dunums
Estimated number of uprooted trees:	1,355,290
Homes demolished:	7761

Homes damaged:	93,842
Unemployment and Poverty:	
Unemployment rate (first quarter of 2005):	26.5%
Poverty rate:	64.6%

Sources:
Palestinian Initiative for the Promotion of Global Dialogue & Democracy (MIFTAH); Palestinian National Information Center; Palestinian Central Bureau of Statistics; Palestinian Ministry of Education and Higher Education; Applied Research Institute Jerusalem (A.R.I.J.); Palestinian Red Crescent Society (P.R.C.S.); Palestinian Center for Human Rights (P.C.H.R.); The Palestine Monitor.

Appendix II
Timeline of Events During the
Second Palestinian Uprising: 2000–05

2000–01

July 25, 2000: Marathon two-week negotiations at Camp David break down without agreement. Israeli Prime Minister, Ehud Barak, places sole blame on the Palestinian Authority President, Yasser Arafat, for allegedly refusing to yield ground on Occupied East Jerusalem.

September 29, 2000: Israeli police injure hundreds of Palestinian protesters at a Jerusalem holy site. Violence breaks out just moments after Israel's hardline opposition leader, Ariel Sharon, enters the Haram al-Sharif compound in Occupied East Jerusalem, surrounded by hundreds of riot police and accompanied by a handful of Likud party colleagues. Protests and subsequent violence soon erupt throughout the Occupied Territories. It is the start of the Al-Aqsa Intifada (the Second Palestinian Uprising).

September 31, 2000: The death of a twelve-year-old Palestinian boy killed by Israeli fire shocks the world. Mohammed al-Durra's death in the arms of his father, Jamal, is captured by French television.

October 2, 2000: The Intifada death-toll climbs to 47 in four days, as the Israeli army deploys helicopter gunships and tanks into Palestinian areas.

October 3, 2000: A truce between Israeli forces and Palestinians lasts just half a day before renewed fighting erupts. The death-toll now stands at 55, including nine "Israeli Arabs"—Palestinians who are Israeli citizens.

October 4, 2000: U.S. Secretary of State, Madeleine Albright, brings Barak and Arafat together to try to get them to return to "the psychology of peacemaking." In a week of strife, more than 60 Palestinians have died.

October 12, 2000: C.I.A. director, George Tenet, flies into the Middle East to set up security talks between the two sides.

October 12, 2000: Israeli helicopters fire rockets into Arafat's residential compound.

October 16, 2000: Barak and Arafat meet warily at an emergency summit in Egypt under the auspices of U.S. President, Bill Clinton, aimed at halting the bloody clashes.

October 17, 2000: The Sharm el-Sheikh agreement, brokered by President Clinton, aims to end the upsurge in violence. It breaks down almost immediately.

October 20, 2000: Fierce fighting in the West Bank claims the lives of ten more Palestinians.

October 21, 2000: Arab League leaders begin their first emergency summit in four years in a bid to form a unified response to the violence between Israelis and Palestinians.

October 22, 2000: Barak announces that he is suspending the peace process.

November 1, 2000: Amnesty International says Israel's violations of human rights could constitute war crimes.

November 9, 2000: Israeli combat helicopters fire rockets onto a truck full of Palestinians, killing one and critically wounding another. Two passers-by are killed and eleven others are injured.

November 20, 2000: Mortar attacks in Occupied Gaza targeting an Israeli bus kill two and wound nine more. Israel carries out a fierce bombing campaign in Palestinian civilian areas, wounding at least 50 people. Egypt recalls its ambassador from Tel Aviv in response.

November 22, 2000: A powerful car bomb explodes in the northern Israeli town of Hadera, killing two people.

November 23, 2000: U.N. agencies warn that half the population of the Occupied Territories—some 1.5 million people—could go hungry if Israel's economic blockade continues.

November 28, 2000: Barak calls for early elections.

December 9, 2000: Barak resigns from his post as Prime Minister, and announces new elections.

December 15, 2000: Israeli troops assassinate Hamas member, Hani Abu Bakr, at a southern Gaza checkpoint. Two others are also wounded. Eyewitnesses said that Abu Bakr was ordered out of his car and shot.

December 30, 2000: Israel seals off the West Bank and Gaza Strip.

January 10, 2001: Israel's Peace Now movement accuses the government and security forces of running a policy of selective assassination of Palestinian leaders.

January 21, 2001: A Jewish settler who bludgeoned a Palestinian child to death with the butt of a rifle is sentenced to six months' community service. Human rights groups around the world express their outrage at the sentence.

January 29, 2001: Barak rules out any contact with Arafat before Israel's February 6 elections and accuses the Palestinian leader of unleashing an "attack of lies" against Israel.

February 6, 2001: Ariel Sharon defeats Barak in a landslide election victory, winning 62.5 percent of the vote.

February 9, 2001: The Administration of U.S. President George W. Bush disowns months of failed efforts by the former Clinton Administration to broker a peace deal in the Middle East. Israel launches the most severe attacks in weeks on Palestinian areas.

February 13, 2001: Israeli helicopter gunships assassinate Palestinian officer, Massoud Ayyad, 54, a major in Force 17, an elite Palestinian security service.

February 14, 2001: Eight Israeli soldiers and civilians are killed when a Palestinian bus driver drives into a crowd of people. Israel responds by reimposing a total blockade on the Occupied Territories. President George Bush condemns the attack, but pointedly refuses to take sides.

February 27, 2001: Veteran Israeli Labor Party leader, Shimon Peres, talks the party into joining Ariel Sharon's right-wing government of national unity. He himself will be Foreign Minister.

March 4, 2001: A Palestinian suicide bomber blows himself up in the Israeli town of Netanya, killing three passers-by, and wounding 60 others.

March 7, 2001: Ariel Sharon formally takes office as Israeli Prime Minister.

March 16, 2001: For the second time in three months, Palestinians press the U.N. Security Council to send a security force into Palestinian Occupied Territories, in the face of staunch opposition from Israel and the United States.

March 23, 2001: Israeli forces assassinate a Palestinian security officer from Yasser Arafat's presidential guard unit. Four others are injured.

March 28, 2001: Israeli helicopters fire rockets into Palestinian police buildings in Gaza and the West Bank town of Ramallah. Israeli ships off the coast of Gaza City open fire on the area of Arafat's office.

April 2, 2001: Palestinian gunmen and Israeli soldiers exchange heavy fire in the West Bank town of Bethlehem.

April 10, 2001: Israel fires rockets at Palestinian targets in the Gaza Strip, killing a Palestinian doctor and injuring 20 others.

April 16, 2001: Israel attacks the Gaza Strip, firing rockets from air, land, and sea. Tensions throughout the Middle East swell.

April 17, 2001: For the first time since the eruption of the Second Palestinian Uprising, Israeli troops seize back land controlled by the Palestinians in the Gaza Strip, and divide the territory into three parts.

April 19, 2001: Israeli tanks and bulldozers re-enter the Gaza Strip and level a Palestinian police station.

May 5, 2001: Former U.S. Senator, George Mitchell, who has been investigating Middle East violence, drafts a report, condemning the expansion of Jewish settlements in the Occupied Territories.

May 8, 2001: Israeli troops shell a Palestinian refugee camp in Gaza, killing four-month-old Iman Hajjo. She becomes the youngest victim of the Intifada. In the West Bank, Israeli troops briefly enter two Palestinian towns—part of a new policy that gives field commanders the authority to decide on such operations on the spot, without waiting for government approval.

May 9, 2001: Two 14-year-old Israeli boys are found bludgeoned to death in a cave near a Jewish West Bank settlement.

May 14, 2001: Five Palestinian policemen are killed in cold blood while manning a checkpoint in the West Bank. Two others are killed in Gaza.

May 16, 2001: A senior Israeli official acknowledges that the killing of the five Palestinian policemen was an error.

May 18, 2001: A Palestinian suicide bomber kills himself and five Israelis in the northern coastal town of Netanya. More than 40 others are wounded. Israel retaliates by bombing the West Bank towns of Nablus and Ramallah with F-16 warplanes—it is the first such use of airpower against the Occupied Territories.

May 21, 2001: Former U.S. Senator Mitchell releases his long anticipated report on the Middle East conflict. The report calls for an immediate ceasefire, to be followed by confidence-building measures and ultimately by renewed peace negotiations. He also dares to endorse an immediate freeze on settlement expansion in the Occupied Territories.

May 22, 2001: The Mitchell report is immediately dismissed by the Sharon government, referring to the settlement expansion in the Occupied Territories as a "vital enterprise."

May 31, 2001: Palestinian leader, Faisal Husseini, dies unexpectedly of a heart attack during a visit to Kuwait.

June 1, 2001: A suicide bomber blows himself up in a Tel Aviv disco, leaving 19 people dead and more than 60 others injured. Islamic Jihad claims responsibility for the attack.

June 10, 2001: Israeli tank shells kill three Palestinian women in the Gaza Strip.

June 13, 2001: C.I.A. Chief, George Tenet, brings senior Israeli and Palestinian security officials together to initiate the implementation of a U.S.-brokered truce which the two sides have accepted.

July 4, 2001: The Israeli security cabinet grants the army liberty to target anyone it deems to be a "potential terrorist" in the West Bank and Gaza.

July 9, 2001: Bulldozers level 14 Palestinian homes.

July 11, 2001: A Palestinian woman in labor who is barred from passing an Israeli military checkpoint for two-and-a-half hours, gives birth in her car. The baby boy dies before reaching a medical clinic. At another checkpoint, an Israeli soldier kills a Palestinian woman after her taxi evades a roadblock trying to take workers to jobs inside Israel.

July 17, 2001: Israeli forces kill four people, including two senior Hamas activists. Israel sends tanks and infantry units into the West Bank.

July 19, 2001: The G8 summit in Genoa calls for international observers to monitor Israel's ceasefire with the Palestinian Authority. Israelis reject the call.

July 19, 2001: Jewish settlers in Hebron kill three Palestinians, including a three-month-old baby.

July 25, 2001: The Israeli army assassinates a Palestinian near Nablus, firing anti-tank missiles.

July 30, 2001: Six Palestinian activists are killed in an explosion in a refugee camp near Nablus.

July 31, 2001: Eight Palestinians are killed when an Israeli helicopter fires rockets into Hamas offices in Nablus. The dead include Jamal Mansour, a leading Hamas figure in the West Bank, and two young children.

August 5, 2001: A Palestinian gunman shoots ten people, most of them soldiers, near Israel's defense ministry in Tel Aviv.

August 7, 2001: Israel announces the names of seven Palestinians targeted for assassination, according to Israel's "pinpoint prevention" list. Since the onset of the Second Palestinian Uprising, some 40 political and paramilitary leaders have been executed without trial.

August 9, 2001: A suicide bombing claims the lives of 25 people and injures more than 90 others. The attack takes place in a busy restaurant in the heart of Jerusalem. Hamas claims responsibility.

August 10, 2001: Israeli forces seize the offices of the P.L.O. at Orient House in Occupied East Jerusalem.

August 15, 2001: About 70 Israeli tanks and hundreds of troops besiege Palestinian government buildings. At least three are killed in the attack.

August 16, 2001: Israeli undercover troops assassinate Palestinian activist, Emad Abu Sneineh, in the town of Hebron.

August 23, 2001: Israeli soldiers shoot and kill four Palestinians in the West Bank.

August 27, 2001: Abu Ali Mustafa, leader of the Popular Front for the Liberation of Palestine, is assassinated when Israel fires rockets into his office. Mustafa is the highest-ranking Palestinian official so far targeted for assassination.

September 7, 2001: An Israeli helicopter fires on two Palestinian activists, killing them both.

September 7, 2001: Israel declares that Palestinians will be forbidden to approach the Green Line unless they obtain a pass from Israeli authorities. Those who disobey—especially at night when a curfew would be in place— could be shot.

September 12, 2001: Israeli tanks invade the town of Jericho in the second invasion of a Palestinian-ruled town in 48 hours. Fighting also rages in Jenin, where at least seven Palestinians, including a young girl, are killed. Palestinian officials accuse Sharon of exploiting the lack of international focus on the region, one day after the terrorist attacks in New York, Washington D.C. and Pennsylvania.

September 16, 2001: Israeli tanks invade Palestinian towns in the West Bank for the second day running. The Israeli incursion into Jericho and Jenin ignites gun battles that leave three Palestinian fighters dead and 21 wounded.

September 19, 2001: In a roadside ambush in the West Bank, Palestinians shoot and kill two Israeli settlers.

September 28, 2001: Palestinians commemorate the first anniversary of their uprising against Israel.

October 5, 2001: Israeli tanks and troops invade Palestinian-controlled areas of Hebron in the West Bank. They kill at least five Palestinians and end the faltering ceasefire between the two sides.

October 8, 2001: Israeli tanks and troops attack Hebron once again, killing five Palestinians.

October 15, 2001: Israelis assassinate a Palestinian activist with a car bomb in Nablus. It is the second targeted assassination carried out by Israel in two days.

October 17, 2001: Israeli Minister of Tourism, Rehavim Ze'evi, dies after being gunned down at close range outside a Jerusalem hotel. The Popular Front for the Liberation of Palestine claims responsibility, saying that the killing is in retaliation for the killing of their leader, Abu Ali Mustafa.

October 25, 2001: Israeli troops withdraw from the West Bank village of Beit Reema after a deadly raid that killed at least 15 Palestinians and injured more then 20 others.

October 26, 2001: The U.S. demands a full and immediate retreat from Palestinian-ruled cities. Israel ignores the call.

November 1, 2001: Israeli missiles kill Jamil Jadallah, a top Hamas commander. Israeli troops kill five more Palestinians.

November 5, 2001: Sharon postpones a planned visit to Washington indefinitely.

November 6, 2001: Three Palestinians and one Israeli soldier are killed in a gunfight near Nablus in the West Bank.

November 7, 2001: Sharon declares plans to bring one million more Jews to Israel.

November 8, 2001: Disguised as Palestinians, Israeli special forces assassinate a Hamas member in the West Bank.

November 13, 2001: Dozens of Israeli troops invade the West Bank, assassinating one Palestinian activist.

November 19, 2001: Israel demolishes Palestinian houses in Gaza and then declares that it plans to build new homes for Jewish settlers in the West Bank city of Hebron.

November 22, 2001: An explosion in a Gaza refugee camp kills five children as they walk to school.

December 1, 2001: A suicide bomber blows himself up in an Israeli bus, killing three Israelis and injuring nine.

December 3, 2001: Sharon cautions Arafat that the uprising could end with Arafat's own demise.

December 4, 2001: Accused of funding Hamas, two Palestinian financial organizations and the largest Islamic charity in the U.S. are shut down and their assets frozen by order of the U.S. Administration.

December 6, 2001: Hundreds of Hamas supporters clash with Palestinian riot police, in response to an intense crackdown imposed by Arafat.

December 8, 2001: Israeli warplanes fire missiles at the Palestinian Authority's main police headquarters in the Gaza Strip, injuring at least 15 people.

December 10, 2001: An Israeli helicopter strike kills two young Palestinians, including a toddler, in the West Bank.

December 11, 2001: Israeli soldiers kill two Palestinians near the West Bank city of Tulkarem.

December 13, 2001: Israeli forces attack the West Bank and Gaza, firing rockets into many buildings in the two regions.

December 14, 2001: Israeli forces invade four West Bank villages with tanks and helicopter gunships, killing eight Palestinians, and arresting more than 40 others.

December 21, 2001: In an attempt to reduce the tension between themselves and the P.A., Hamas calls for a halt to suicide bombings and mortar attacks in Israel.

December 24, 2001: Arafat is forbidden to travel to Bethlehem to attend Christmas Eve midnight mass at the Church of the Nativity.

2002

January 3, 2002: Israel announces plans to pull out of West Bank towns. Palestinians dismiss the announcement as propaganda. Meanwhile Israeli tanks remain stationed within 100 meters of Arafat's offices in Ramallah. These events coincide with a visit from U.S. Special Envoy, Anthony Zinni.

January 11, 2002: Israeli bulldozers destroy the runway of the Palestinian-run Gaza Airport. Twenty-one tanks, armored vehicles, and bulldozers break through the Airport's fence and tear up its entire 3.5-kilometer-long runway.

January 15, 2002: Israel assassinates Raed al-Karmi, 28, a Palestinian leader in the Al-Aqsa Brigades. The Al-Aqsa Brigades retaliates by killing a Jewish settler near Nablus.

January 17, 2002: Six people are killed and 30 wounded when a Palestinian gunman opens fire on a group of Israelis in the northern Israeli town of Hadera.

January 20, 2002: Israeli tanks and troops invade the West Bank town of Tulkarem, killing one Palestinian.

January 22, 2002: Israeli troops kill four Palestinians, accusing the men of being Hamas activists and claiming that their house was a bomb factory.

January 24, 2002: An Israeli tank shell kills two Palestinians east of the illegal Kfar Darom settlement in the central Gaza Strip.

January 25, 2002: Israeli helicopter crews kill one Hamas member and two bystanders in the Gaza Strip.

February 1, 2002: Sharon tells the Israeli newspaper *Maariv* that he regrets not having "eliminated" Arafat 20 years ago when he had the chance during the invasion of Lebanon.

February 8, 2002: A Palestinian gunman kills an Israeli soldier. An Israeli settler and her daughter are also killed in the gun battle. Israeli F-16 warplanes fire two missiles into a prison and government complex in the West Bank town of Nablus, wounding eleven Palestinians.

February 11, 2002: Two Palestinian gunmen kill two Israeli soldiers in the southern city of Beersheba.

February 12, 2002: Israeli troops raid a West Bank town, killing a Palestinian and destroying a house.

February 13, 2002: In a midnight assault, Israeli forces carry out one of the most ruthless attacks since the onset of the Palestinian uprising. British Foreign Minister, Jack Straw, visits the Middle East, saying that Arafat must take more responsibility in controlling acts of terrorism against Israel. Israeli forces kill five Palestinian policemen in the Gaza Strip after threatening to carve out "security zones" in Palestinian areas.

February 19, 2002: Israeli forces kill eight Palestinians in missile strikes, bombing raids and gun battles.

February 19–20, 2002: Six Israeli soldiers are killed in a commando-style raid by Palestinian fighters on an Israeli army checkpoint at Ein Ariq, near Ramallah. Reprisal strikes leave 16 Palestinians dead.

February 20, 2002: Palestinians detonate a bomb in Gaza, destroying a tank and killing three soldiers. A few hours later, Israeli forces attack a West Bank village killing one Palestinian. Sharon promises a "different course of action" against the new-style raids.

February 23, 2002: Israeli helicopter gunships fire missiles into Arafat's West Bank compound. Palestinian fighters kill six Israeli soldiers at a West Bank checkpoint. Israel kills 13 Palestinians in night raids.

February 24, 2002: Five Palestinians are killed and 50 are injured during widespread Israeli army invasions in the eastern and southern Gaza Strip.

February 25, 2002: Israeli forces shoot and kill a 15-year-old Palestinian girl allegedly wielding a knife at an Israeli checkpoint near the West Bank town of Tulkarem.

February 26, 2002: Israelis and Palestinians agree to resume peace talks as interest grows in a Saudi peace plan.

February 28, 2002: Israeli troops launch a major assault on the West Bank's Balata and Jenin refugee camps. Eight Palestinians are killed, and more than 90 are wounded. The military strike comes just hours after 21-year-old Dareen Abu Aisheh blew herself up at an Israeli checkpoint.

March 3, 2002: Ten Israelis—including seven soldiers—are shot dead by a lone Palestinian sniper. Another Israeli soldier is killed and four others injured in an attack in the Gaza Strip.

March 4, 2002: Israeli forces kill 17 Palestinians, including five children, in the West Bank city of Ramallah. Six Palestinians, including two children, die when a car belonging to a Hamas leader is hit by Israeli gunships. The Israeli attack on the Jenin and Rafah refugee camps claims eleven lives.

March 5, 2002: Israel launches new air strikes on the West Bank city of Ramallah.

March 6, 2002: Israeli raids kill more than 17 Palestinians, including the wife and three children of a Hamas activist.

March 8, 2002: The bloodiest day of the Intifada so far sees 45 people killed, mostly Palestinians.

March 10, 2002: Eleven Israelis are killed and 50 are wounded when a suicide bomber blows himself up in a Jerusalem cafe. Israel responds by destroying Arafat's headquarters in Gaza City.

March 11, 2002: Israeli tanks and troops storm a Palestinian refugee camp in the Gaza Strip, unleashing a ferocious firefight. Seventeen Palestinians are killed and more than 50 are wounded.

March 12, 2002: Twenty-three Palestinians are killed when Israelis forces invade several Palestinian towns and villages. Thousands of Israeli troops invade refugee camps in the Gaza Strip and reoccupy the West Bank town of Ramallah. At least 31 Palestinians are killed and hundreds more are ordered out of their homes. Seven Israelis are killed when a Palestinian gunman opens fire on a kibbutz near the border with Lebanon.

March 15, 2002: The United Nations passes a resolution calling for the creation of a Palestinian state.

March 26, 2002: Ariel Sharon declares that, with U.S. support, he will exile P.A. President Arafat if there are further terrorist attacks while he is at an Arab summit in Beirut. As a result, Arafat announces that he will not attend the summit.

March 27, 2002: In the Israeli resort of Netanya, a suicide bomber blows himself up, killing 19 Israelis.

March 28, 2002: The Arab League summit comes to a final agreement: it promises Israel peace, security, and normal relations in return for a full withdrawal from Arab lands occupied since 1967, the establishment of a Palestinian state with East Jerusalem as its capital and a "fair solution" for the 3.8 million Palestinian refugees. Israel refuses.

March 29, 2002: Israel begins a massive military assault on the West Bank. Arafat's Ramallah headquarters are targeted and Palestinians take refuge in the Church of the Nativity in Bethlehem. Heavy fighting goes on for days in the northern West Bank town of Jenin. Scores of Palestinians are reported killed.

March 30, 2002: While Arafat is still under siege, President Bush presses the P.A. to root out terrorism.

March 31, 2002: Sixteen Israelis are killed in a suicide bombing in the northern city of Haifa, and four more are wounded in another suicide attack on the Efrat Settlement. Israelis retaliate by storming the town of Qalqilya, on the edges of the West Bank. Sharon says that Arafat is an "enemy of Israel."

April 1, 2002: Israeli tanks and thousands of troops attack the Palestinian town of Qalqilya in the northern part of the West Bank.

April 2, 2002: Italian priest, Jacques Amateis, 65, is killed and a number of nuns are wounded inside the Church of the Nativity when Israeli helicopter gunships and artillery bombard the area.

April 3, 2002: The attack on Bethlehem and the siege of Ramallah continue as diplomatic tensions grow. The Vatican denounces the deadly military operation on the West Bank and Egypt limits its ties with Israel.

April 5, 2002: The Israeli army assassinates six Palestinians in the West Bank village of Tubas, near Nablus.

April 6, 2002: Israeli forces carry out artillery attacks and air raids in South Lebanon and fierce assaults continue in many West Bank towns. President Bush urges Israel to withdraw "without delay" from the West Bank cities.

April 7, 2002: Refugees of the Jenin refugee camp under siege for the fifth consecutive day report that Israeli forces are bombarding their homes with Apache helicopters, inflicting heavy casualties among civilians. According to a Nablus hospital report, more than 15 people are killed and scores are wounded in the Nablus area.

April 8, 2002: Determined to destroy Arafat's "regime of terror," Israeli forces continue their siege unhindered, defying U.S. calls to leave the West Bank without delay. Israeli forces once again open fire on Bethlehem's Church of the Nativity.

April 9, 2002: Israeli Foreign Minister, Shimon Peres, reportedly admits that the Israeli army carried out a massacre of civilians in the Jenin refugee camp. The Israeli army adamantly refuses to allow medics and rescue teams to reach the camp to transfer the wounded to neighboring hospitals.

April 9, 2002: Thirteen soldiers are killed in a West Bank battle, the Israeli army's single biggest loss of life since the fighting began 18 months ago.

April 10, 2002: A Palestinian suicide bomber kills eight Israelis in an attack on a crowded bus, as Israeli forces move deeper into two West Bank refugee camps. Meanwhile, an Armenian Orthodox monk is shot and seriously wounded in the Church of the Nativity compound, where more than 200 Palestinians and many expatriates are besieged by the Israeli army.

April 15, 2002: Marwan Barghouti is seized by Israeli special forces. Journalists are finally allowed to enter the Jenin refugee camp, and report seeing a "silent wasteland." In the course of twelve days over 60 Palestinians are killed, 300 wounded, and hundreds arrested. The rest of the population becomes homeless when they are forced by the Israeli army to leave the camp.

April 23, 2002: The Israeli army assassinates Marwan Zalloum, a prominent local resistance activist, and his aide, Samir Abu Rajab.

April 28, 2002: Israeli soldiers shoot and kill a Palestinian boy as he tries to avoid a roadblock on his way back to his village.

April 29, 2002: More than a hundred Israeli tanks and armored personnel carriers, backed by helicopter gunships, attack the West Bank city of Hebron and open fire with heavy machine guns, killing and wounding scores of Palestinians, mostly civilians.

April 30, 2002: The United Nations presses for entry into the Jenin refugee camp to investigate the fighting there. Israel denies access.

May 3, 2002: Two Palestinians and an Israeli army commander are killed during an Israeli military incursion into the northern West Bank city of Nablus.

May 7, 2002: The mayor of Bethlehem announces that a deal has been reached to end the stand-off at the Church of the Nativity.

May 8, 2002: A Palestinian bomber detonates explosives at a pool hall near Tel Aviv, killing at least 16 people, and wounding more than 60.

May 14, 2002: An Israeli human rights group releases a report claiming that Israel has secretly confiscated 42 percent of Palestinian land for illegal settlement construction.

May 15, 2002: Israeli forces stage three pre-dawn raids into West Bank villages, killing two Palestinian intelligence officers and arresting 13 others.

May 16, 2002: Israeli army units enter Palestinian-ruled areas near the West Bank town of Ramallah, killing one Palestinian and arresting others.

May 17, 2002: Israel carries out a deadly raid on the Jenin refugee camp.

May 19, 2002: Three Israelis are killed in a suicide bombing in Netanya.

May 29, 2002: Three Jewish settlers are shot and killed by a Palestinian fighter in the West Bank.

May 31, 2002: Israeli forces invade the West Bank town of Nablus, reoccupying most of the Palestinian-ruled town and the nearby Balata refugee camp.

June 4, 2002: Israeli forces raid the center of the Palestinian autonomous area of Hebron, the largest city in the southern West Bank, imposing a curfew and closing down shops. Earlier in the day, the army raids the town of Jenin in the far north of the West Bank, and the city of Nablus is occupied for the fifth straight day.

June 5, 2002: At least 18 Israeli soldiers and settlers are killed and 30 others injured when a car bomb explodes near an Israeli bus.

June 6, 2002: A massive assault carried out by the Israeli army completely destroys Arafat's headquarters in Ramallah. More than 50 tanks and armored vehicles leave the compound in ruins. One building barely remains standing.

June 9, 2002: Amidst international calls for reform within the P.A., Arafat dismisses more than half his cabinet. This takes place the night before a meeting between Sharon and President Bush in Washington.

June 10, 2002: Israeli tanks and troops make a pre-dawn raid on Ramallah and declare a curfew. In Washington, George Bush backs Israel's demand that the Palestinian leadership be overhauled before meaningful peace talks can begin. Bush refuses to propose a timetable for the creation of a Palestinian state.

June 12, 2002: Five Palestinians are killed in an Israeli bombardment of the Mughraqa neighborhood in the Gaza Strip.

June 16, 2002: At least two Israeli soldiers are killed and four others injured in a Palestinian attack on Israeli forces in the Gaza Strip.

June 16, 2002: Israel begins construction of its West Bank Separation Wall, a 640-kilometer (440-mile) structure allegedly designed to keep Palestinian suicide bombers out of Israel.

June 17, 2002: U.S. National Security Advisor, Condoleezza Rice, condemns the Palestinian Authority, accusing it of collaborating with terrorists.

June 18, 2002: At least 19 Israeli settlers and soldiers are killed and more than 30 injured in an early morning bus bomb attack on the West Bank Jewish settlement of Gilo south of Jerusalem.

June 19, 2002: At least seven Jewish settlers are killed and 20 others injured in a bomb attack in Jerusalem.

June 20, 2002: Arafat calls on his people not to attack Israeli civilians. He says that recent suicide bombs "have given the Israeli government the excuse to reoccupy our land."

June 24, 2002: At least six Palestinians are killed and eleven others wounded when an Israeli helicopter gunship fires several missiles at three taxicabs in Rafah.

June 27, 2002: Fifteen Palestinian fighters taking refuge in an old British military base in Hebron are bombarded by helicopter gunships. Israeli forces topple the building with the men inside, and then destroy the ruins with explosives. All 15 men are believed dead.

July 1, 2002: Israeli tanks, artillery shells, and heavy gunfire attack civilian areas in the southern parts of the Gaza Strip.

July 7, 2002: Reports reveal that Britain is selling arms to Israel by trading through the U.S., despite a British embargo.

July 9, 2002: Israeli policemen fire indiscriminately on Palestinian bystanders in Jerusalem, killing a 70-year-old man and injuring a number of other people.

July 16, 2002: At least seven Jewish settlers are killed and 30 others injured when a roadside bomb explodes close to their bus near the northern West Bank town of Qalqilya.

July 19, 2002: Israeli forces arrest 21 Palestinians—all relatives of suspected militants—for exile. After arresting the individuals, the army destroys their homes with bulldozers and explosives.

July 22, 2002: Israel kills Hamas military commander, Salah Shehada, and 14 others, including nine children, with aircraft bombs dropped on his Gaza housing block. Ariel Sharon hails the raid as a great success.

July 26, 2002: Four Jewish settlers are killed when their cars are ambushed by Palestinian fighters in the town of Yatta, 20 kilometers southwest of Hebron.

July 30, 2002: A suicide bomber blows himself up in Jerusalem, killing two. Hamas claims responsibility.

August 10, 2002: An Israeli tank kills one Palestinian in the West Bank town of Tulkarem.

August 20, 2002: Scores of Israeli armored personnel carriers and hundreds of soldiers backed by helicopter gunships attack the Tulkarem refugee camp.

August 21, 2002: Israeli forces, backed by armored personnel carriers and helicopter gunships, attack a Palestinian refugee camp south of Gaza, killing a Palestinian civilian and injuring five others.

August 22, 2002: Israeli forces demolish more than 21 Palestinian homes in the Gaza Strip, leaving 450 people homeless.

August 26, 2002: Israeli troops, backed by tanks and armored personnel carriers, attack the town of Jenin and its refugee camp.

August 28, 2002: Israeli forces shell the coastal village of Sheikh Ijleen, near Gaza City, killing four Palestinians, including a mother and her two children.

August 31, 2002: At least five Palestinians are killed and many others wounded when Israeli helicopter gunships attack a passenger car in the West Bank village of Tubas.

September 5, 2002: Israel rejects a peace plan prepared by the European Union and presented to Israeli and Palestinian leaders by the visiting Danish Foreign Minister.

September 12, 2002: Israeli tanks invade the Shujaiya neighborhood in eastern Gaza, destroying and vandalizing civilian property.

September 17, 2002: Jewish settlers near Hebron detonate a bomb in a Palestinian primary school, injuring at least five children.

September 19, 2002: A Palestinian bomber blows himself up inside a passenger bus in Tel Aviv, killing five other people. Another Palestinian suicide bombing, near the town of Um el-Fahm, kills one Israeli soldier and wounds two others.

September 20, 2002: Israeli tanks and bulldozers smash their way through Arafat's compound in Ramallah, destroying half of the last building still standing.

September 24, 2002: Israeli forces kill nine Palestinians in the Gaza Strip.

September 25, 2002: Israeli forces dynamite the family home of the former Mayor of Dura, in Hebron, as a reprisal for his son's involvement in attacks on Israeli troops.

September 28, 2002: Thousands of Palestinians march in the streets of the West Bank and Gaza Strip, commemorating the second anniversary of the Palestinian Uprising.

September 30, 2002: Israeli occupation soldiers shoot and kill a Palestinian child in the Balata refugee camp.

October 3, 2002: Sharon expresses hopes of accommodating one million Russian Jews over the next few years in illegal settlements in the Occupied Territories.

October 7, 2002: At least ten Palestinian civilians are killed and more than 80 others are wounded before dawn when an Israeli helicopter gunship fires missiles at civilians in Khan Yunis, in the Gaza Strip.

October 10, 2002: One woman is killed and ten others wounded in Tel Aviv when a Palestinian suicide bomber attacks an Israeli bus carrying soldiers to their base.

October 16, 2002: A report issued by the Israeli human rights group, B'tselem, points out that more than 80 percent of Palestinian civilians killed by Israeli occupation troops during curfew-enforcing activity were children.

October 17, 2002: Israeli tanks fire on several Palestinian houses in Rafah; at least eight Palestinians are killed in the southern Gaza town near the Egyptian border.

October 22, 2002: Two Palestinian bombers blow themselves up inside Israel; hospital sources say at least 14 people, including the two bombers, were killed.

October 23, 2002: At least 13 Palestinians are injured when an Israeli army unit detonates a remote-controlled bomb inside a bus in the Balata refugee camp.

October 24, 2002: U.S. Envoy, William Burns, is dispatched to the area to deliver a message to the Palestinians. He tells them that no negotiations will take place and Palestinians will have no hope of statehood until they take extreme measures to uproot terrorism.

October 27, 2002: At least three Israeli soldiers are killed and more than 30 others injured by a Palestinian suicide bomber at a gas station on a Jewish settlement in the West Bank.

October 29, 2002: Arafat appoints a new cabinet.

October 30, 2002: Israel's coalition cabinet collapses. One Palestinian fighter and three Jewish settlers are killed in a shootout on a settlement north of Nablus.

November 3, 2002: Israeli forces blow up two Palestinian homes with dynamite.

November 4, 2002: At least two people are killed and over 20 others injured when a bomb goes off inside a shop in the Israeli town of Kfar Saba, northeast of Tel Aviv.

November 6, 2002: At least two Palestinians are killed in two separate shooting incidents in the southern and central parts of the Gaza Strip.

November 10, 2002: At least five Jewish settlers are killed and ten injured when Palestinian fighters attack a Jewish settlement in the northern West Bank.

November 12, 2002: Israeli forces attack Tulkarem and Nablus. They shoot dead a two-year-old child.

November 15, 2002: Palestinian fighters attack a Jewish settlement in Hebron, killing twelve settlers.

November 19, 2002: Five Palestinians are killed as Israeli soldiers sweep through Tulkarem.

November 21, 2002: A Palestinian detonates a bomb aboard an Israeli bus in the heart of West Jerusalem, killing at least ten Israeli settlers, including several children, and injuring 30 others.

November 22, 2002: British United Nations worker, Ian Hook, and an eleven-year-old Palestinian boy, are shot and killed by Israeli soldiers in Jenin.

November 27, 2002: Israeli helicopter gunships shoot rockets into a building in the Jenin refugee camp, killing two people.

November 28, 2002: At least seven people are killed and more than 15 others injured when Palestinian fighters open fire on Israeli soldiers and settlers in the city of Bisan, 120 kilometers northwest of Jerusalem.

November 29, 2002: Ariel Sharon emerges victorious from a Likud leadership challenge.

December 1, 2002: As many as 30 Israeli tanks and armored vehicles, backed by helicopter gunships, attack a town in the northern Gaza Strip.

December 3, 2002: Israel's ambassador to the United Nations states that Palestinians should have their own state. Sharon denounces the remarks.

December 4, 2002: Israeli forces kill a 95-year-old Palestinian woman near Ramallah after opening fire on a minibus taxi. Three Palestinians are also killed in two separate attacks in Hebron and the Gaza Strip.

December 6, 2002: Israeli forces attack a refugee camp in the Gaza Strip, killing more than ten civilians.

December 10, 2002: Israeli forces bulldoze three more Palestinian homes in Rafah.

December 11, 2002: Israeli forces shoot and kill five Palestinians in the Gaza Strip.

December 12, 2002: Two Jewish settlers are killed in Hebron.

December 15, 2002: Israeli forces demolish 16 houses and destroy eight greenhouses in the Rafah area.

December 22, 2002: Palestinian presidential elections are delayed, as officials say that a fair vote is impossible under Israeli occupation.

December 26, 2002: Israel speeds up its assassination policy, killing more than seven Palestinians in one day.

December 30, 2002: The Israeli Knesset attempts to prevent Arab members voting in the general election, saying that they should lose the right to vote since they sympathize with the Palestinian resistance.

2003

January 2, 2003: Israeli forces kill three boys in a Gaza night raid.

January 5, 2003: Two suicide bombers kill more than 23 people and wound 100 others in Tel Aviv.

January 19, 2003: Sharon disregards European diplomatic attempts to forge a lasting ceasefire with the Palestinians. He charges the Europeans with anti-Semitism and claims that the only honest partner is the U.S.

January 26, 2003: Israeli forces launch a major attack on the Gaza Strip, killing twelve and injuring eight Palestinians.

February 11, 2003: According to U.N.R.W.A., the problem of unemployment and hunger in Palestinian areas is reaching alarming levels, similar to Congo. They place the responsibility on Western governments who haven't heeded the U.N.'s call for additional relief funding.

February 14, 2003: The Belgian Supreme Court charges that Sharon could be tried for war crimes committed against Palestinians in South Lebanon in 1982.

February 20, 2003: Israel launches new attacks on the Gaza Strip, killing more than eleven people in one day.

March 3, 2003: Israeli soldiers kill eight people, including a pregnant woman in the Gaza Strip.

March 5, 2003: A suicide bomber blows himself up in Haifa, killing 15 Israelis.

March 6, 2003: Israeli forces kill at least eleven Palestinians in a major raid in the Gaza Strip.

March 16, 2003: Twenty-three-year-old Rachel Corrie, a peace activist from the United States, is deliberately crushed to death by an Israeli bulldozer, while peacefully protesting the demolition of a Palestinian home in Gaza.

March 19, 2003: Mahmoud Abbas agrees to become the first Palestinian Prime Minister.

April 2, 2003: Six Palestinians are killed and more than a thousand boys and men are arrested by Israeli forces in the West Bank and Gaza.

April 9, 2003: More than 20 Palestinian children are wounded when Jewish extremists detonate a bomb on a school playground near Jenin.

April 20, 2003: Six Palestinians are killed and 48 are wounded in Rafah by Israeli forces.

April 30, 2003: The Quartet—the E.U., U.N., Russia, and the U.S.—launches the Road Map Peace Plan.

May 1, 2003: Israeli forces raid a home in Gaza, killing 14 Palestinians, including two children. Israelis justify the raid saying that the house was a bomb factory.

May 7, 2003: Israeli soldiers kill one Palestinian in Nablus.

May 18, 2003: A suicide bomber kills seven passengers on an Israeli bus.

May 25, 2003: The U.S. brokered Road Map for Peace Plan is accepted by the Israelis with much hesitance, and an exhaustive attachment of conditions demanded by Israel of Palestinians.

June 4, 2003: In a summit between Sharon, Bush, and Abbas, the new Palestinian Prime Minister declares that armed resistance against the occupation must be eliminated.

June 6, 2003: Hamas said it was breaking off talks with Abbas on ending its retaliatory attacks on Israelis, in a strong challenge to pledges Abbas made at a U.S.-led summit.

June 10, 2003: Israel carries out air strikes in Gaza, targeting Hamas leader, Abdelaziz Rantisi. The strike is unsuccessful.

June 11, 2003: Sixteen people are killed in a bus bomb in Jerusalem.

June 13, 2003: Israel pledges a "war to the bitter end" against Hamas.

June 17, 2003: An Israeli settler girl is killed by Palestinian fighters in the West Bank.

June 22, 2003: Israel kills a top Hamas leader in one of its "targeted assassinations."

June 25, 2003: Israeli troops kill two Palestinians in the Gaza Strip.

June 27, 2003: Israeli troops kill four Palestinians.

June 27, 2003: Palestinian factions agree with the Palestinian Authority to temporarily halt attacks on Israelis. The one-sided ceasefire lasts for seven weeks. During this period, scores of Palestinians are killed and seriously wounded by Israeli forces.

June 30, 2003: Israel returns the Gaza Strip's main highway to Palestinian control, temporarily ending a 30-month blockade.

July 1, 2003: The B.B.C. airs a controversial documentary about Israel. The Israeli government in turn accuses the B.B.C. of anti-Semitism and severs ties with the British network.

July 25, 2003: Israeli forces invade the West Bank, killing a four-year-old boy and injuring two other children with machine gun fire.

July 25, 2003: Abbas meets with Bush in the White House for the first time, in an attempt to jump-start the peace process.

July 29, 2003: President Bush requests a halt to the construction of the Separation Wall; his calls go ignored by Sharon.

August 6, 2003: Israel initiates a process to release more than 300 Palestinian prisoners.

August 14, 2003: Israeli troops kill one Palestinian.

August 20, 2003: A suicide bomber attacks a bus in Jerusalem, killing at least 18 people.

August 21, 2003: A senior Hamas official cancels the ceasefire after Israeli helicopter missiles kill the moderate Hamas leader, Ismail Abu Shanab.

September 5, 2003: Israeli commandos kill a leading Palestinian activist in the West Bank.

September 6, 2003: Abbas resigns after clashing with Arafat over the reform of security services.

September 8, 2003: Arafat's nominee for Prime Minister, Ahmed Qorei, requires assurances from Washington and Europe that their policies regarding Israel's poor treatment of Palestinians will change before he assumes the role of Prime Minister.

September 9, 2003: A suicide bomber kills 15 Israeli soldiers.

September 10, 2003: Senior Hamas leader, Mahmoud Zahar, is wounded along with his wife, and his son is killed, when Israeli warplanes attack his home with rockets.

September 14, 2003: The Israeli government declares that it is considering killing Arafat, as he has become a liability in the peace process, according to Israeli officials.

September 16, 2003: A U.N. resolution which presses Israel not to harm Arafat in any way is vetoed by the U.S. in the Security Council.

September 25, 2003: One of the most prominent Palestinian intellectuals, Professor Edward Said of Columbia University, dies in a New York hospital after a battle with leukemia that lasted several years.

October 1, 2003: The Israeli cabinet votes in favor of extending the West Bank Separation Wall.

October 4, 2003: A female suicide bomber blows herself up in a Haifa cafe, killing 20.

October 5, 2003: Israel takes its battle against the Palestinians to Syria, bombing near the capital Damascus for the first time in decades. Israel justifies its actions by saying that Syria is hosting terrorist organizations.

October 10, 2003: An eight-year-old Palestinian boy is killed by Israeli troops in the southern Gaza Strip.

October 11, 2003: An Israeli attack on the Rafah refugee camp destroys over 100 homes, rendering nearly 1500 people homeless. Israeli forces also destroy water tanks and pipes, uproot trees, and confine the camp's residents to their homes for days.

October 12, 2003: Ten Palestinians are killed and 51 wounded when Israeli forces launch a massive military invasion on the Yubna refugee camp near Rafah.

October 13, 2003: The Geneva Accords, an alternative peace-plan negotiated by prominent ex-Israeli and Palestinian officials, is unveiled. Israel and some

Palestinian groups quickly reject the plan, saying that it contains too many compromises. The plan fails to adequately address the issue of the right of return for Palestinian refugees.

October 21, 2003: Twelve Palestinians are killed and more than 100 injured when Israeli military jets and gunships carry out five consecutive air raids on Gaza City and a densely populated refugee camp.

October 22, 2003: In a decision seen as a sharp rebuke to Israel, the U.N. General Assembly overwhelmingly approves a resolution demanding the Jewish State "stop and reverse" the construction of the unilateral Separation Wall it is building on Palestinian land. Israel says it will ignore the resolution.

October 24, 2003: Palestinian fighters kill three Israeli soldiers in an illegal Jewish settlement in the Gaza Strip.

October 26, 2003: Thousands of Palestinians living near the construction of the Separation Wall are required by the Israeli government to obtain permits, granting them permission to continue to live in their own homes.

October 30, 2003: Israeli forces shoot dead two boys aged 12 and 16 in the West Bank and an armed Palestinian man in the Gaza Strip. The killings come only days after the killing of an eleven-year-old Palestinian boy near a Jewish settlement in Gaza.

November 2, 2003: According to a European Commission poll of more than 7000 Europeans, Israel is considered a greater threat to world peace than North Korea, Afghanistan, and Iran.

November 8, 2003: Six Palestinians are killed and more than ten others injured by Israeli forces in the West Bank and the Gaza Strip.

November 18, 2003: A Palestinian gunman kills two Israelis at a West Bank roadblock.

November 23, 2003: Israeli forces shoot dead two Palestinians in the West Bank and the Gaza Strip.

November 28, 2003: Israel receives harsh criticism from U.N. Secretary General, Kofi Annan, regarding the Separation Wall. According to Annan, the wall violates international law and must be taken down.

November 29, 2003: Israeli forces shoot dead six Palestinians in the West Bank and Gaza Strip during a major Muslim feast.

December 1, 2003: Israeli forces launch a large-scale invasion of the West Bank cities of Ramallah and al-Bireh, killing three Palestinians including a nine-year-old boy.

December 7, 2003: Israeli forces shoot dead three Palestinian youth.

December 11, 2003: Six Palestinians are killed in a major Israeli attack in southern Gaza.

December 18, 2003: Israeli forces shoot dead seven Palestinians in the West Bank and the Gaza Strip.

December 23, 2003: At least seven Palestinians are killed and some 30 others wounded in an Israeli military raid on the southern Gaza Strip town of Rafah, a few days after troops kill four Palestinians in the West Bank refugee camp of Balata.

December 25, 2003: Five Palestinians, including three members of Islamic Jihad, are killed in an Israeli air strike in Gaza. Shortly after, four Israelis are killed by a suicide bombing near Tel Aviv.

December 31, 2003: Israel approves a plan to double the number of settlements in the occupied Syrian Golan Heights.

2004

January 3, 2004: Israeli soldiers shoot dead five Palestinians in Nablus and Gaza.

January 8, 2004: The Israeli army steps up its raids in the West Bank, killing three Palestinians and arresting 19.

January 9, 2004: Palestinian Prime Minister, Ahmed Qorei, says that he will seek a one-state solution if Sharon annexes parts of the West Bank and imposes borders on Palestinians.

January 14, 2004: In the past week, three Palestinians are killed, six others wounded, and eleven houses demolished. A Jewish settler and four Israeli soldiers are killed and ten others are wounded in Palestinian attacks.

January 28, 2004: One week before the Muslim feast of Eid Al-Adha, 13 Palestinians are killed by Israeli forces in Gaza.

January 29, 2004: A Palestinian suicide bomber kills ten on a West Jerusalem bus.

February 2, 2004: Israeli forces raid the Rafah refugee camp in southern Gaza Strip, killing four Palestinians.

February 2, 2004: The Sharon government unveils the Disengagement Plan, to empty all settlements in the Gaza Strip, citing the need to fortify their settlement project in the West Bank.

February 7, 2004: Israeli forces assassinate a top Islamic Jihad leader in Gaza, and a twelve-year-old bystander, after launching rockets from a helicopter gunship.

February 9, 2004: Legal action is taken against the Sharon government by several Israeli human rights groups in regard to the Separation Wall, built illegally on Palestinian land, stating that it infringes on the human rights of Palestinians affected by its construction.

February 11, 2004: Israeli forces storm a Palestinian neighborhood in the Gaza Strip, killing 15 Palestinians.

February 12, 2004: The international court of human rights in The Hague holds hearings on the legality of the Separation Wall. In protest, Israel refuses to send representatives to the hearings, saying that no one has the right to interfere in Israel's internal affairs.

February 18, 2004: The International Committee of the Red Cross calls on Israel to halt construction of the steel and concrete "security fence" through the West Bank because it breaches international law and is causing widespread harm to Palestinians.

February 22, 2004: A Palestinian bomber kills eight people on a crowded Jerusalem bus.

February 25, 2004: Israeli forces raid Palestinian financial institutions in Ramallah, seizing large sums of money.

February 29, 2004: An Israeli helicopter fires two rockets at a car in the Gaza Strip, killing three people, including an Islamic Jihad member, and wounding 15 others.

March 3, 2004: Israel kills three members of Hamas in an air strike in the Gaza Strip.

March 6, 2004: Israeli forces kill a 19-year-old Palestinian policeman, two Palestinian children die and a third is critically wounded.

March 7, 2004: Israeli forces invade Gaza, killing 14 Palestinians, three of them children.

March 10, 2004: Five members of Al-Aqsa Martyrs Brigades are killed in the town of Jenin.

March 14, 2004: Two Palestinian suicide bombers kill at least seven people in a double-attack at Israel's port town of Ashdod.

March 17, 2004: Israelis kill four Palestinians in Rafah, demolishing five houses and wounding nine people, one critically.

March 21, 2004: Israeli forces kill three Palestinian activists and three bystanders in A'basan village east of the central Gaza Strip.

March 21, 2004: Israeli helicopter gunships assassinate Hamas spiritual leader, Sheikh Ahmed Yassin. Six bystanders are also killed.

March 24, 2004: Top Hamas leader, Dr. Abdelaziz Rantisi, is chosen as the new supreme head of the Palestinian Islamic group Hamas to succeed Sheikh Ahmed Yassin.

April 5, 2004: Three Palestinians are killed in the heart of the Gaza Strip by several Israeli missiles.

April 10, 2004: A twelve-year-old Palestinian girl is shot dead in Khan Yunis.

April 12, 2004: Israeli forces kill three Palestinians, northwest of the Jewish settlement of Nitzarim.

April 17, 2004: Abdelaziz Rantisi is assassinated by Israeli forces when a helicopter fires rockets onto his car in Gaza.

April 20, 2004: Five Palestinians are killed in an Israeli raid on northern Gaza.

April 20, 2004: After 18 years, Israeli whistle-blower Mordechai Vananu is released from an Israeli prison. Vanunu was imprisoned for exposing Israel's position as one of the world's greatest nuclear powers.

April 22, 2004: At least nine Palestinians are killed as Israeli troops raid a Gaza Strip town.

April 23, 2004: Sharon warns that Arafat may be the next on the list of Israel's "targeted killings."

April 27, 2004: Israeli troops kill five Palestinians throughout the Occupied Territories.

April 29, 2004: One Hamas fighter is killed and four Israeli soldiers are wounded in a car bombing on a Gaza Strip settlement.

May 2, 2004: Israeli missiles kill four members of the Palestinian resistance in a strike on a car in the West Bank city of Nablus.

May 4, 2004: Two Palestinians are killed and 30 homes are demolished by Israeli forces in Khan Yunis.

May 10, 2004: Israeli forces kill one Palestinian in Khan Yunis and one near Occupied East Jerusalem.

May 13, 2004: A powerful explosion rips apart an Israeli armored personnel carrier, killing five soldiers in Gaza.

May 14, 2004: Israel kills twelve Palestinians in revenge raids on the Gaza Strip. Eleven Palestinians are killed in helicopter missile strikes in the Rafah refugee camp.

May 18, 2004: Israeli forces attack the Rafah refugee camp, killing at least 20 people. Three of the victims are children.

May 19, 2004: Israeli forces kill at least ten Palestinians in Gaza.

May 20, 2004: The Israeli forces kill six Palestinians in Rafah city.

May 20, 2004: Palestinian popular leader, Marwan Barghouti, is found guilty of murder in an Israeli court.

June 2, 2004: Two Palestinians are killed by Israeli forces in Gaza.

June 6, 2004: An Israeli court sentences Marwan Barghouti to life in prison for the charge of murder.

June 7, 2004: Israeli forces kill two Palestinians and wound five others in different parts of the Occupied Territories.

June 15, 2004: Israeli forces kill two Palestinians, including a leader of the Al-Aqsa Martyrs Brigades, in the West Bank city of Nablus.

June 23, 2004: Three Palestinians are killed in a northern Gaza Strip town.

June 24, 2004: Israeli forces impose a curfew on parts of the West Bank. Three Palestinians are killed in the Gaza Strip.

June 28, 2004: Palestinian rockets kill two people. Palestinian fighters blow up an army post in the Gaza Strip, killing one Israeli soldier.

June 28, 2004: Israeli forces kill three Palestinians in Khan Yunis.

July 1, 2004: Israeli forces seal off and impose a curfew on Jericho and Nablus. They continue their siege of the northern Gaza Strip town of Beit Hanoun, where they begin bulldozing a five-kilometer-deep "security zone."

July 2, 2004: Israeli forces kill three Palestinians in the Gaza Strip.

July 5, 2004: Israeli forces kill a Palestinian security officer in Rafah.

July 6, 2004: Israeli forces kill four in Nablus.

July 9, 2004: Members of an Israeli undercover unit break into several houses in Gaza, killing seven Palestinians.

July 9, 2004: The International Court of Justice rules that the West Bank Separation Wall is illegal and that construction must be halted. It brands Israel's vast barrier through the West Bank a de facto land-grab and tells Israel to tear it down and compensate the victims.

July 11, 2004: Sharon says the world court's ruling regarding the Separation Wall enables terrorists.

July 14, 2004: 110 Palestinian children in the West Bank city of Hebron survive death after drinking poisoned water taken from a well apparently spoiled by a group of Israeli settlers.

July 18, 2004: Sharon presses French Jews to immigrate to Israel to evade the problem of anti-Semitism.

July 21, 2004: The U.N. General Assembly overwhelmingly adopts a resolution by 150–6 votes, with ten abstentions, demanding that Israel comply with the International Court of Justice "advisory opinion" on the Separation Wall. Israel and the United States vote against. All 25 members of the European Union vote in favor. Israel accuses the E.U. of "encouraging Palestinian terrorism."

July 31, 2004: Eight Palestinians are killed by Israeli forces, who also extra-judicially execute three activists.

August 3, 2004: Israeli gunships fire missiles, killing three Palestinians in a Rafah refugee camp.

August 5, 2004: Israeli forces kill five Palestinians in the northern Gaza Strip.

August 11, 2004: A car bomb explodes between two Israeli army checkpoints on a busy transit route outside Jerusalem, killing two Palestinians.

August 15, 2004: Palestinian prisoners protest inhumane prison conditions by instituting a 1600-participant hunger strike.

August 17, 2004: Israel announces plans to construct another 1000 settlement units in the West Bank.

August 18, 2004: Israeli attempts to assassinate a leading Hamas figure in Gaza are foiled. But, five bystanders are killed and twelve are seriously wounded.

August 23, 2004: Israel declares that it plans to build another 530 settlement units in the West Bank, following a shift in U.S. policy regarding the settlement issue.

August 29, 2004: Rumors of an F.B.I. investigation into Israeli espionage in the Pentagon are revealed. Israel denies any such charges.

August 31, 2004: Sixteen people are killed in suicide bombings on two buses in the Israeli town of Beersheba.

September 4, 2004: Israeli forces kill two Palestinians in Gaza and Rafah.

September 6, 2004: Israeli forces kill 14 Palestinians in Gaza.

September 8, 2004: Israeli plans to expand settlements and confiscate 8000 more acres of Palestinian land are announced by Israeli Agricultural Minister, Israel Katz.

September 30, 2004: Israeli forces kill at least 23 Palestinians in a major onslaught in the Gaza Strip.

October 5, 2004: Israeli forces invade Gaza, demolish hundreds of homes, and destroy scores of acres of agricultural land.

October 14, 2004: Israel's Foreign Minister cautions the Sharon government, saying that Israel risks being branded like apartheid South Africa if the Israelis continue assaulting Palestinians.

October 27, 2004: Israeli legislators vote in favor of the Disengagement Plan, a controversial plan to withdraw Jewish settlers from Gaza.

October 29, 2004: Arafat is stricken with poor and suspicious health problems and is flown to Paris for medical treatment.

November 11, 2004: Arafat dies in France aged 75. Israel welcomes his death, saying that it may be a turning point for peace in the Middle East. Mahmoud Abbas is elected head of the Palestine Liberation Organization.

November 22, 2004: The U.S. Secretary of State, Colin Powell, travels to Israel and the West Bank.

November 25, 2004: Abbas vows to bring Palestinian militants to their knees.

December 1, 2004: Jailed popular leader, Marwan Barghouti, decides not to run against Abbas in upcoming elections.

December 12, 2004: Barghouti officially drops out of the Palestinian presidential race and expresses his support for Abbas.

December 14, 2004: Abbas condemns the Palestinian uprising, saying it was a mistake and must come to an end immediately.

2005

January 3, 2005: An Israeli soldier is arrested after calling on his comrades to refuse to evacuate a West Bank settlement outpost.

January 4, 2005: Mahmoud Abbas condemns "the Zionist enemy" after seven children on their way to pick strawberries are killed by Israeli tank shells.

January 5, 2005: Sharon vows to use the full force of government power against any Jewish settlers who violently resist his planned withdrawal from Gaza.

January 9, 2005: Palestinians elect Abbas to succeed Yasser Arafat as chairman of the Palestinian Authority.

January 10, 2005: Israel's parliament backs a new coalition government, giving Sharon a firm basis to implement his Gaza pull-out plan.

January 10, 2005: Abbas is confirmed as winner of the Palestinian presidential elections. He gains the support of Palestinian groups, despite concerns over electoral irregularities.

January 11, 2005: Sharon telephones Abbas to congratulate him on his election victory, while Arafat's former security advisor resigns in a move seen as pre-empting a security forces shake-up.

January 13, 2005: Members of a Palestinian faction detonate a bomb on the edge of the Gaza Strip, killing at least five Israelis.

January 14, 2005: Israel seals off the Gaza Strip.

January 15, 2005: Abbas is sworn in as the new President of the Palestinian Authority in the West Bank town of Ramallah. He uses his inauguration speech to call for a ceasefire between Israel and Palestinian groups.

January 21, 2005: Hundreds of Palestinian Authority police take up positions in the northern Gaza Strip to stop members of various Palestinian factions from firing rockets on Israeli targets.

January 21, 2005: Abbas presents Hamas and other Palestinian factions with proposals to end their military struggle against Israel in return for international guarantees of a ceasefire.

January 23, 2005: Hamas and Islamic Jihad agree to suspend attacks on Israel in order to give Abbas time to secure international guarantees for a comprehensive ceasefire that would end more than four years of Intifada.

January 24, 2005: Following a week of talks between Abbas and Palestinian opposition leaders, the groups say they have agreed to a ceasefire.

January 30, 2005: Israel says it is prepared to transfer responsibility for security in several West Bank towns to the new Palestinian leadership in the latest measure aimed at securing a permanent ceasefire.

February 3, 2005: Israel approves a plan to free hundreds of jailed Palestinians and to withdraw forces from West Bank cities.

February 8, 2005: After a summit at the Egyptian resort of Sharm el-Sheikh, Abbas and Sharon declare a truce. Both express hopes that the informal ceasefire will lead to a new era of hope for the region.

February 9, 2005: Israel says it will lift roadblocks around some West Bank cities to allow freer movement and will take other steps to ease controls on Palestinians as both sides seek to build on the newly announced ceasefire.

February 15, 2005: Israel will not give up the main Jewish settlements in the West Bank as part of a final peace deal with the Palestinians, Sharon says. He tells a press conference that Jewish "population blocks" have been there for many years and that they "will be part of the Jewish state in the future."

February 17, 2005: Israel's Attorney-General lifts the threat of indictment against Sharon in a scandal over illegal campaign funds, but charges the Prime Minister's son, Omri, with fraud and other crimes in the same case.

February 24, 2005: The Palestinian parliament approves a new line-up of ministers in which technocrats replace loyalists of the late Yasser Arafat.

February 25, 2005: A Palestinian suicide bomber blows himself up outside a seafront nightclub in Tel Aviv, killing at least four people and wounding dozens.

March 1, 2005: A ripple of change is running through the Middle East, says the British Prime Minister, Tony Blair as he hosts a Middle East conference in London.

March 15, 2005: Palestinians prepare to assume responsibility for security in Jericho; the Israeli army announces a planned withdrawal from Tulkarem and Qalqilya within days.

March 15, 2005: Israel announces plans to annex large Palestinian areas around Jerusalem; 26,000 Palestinian homes are set for demolition.

March 19, 2005: The Palestinian Authority probes alleged selling of "Orthodox property" in Jerusalem; the Greek Orthodox Church says the reported deal is "null and void."

March 20, 2005: Arab foreign ministers reach a consensus on redrafting a Jordanian proposal which was harshly criticized for offering unconditional normalization with Israel.

March 21, 2005: Shaul Mofaz approves the expansion of the illegal Jewish settlement of Maale Adumim in East Jerusalem by 3500 units.

March 22, 2005: The Israeli military hands over the West Bank town of Tulkarem to the Palestinian Authority but three adjacent villages remain occupied.

March 22, 2005: Israel rejects the Arab countries' call for peace as Abbas proposes that an Arab delegation visit Washington.

March 22, 2005: Outraged Palestinians urge Bush and Blair to intervene to stop proposed Israeli expansions of the Maale Adumim settlement block, aimed at isolating Arab East Jerusalem.

March 24, 2005: In an Arab League summit held in Algeria, Arab leaders reject the resettlement of Palestinian refugees in host countries. They reactivate the Arab peace initiative.

March 27, 2005: Palestinians respond angrily to what they perceive as a contradictory American position regarding Israeli settlements. The Palestinian Authority says the U.S. cannot decide on behalf of Palestinians, asserting that all Jewish settlements are illegal under international law.

March 28, 2005: Palestinian officials say Palestinian–Israeli relations "are headed towards a real crisis" because of Israel's wavering on the implementation of the Road Map.

April 3, 2005: Abbas makes sweeping security changes and a state of alert is declared in the West Bank as several security chiefs announce "retirement."

April 5, 2005: The Palestinian Authority announces that it will report Israeli garbage dumping to the World Health Organization, saying Israel is purposely polluting West Bank aquifers and is damaging fertile land.

April 6, 2005: Bush urges Israel to commit to the Road Map and to stop settlement expansion.

April 10, 2005: The Israeli army shoots dead three Palestinian boys in the Gaza Strip. Eyewitnesses say that the victims were playing soccer when the soldiers opened fire.

April 13, 2005: Palestinian official, Saeb Erekat, says unilateral withdrawal will turn Gaza into the "biggest prison in history."

April 16, 2005: Thousands of Palestinian detainees go on a hunger strike to protest inhuman prison conditions.

April 17, 2005: Abbas declares that Palestinian legislative elections will be held on time; Hamas is apprehensive.

April 19, 2005: Sharon's office outlines the Gaza "Disengagement Plan" which stipulates that Israel will maintain control of the border perimeter, air space, and coast security.

April 20, 2005: Abbas says Israel is undermining his authority and the legitimacy of the Palestinian Authority.

April 23, 2005: Abbas and Sharon agree to meet in near future, according to official Israeli sources.

April 27, 2005: Abbas issues four presidential reform decrees, and appoints a new preventive security service chief.

April 27, 2005: Palestinian Prime Minister, Ahmed Qorei, says the P.A. is ready to control Gaza after the Israeli withdrawal.

April 28, 2005: Palestinian officials welcome a proposal by Russian President Putin to host an international conference in Moscow on the Middle East. The U.S. and Israel reject the Russian proposal.

May 4, 2005: The Israeli group, Peace Now, decries Israel's settlement expansion.

May 5, 2005: The Israeli army shoots dead two Palestinian boys protesting the Separation Wall. The second stage of local Palestinian elections is launched.

May 7, 2005: U.S. Congress channels U.S. aid to Palestinians through Israel and N.G.O.s.

May 9, 2005: The Grand Mufti of Jerusalem calls on Palestinians to defend the city's holy sites against the threat of Jewish extremists.

May 10, 2005: Preliminary official results of Palestinian local polls announce that 86 percent of registered voters cast their ballots.

May 11, 2005: The "Declaration of Brasilia" asserts the right to resist occupation; Abbas questions Israel's democracy while Brazilian President Lula praises Palestinian patience.

May 11, 2005: Israel closes Palestinian election offices in East Jerusalem.

May 16, 2005: Abbas calls for a just solution to the refugee problem; Qorei says Palestinians will never give up the right of return.

May 19, 2005: Israel returns to extra-judicial killings by air strikes, seriously wounding a Palestinian in the Gaza Strip.

May 21, 2005: Abbas urges Palestinian factions to remain committed to the Sharm el-Sheikh truce. Israeli military escalation claims three more Palestinian lives.

May 23, 2005: Israel agrees to hand control of the Rafah border post to Egypt; the latter says it plans to deploy troops to both sides of the crossing.

May 25, 2005: Abbas travels to the U.S., seeking American political support and financial assistance.

May 26, 2005: Amnesty International decries Israeli war crimes and crimes against humanity. They say that Israeli forces continue to carry out extrajudicial executions and home demolitions.

May 28, 2005: President Bush says Israel should not prejudice final status negotiations on Jerusalem. Canada's Prime Minister, Paul Martin, pledges $9.7 million in aid for Palestinians.

May 29, 2005: Israeli troops shoot dead two Palestinians in the West Bank and Gaza; an elderly man dies after being denied access to the hospital.

May 31, 2005: The Israeli cabinet votes in favor of releasing 400 Palestinian prisoners; the P.A. says that the move is not enough.

June 5, 2005: Palestinian factions wrangle over the election date: Fatah recommends changing the electoral law as Hamas rejects postponement of elections.

June 8, 2005: Israeli forces kill six Palestinians; the P.A. warns that the Israeli military escalation endangers the fragile truce.

June 9, 2005: Abbas calls for a complete and coordinated Israeli withdrawal from Gaza. British Foreign Minister, Jack Straw, says peace, the creation of a Palestinian state, and security are in the Palestinian leader's hands.

June 18, 2005: Israel reportedly starts building a sea wall off the Gaza Strip; Erekat protests "Israel's barriers mentality."

June 21, 2005: The Palestinian Interior Minister says the Palestinian Authority will act against those who undermine the truce.

June 23, 2005: The Israeli army resumes its assassination policy; Palestinian officials appeal to the U.S. and the E.U. to save the fragile truce.

June 29, 2005: Qorei declares "emergency measures" to ease Israeli withdrawal from Gaza.

June 30, 2005: Eight Palestinian women are nominated for the Noble Peace Prize 2005.

July 12, 2005: The P.L.O. says Israel is transferring the Palestinian population of Jerusalem and strongly criticizes Israel's "land-grab in broad daylight."

July 13, 2005: The Palestinian Authority condemns a suicide bombing in the Israeli city of Netanya. The bomber kills himself and three Israelis, including two teenage girls.

July 14, 2005: Israel cancels all contact with Palestinians.

July 19, 2005: Hamas and Islamic Jihad demand a "reciprocal" ceasefire from Israel.

July 21, 2005: Serious disagreements arise between Hamas and the Palestinian Authority as U.S. Secretary of State, Condoleezza Rice, embarks on a visit to the region. Jewish settlers stab a twelve-year-old Palestinian boy to death.

July 23, 2005: One Palestinian youth is shot dead in Hebron.

July 25, 2005: Sharon orders his army to "stand by for a major operation."

July 26, 2005: Abbas declares Gaza the new base of the Palestinian Authority Cabinet.

July 27, 2005: The Israeli government is reportedly planning a new illegal settlement in the heart of East Jerusalem.

July 28, 2005: Eighteen days ahead of the beginning of the Israeli withdrawal from the Gaza Strip, Abbas says that real peace can only be achieved with the complete end of Israeli military dominance over the Occupied Territories.

July 31, 2005: Palestinians claim the Israeli withdrawal from Gaza is a victory for resistance.

August 1, 2005: Israel threatens another "Operation Defensive Shield"; Palestinians slam renewed Israeli threats.

August 9, 2005: The Israeli government decides to keep Gaza sealed off after the pull-out; Palestinians say Israel will remain an occupying power.

August 10, 2005: Israel says it will retain security control over the northern West Bank, where four isolated settlements were readied for evacuation.

August 13, 2005: Sharon renews his commitment to the settlement project in the Occupied West Bank and East Jerusalem.

August 15, 2005: Palestinian officials describe the Israeli withdrawal as evacuation, not liberation, as settlers continue rioting in protest.

August 16, 2005: The Palestinian Authority sets January 21, 2006, as the date for Palestinian legislative elections.

August 17, 2005: Hundreds of Israeli troops escorted by bulldozers march in formation through the largest settlement in the Gaza Strip, in what the army said was the start of the forcible removal of settlers.

August 21, 2005: Evacuated Gaza settlers resettle in Jerusalem and Hebron. The Israeli government offers additional large financial incentives to those who choose to settle in Jerusalem.

August 22, 2005: Abbas urges the implementation of Bush's two-state vision as Israel launches its largest ever settlement expansion project in Jerusalem; 62,000 dunums of Palestinian land are confiscated to expand the illegal Maale Adumim settlement.

August 23, 2005: Israeli troops enter unopposed into the Gaza Strip's last Jewish settlement to complete the evacuation of the territory after nearly four decades of occupation.

August 24, 2005: Israel pushes Maale Adumim 35 kilometers deep into the West Bank. Bush rules out jumpstarting the Road Map after the Gaza evacuation.

August 25, 2005: Israeli soldiers shoot dead five Palestinians, including two teenagers. An official Palestinian Authority spokesperson describes the killing as "an ugly massacre that was committed in cold blood."

August 27, 2005: The Bush administration stays silent on Israeli settlement expansion in the West Bank.

August 27, 2005: Twelve thousand newcomers increase the population of Jewish settlers in the West Bank to 246,000.

September 3, 2005: Egypt and Israel sign the Philadelphi route pact, amending a 1978 treaty. The pact designates a new role for Egypt in monitoring the Gaza border.

September 4, 2005: Abbas is to meet Bush, Putin, and Blair in New York. Abbas insists that any meeting with Sharon must be an official part of peace negotiations.

September 6, 2005: Israeli officials report the wide interest of Arab and Muslim countries in normalizing relations with Israel, following talks with Pakistan.

September 7, 2005: The Palestinian Authority rejects Israel's supreme court decision to "preserve" 38 synagogues in newly evacuated Gaza. Mousa Arafat, a cousin of Yasser Arafat and founder of the military intelligence unit in the P.A., is murdered after a fierce gun battle. Abbas is outraged.

September 8, 2005: Israel says it will close Gaza's Rafah border for at least six months.

September 9, 2005: Abbas cuts short a U.N. trip to attend to security chaos in Gaza, following the murder of Mousa Arafat.

September 10, 2005: Mousa Arafat is laid to rest with a military funeral as Palestinian factions denounce his murder. Israeli forces blow up their last military posts in Gaza.

September 11, 2005: Palestinians say that Washington's "verbal" objection to Israel's settlement expansion is not enough.

September 12, 2005: The P.L.O. and the P.A. decide Gaza is still occupied.

September 14, 2005: Abbas wants to "engage immediately" in final status negotiations; the U.S. and Israel announce there will be no peace talks until Palestinians prove capable of governing Gaza.

September 17, 2005: Mofaz orders the creation of an Israeli "security zone" inside northern Gaza.

September 19, 2005: Israel decides not to prosecute police responsible for the murder of 13 Palestinian citizens inside Israel in the early months of the uprising. "Israeli Arabs" protest the decision.

September 20, 2002: Media reports say that Israel has agreed in principle to an E.U. role in policing the Gaza–Egypt border.

September 21, 2005: An Israeli official calls for the annexation of 28 Palestinian towns into Israeli territory.

September 22, 2005: Palestinians come under heavy U.S. and Israeli pressure to disarm Palestinian factions; Abbas says disarming is "an internal affair."

September 23, 2005: An extremist Jewish group, Ateret Cohanim, is reportedly digging 80 meters away from the Al-Aqsa Mosque in Jerusalem; Palestinian's fear for the mosque's foundation.

September 24, 2005: Nineteen Palestinians are reportedly killed in a large explosion in a Gaza refugee camp. The blast takes place during a Hamas rally celebrating the Israeli withdrawal from the Gaza Strip. Hamas blames Israeli airplanes for firing missiles into the crowd, a claim supported by eyewitnesses. Israel and the P.A. blame Hamas' own explosives for triggering the blast. Meanwhile, Israel kills three Islamic Jihad activists, setting off a barrage of Palestinian rockets fired by the Palestinian group into Israel.

September 25, 2005: The P.L.O. holds Israel responsible for military escalation in Gaza, which eventually extends to the West Bank. Israel conducts many raids at various parts of the Gaza Strip, wounding many Palestinians and destroying schools, homes, and shops. Israel declares a "new order" in Gaza.

September 26, 2005: Abbas cancels a meeting with Sharon as Israeli bombardments continue. While Hamas renews its commitment to the February ceasefire, the Islamic Jihad says a truce is void as long as Israel is launching a war on Palestinians.

September 27, 2005: The U.S. and Britain renew their commitment to Israel's "security." Bush says Israel has the right to defend itself.

September 28, 2005: Israel presses on with its military offensive against Gaza. Massive arrest raids are underway in the West Bank targeting potential Hamas candidates for Palestinian parliamentary elections, scheduled for January 2006.

September 29, 2005: Palestinians commemorate the fifth anniversary of the Second Palestinian Uprising, the Al-Aqsa Intifada. 4166 Palestinians were reportedly killed and 45,538 were wounded during the past five years. 1113 Israelis were also killed during the same period. All Palestinian factions announce their commitment to the struggle; they say they will carry on until the establishment of an independent and free Palestine.

SOURCES

The Guardian (guardian.co.uk); *BBC News Online* (news.bbc.co.uk); Palestine Media Center (www.palestine-pmc.com); www.Aljazeera.net; www. palestinehistory.com; www.phrmg.org/aqsa.html; www.palestinemonitor. org; en.wikipedia.org; www.emergency.com/2000/intifada2000.html.

Notes

FOREWORD

1. Charles D. Smith, *Palestine and the Arab Israeli Conflict* (New York: St. Martin's Press, 1996), pp. 144–7.
2. Numerous studies have been conducted, all pointing to the same conclusion. Two excellent sources that either completed their own studies or highlighted the work of others on this subject are: http://ifamericansknew.org and http://www.pmwatch.org/pmw/index.asp.

1   THE INTIFADA TAKES OFF (2000–01)

1. Eytan Bentsur, "Israel's Withdrawal from Lebanon," *Israeli Ministry of Foreign Affairs website*, www.mfa.gov.il/MFA/Government/Speeches+by+Israeli+leaders/2000/Op-ed+Article+on+Israel-s+Withdrawal+from+Lebanon.htm, accessed August 29, 2005.
2. Suzanne Goldenberg, "Peace Talks Called off," *Guardian* (May 22, 2000), www.guardian.co.uk/israel/Story/0,2763,223627,00.html.
3. Suzanne Goldenberg, "Barak's Deal Puts Peace in Jeopardy," *Guardian* (June 23, 2000), www.guardian.co.uk/israel/Story/0,2763,335454,00.html.
4. Daniel Pipes, "Israel's Lebanon Lesson," *Jerusalem Post* (May 23, 2001), p. 8.
5. "Memorandum of Agreement between the Governments of the United States of America and the State of Israel," *Jewish Virtual Library*, www.jewishvirtuallibrary.org/jsource/Peace/moa.html, accessed August 29, 2005.
6. Noam Chomsky, "Limited War in Lebanon," *Z Magazine* (September 1993), www.chomsky.info/articles/199309--.htm.
7. Hussein Agha and Robert Malley, "Camp David: The Tragedy of Errors," *New York Review of Books*, Vol. 48, No. 13 (August 2001), www.nybooks.com/articles/14380.
8. Akiva Eldar, "Military Intelligence Presented Erroneous Assumption on Palestinians," *Haaretz* (June 10, 2004).
9. Jumana Odeh, "Who Will Protect Palestine's Children?" *International Herald Tribune* (October 27, 2000), www.commondreams.org/views/102700-107.htm.
10. Bassem Eid, "A Better Intifada," *New York Times* (February 22, 2001), www.nytimes.com/2001/02/22/opinion/22EID.html?ex=1125460800&en=fd31e1860bc296e4&ei=5070.
11. Ali S. Zaghal and Abdel Baset A. Athamneh, "The Humanitarian Aspects of Conflict: The Case of Palestinian Refugees in Jordan" (A study sponsored by UNESCO and The American University in Cairo, Yarmouk University, 2000), www.aucegypt.edu/unescounitwin/paper1.pdf.

12. Jonathan Cook, "Vale of Tears: Tear or Poison Gas?," *Al-Ahram Weekly*, No. 528 (April 5–11, 2001), http://weekly.ahram.org.eg/2001/528/re3. htm.

13. "Tanks Attack Palestinian Refugee Site," *Guardian* (April 11, 2001), www. guardian.co.uk/israel/Story/0,2763,471931,00.html.

14. Ibid.

15. Derek Brown, "Middle East Timeline: 2001," *Guardian* (October 17, 2001), www.guardian.co.uk/israel/Story/0,2763,554603,00.html.

16. Ibid.

17. "Four Palestinians Killed in Gun Battle," *Guardian* (August 22, 2001), www.guardian.co.uk/israel/Story/0,2763,540792,00.html.

18. Emad Gad, "From Israel: Playing with the Dead," *Al-Ahram Weekly*, No. 728 (February 3–9, 2005), http://weekly.ahram.org.eg/2005/728/pr3. htm.

19. Daniel Williams, "Conflict Deepens Despair for Palestinians in Gaza," *Washington Post* (August 20, 2001), p. A07.

20. "Israel Kills Key Palestinian Leader," *BBC News Online* (August 27, 2001), http://news.bbc.co.uk/1/hi/world/middle_east/1511515.stm.

21. "World Welcomes Milosevic Handover," *CNN.com* (July 2, 2001), http:// edition.cnn.com/2001/WORLD/europe/06/28/milosevic.reax.

22. "Panorama: The Accused," *BBC News Online* (June 17, 2001), http://news. bbc.co.uk/1/hi/programmes/panorama/1381328.stm.

23. Hugh Muir, "Sharon is war criminal says Livingstone," *Guardian* (March 4, 2005), http://politics.guardian.co.uk/gla/story/0,9061,1430317,00. html.

24. "UN Security Council Meeting Held on 27 October 1953," United Nations Information System on the Question of Palestine website, http:// domino.un.org/UNISP.A.L.NSF/0/017eefb458011c9d05256722005e5499? OpenDocument, accessed August 30, 2006.

25. See Nur Farahat, "The Force of Law, Not the Law of Force," *Al-Ahram Weekly*, No. 542 (July 12–18, 2001), http://weekly.ahram.org.eg/2001/542/ fo4.htm.

26. "Return of the Terrorist: The Crimes of Ariel Sharon," *CounterPunch.org* (February 7, 2001), www.counterpunch.org/sharon.html.

27. "Panorama: The Accused," *BBC News Online* (June 17, 2001), http:// news.bbc.co.uk/hi/english/static/audio_video/programmes/panorama/ transcripts/transcript_17_06_01.txt.

28. Mike Zmolek, "Ignore the Distractions: Bush Means War," *CommonDreams. org* (September 9, 2002), www.commondreams.org/views02/0909-06.htm.

29. "U.S. Financial Aid To Israel: Figures, Facts, and Impact," *Washington Report on Middle East Affairs*, www.wrmea.com/html/us_aid_to_israel. htm, last accessed October 15, 2005.

30. "Palestinian Refugees: The Right of Return," *Council for the Advancement of Arab-British Understanding* (September 2003), www.caabu.org/press/ factsheets/refugees.pdf, accessed August 29, 2005.

31. "Lessons from Palestinian Diaspora," *Berkeley Journal of International Law*, Vol. 18, No. 2 (2000), www.law.berkeley.edu/journals/bjil/pastissues/18-2.htm.

32. Daryl Lindsey, "The Children's' War, again," *Salon.com* (May 11, 2001), www.salon.com/news/feature/2001/05/11/middle_east.
33. "Former Israeli Soldier: We Behaved Like Animals, Criminals, Thieves toward Palestinians," *MIFTAH.org* (December 1, 2003), http://miftah.org/Display.cfm?DocId=2789&CategoryId=12.
34. "Vatican Outrage Over Church Siege," *BBC News Online* (April 8, 2002), http://news.bbc.co.uk/1/hi/world/middle_east/1916580.stm.
35. "Palestinian Prisoners' Day: Thousands of Palestinians Blindfolded, Handcuffed and Tortured," *Prison Art Newsletter*, Vol. 2, No. 5 (May 2002), www.prisonart.org/pdf/Vol2-No5.pdf.
36. Ran HaCohen, "The Apartheid Wall," *AntiWar.com* (May 21, 2003), www.antiwar.com/hacohen/h052103.html.
37. "Israel Poisoning West Bank with Nuclear and Toxic Waste, Say Palestinians," *Crescent International* (October 1–15 1999), www.muslimedia.com/archives/oaw99/pal-toxic.htm.

2   INTIFADA INTERNATIONAL (2002)

1. Carolyn LaFave, "Bearing Witness: Homegrown Activist Founds Group for Palestinian Rights, Peace," *Metro Times* (July 23, 2003), www.metrotimes.com/editorial/story.asp?id=5178.
2. Nidal al-Mughrabi, "Palestinians Slam U.S. Veto in United Nations," *Reuters* (March 28, 2001), www.themodernreligion.com/jihad/veto-pal.html.
3. Ibid.
4. "Stun Grenades Used on West Bank," *Daily Telegraph* (December 28, 2001), http://nucnews.net/nucnews/2001nn/0112nn/011228nn.htm.
5. Ramzy Baroud (ed.), *Searching Jenin: Eyewitness Accounts of the Israeli Invasion* (Seattle: Cune Press, 2002), p. 23.
6. "United Nations General Assembly Resolution 194 of December 1948," United Nations Information System on the Question of Palestine website, http://domino.un.org/UNISP.A.L.NSF/0/c758572b78d1cd0085256bcf00 77e51a?OpenDocument, accessed 27 September 2005.
7. Justin Podur, "What Happened in Jenin?" *Z Magazine*, Vol. 15, No. 8 (September 2002), www.zmag.org/ZMag/articles/sep02podur.html.
8. "Mofaz to Destroy Palestinian Refugee Camp," *Al-Jazeera Satellite Channel Arabic Website* (April 6, 2002); translated from Arabic for *Z Magazine* by Eric Mueller, www.zmag.org/content/Mideast/aljazeera_jenin_april6-2002.cfm.
9. Justin Huggler, "Jenin: The Camp That Became a Slaughterhouse," *Independent* (April 14, 2002), www.commondreams.org/headlines02/0414-06. htm.
10. Katie Barlow, "Courage Under Fire," *Guardian* (November 17, 2005), www.guardian.co.uk/g2/story/0,3604,848369,00.html.
11. Ibid.
12. Ibid.
13. Ibid.
14. See *The American Heritage Dictionary of the English Language*, 4th edn (Boston: Houghton Mifflin Company, 2000).

15. Eyad Sarraj, "Why We Blow Ourselves Up: A Palestinian Doctor Explains Why So Many of His People Want to Be Martyrs," *Time Magazine*, Vol. 159, No. 14 (April 8, 2002), p. 39.
16. Baruch Kra, Amira Hass, and Nadav Shragai, "IAF Strike Kills Five, Including Two Children," *Haaretz* (September 1, 2002), www.haaretzdaily. com/hasen/pages/ShArt.jhtml?itemNo=203532&contrassID=2&subCon trassID=1&sbSubContrassID=0&listSrc=Y.
17. "A New Berlin Wall?," American-Arab Anti-Discrimination Committee (August 30, 2005), www.adc.org/index.php?id=2085.
18. Paul de Rooij, "Identity Under Siege," *CounterPunch.org* (November 20, 2002), www.counterpunch.org/rooij1120.html.
19. Suzanne Goldenberg, "Israel Descends into Chaos," *Guardian* (March 9, 2002), www.guardian.co.uk/Archive/Article/0,4273,4371161,00.html.
20. Simon Jeffery, "Middle East Timeline 2002: July to October," *Guardian* (September 20, 2002), www.guardian.co.uk/israel/Story/0,2763,758250,00. html.
21. See Human Rights Watch website coverage of the Russia–Chechnya conflict, www.hrw.org/campaigns/russia/chechnya, accessed August 30, 2005.
22. "World Relieved that Crisis is Over," *BBC News Online* (October 27, 2002), http://news.bbc.co.uk/2/hi/world/europe/2364257.stm.

3   CALLS FOR REFORM (2003)

1. Ramzy Baroud, "Condemned to Violence," *Washington Post* (December 2, 2002), p. A21.
2. Interestingly, much of the content of Wolf's response is standardized in a letter to the editor format that is used frequently by the A.D.L. See Abraham H. Foxman, "ADL Letter to The Washington Post," www.adl. org/media_watch/newspapers/letter_washington_post22.htm, accessed September 27, 2005.
3. "U.N., EU Slam Israel over Al-Bureij Massacre," *Palestine Media Center*, www.palestine-pmc.com/details.asp?cat=1&id=344, accessed September 27, 2005.
4. Theodore Roosevelt, *The Winning of the West* (New York: Putnam, 1889–96).
5. Avi Shlaim, *The Iron Wall: Israel and the Arab World* (New York: W. W. Norton & Company, 2001), p. 311.
6. Walid Khalidi (ed.), *All That Remains: The Palestinian Villages Occupied and Depopulated by Israel in 1948* (Beirut: Institute for Palestine Studies, 1992).
7. "Law of Return 5710–1950," *Jewish Virtual Library*, www.jewishvirtual library.org/jsource/Immigration/Text_of_Law_of_Return.html, accessed September 1, 2005.
8. "The Jenin Inquiry Report," www.jenininquiry.org, accessed September 1, 2005.
9. "I Made Them a Stadium in the Middle of the Camp," *If Americans Knew*, www.ifamericansknew.org/cur_sit/stadium.html, accessed September 1, 2005.

10. Ben Lynfield and Rory Macmillan, "Are the Israelis Guilty of Mass Murder?," *Scotsman* (April 19, 2002), http://news.scotsman.com/international.cfm?id=417052002.
11. "From the 1927 Grand Council of American Indians," www.ilhawaii.net/~stony/quotes.html, accessed September 1, 2005.
12. See Ramzy Baroud, *Searching Jenin: Eyewitness Accounts of the Israeli Invasion* (Seattle: Cune Press, 2002).
13. "Human Rights Watch: Suicide Bombers War Criminals," *CNN. com* (November 1, 2002), http://archives.cnn.com/2002/WORLD/meast/11/01/human.rights.Palestinians, accessed September 27, 2005.
14. See "Charter of the United Nations: Chapter VII," www.unhchr.ch/html/menu3/b/ch-chp7.htm, accessed September 1, 2005.
15. See "The Universal Declaration of Human Rights," United Nations website, www.un.org/Overview/rights.html, accessed September 1, 2005.
16. See "Resolutions Adopted by the General Assembly During Its Twentieth Session," United Nations website, www.un.org/documents/ga/res/20/ares20.htm, accessed September 1, 2005.
17. See "Commissioner-General's Address to the Second International Academic Conference," U.N.R.W.A. website, www.un.org/unrwa/news/statements/miftah-jan04.html, accessed September 1, 2005.
18. "Protocol Additional to the Geneva Conventions of 12 August 1949," Office of the United Nations High Commissioner for Human Rights website, www.unhchr.ch/html/menu3/b/93.htm, accessed September 1, 2005.
19. See Baroud, *Searching Jenin*.
20. "Convention (IV) Relative to the Protection of Civilian Persons in Time of War," International Committee of the Red Cross website, www.icrc.org/ihl.nsf/0/6756482d86146898c125641e004aa3c5?OpenDocument, accessed September 1, 2005.
21. See United Nations Information System on the Question of Palestine website, "General Assembly Resolution 181 (II)," http://domino.un.org/UNISP.A.L.NSF/a06f2943c226015c85256c40005d359c/7f0af2bd897689b785256c330061d253!OpenDocument, and "Resolution 194 (III)," http://domino.un.org/UNISP.A.L.NSF/a06f2943c226015c85256c40005d359c/c758572b78d1cd0085256bcf0077e51a!OpenDocument, accessed September 1, 2005.
22. Nicole Gaouette, "American Killed in Gaza," *Christian Science Monitor* (March 18, 2003), www.csmonitor.com/2003/0318/p25s01-wome.html.
23. Steve Niva, "One Year Later: Rachel Corrie's Critics Fire Blanks," *Electronic Intifada* (March 16, 2004), http://electronicintifada.net/cgi-bin/artman/exec/view.cgi/10/2506.
24. J. Edward Tremlett, Columnist, "Rachel Corrie: Bravery or Stupidity?," *American Partisan* (April 22, 2003), www.american-partisan.com/cols/2003/tremlett/qtr2/0422.htm.
25. Associated Press, "Students Protest Cartoon of Rachel Corrie: Newspaper's Editors Refuse to Apologize for Running It," *Seattle Post Intelligencer* (March 21, 2003), http://seattlepi.nwsource.com/local/113561_cartoon21.shtml.

26. Joseph Smith, "Rachel Corrie: Detailed Eyewitness Account, Remembrance, and Thoughts about the Future," *Electronic Intifada* (March 21, 2003), http://electronicintifada.net/cgi-bin/artman/exec/view.cgi/7/1284.

27. See Ramzy Baroud, "Rest in Peace, Rachel Corrie," *CounterPunch.org* (March 17, 2003), www.counterpunch.org/baroud03172003.html.

28. Carl Arrindell, "Tom Hurndall: An Aspiring Photojournalist and Committed Peace Activist," *Guardian* (January 22, 2004), www.guardian.co.uk/obituaries/story/0,3604,1128176,00.html.

29. "A Performance-Based Roadmap to a Permanent Two-State Solution to the Israeli-Palestinian Conflict," U.S. Department of State website (April 30, 2003), www.state.gov/r/pa/prs/ps/2003/20062.htm, accessed September 27, 2005.

30. Edward Said, "Archaeology of the Roadmap," *Al-Ahram Weekly*, No. 642 (June 12–18, 2003), http://weekly.ahram.org.eg/2003/642/op10.htm.

31. "Abbas Calls for End to Violence," *BBC News Online* (December 14, 2004), http://news.bbc.co.uk/2/hi/middle_east/4096783.stm.

32. "President Bush Calls for New Palestinian Leadership," White House website, www.whitehouse.gov/news/releases/2002/06/20020624-3.html, accessed September 27, 2005.

33. "Road Map May be Last Chance at Middle East Peace for Long Time," *U.N. News Center* (May 19, 2003), www.un.org/apps/news/story.asp?NewsID=7116&Cr=palestin&Cr1=, accessed September 27, 2005.

34. Palestine Red Crescent Society Database, www.palestinercs.org/Database/index.htm, accessed on October 17, 2005.

35. See Appendix I.

36. "Powell, Rice Acknowledge Israeli Concerns about Roadmap," American Embassy in Israel website (May 23, 2003), www.usembassy-israel.org.il/publish/press/2003/may/052401.html, accessed September 27, 2005.

37. "Bush Criticizes Israel Security Wall," *The Age* (July 26, 2003), www.theage.com.au/articles/2003/07/26/1059084248111.html.

38. "Bush Warns Israel of Consequences of Actions," *People's Daily* (July 30, 2003), http://english.people.com.cn/200307/30/eng20030730_121226.shtml.

39. "Powell Urges Youngsters from Israel, Arab Countries to Work for Peace," U.S. International Information Program website, http://usinfo.state.gov/mena/Archive/2004/Apr/12-872286.html, accessed September 27, 2005.

40. "Israel Will Work to Remove Arafat," *CNN.com* (September 12, 2003), http://edition.cnn.com/2003/WORLD/meast/09/11/mideast.

41. "Security Council Fails to Adopt Text on Palestinian Leader's Deportation, as United States Casts Negative Vote," United Nations website, www.un.org/News/Press/docs/2003/sc7875.doc.htm, accessed September 27, 2003.

42. See Donald Neff, "List of Vetoes Cast by the United States to Shield Israel from Criticism," *Washington Report on Middle East Affairs* (May 2005), p.14, www.wrmea.com/archives/May-June_2005/0505014.html.

43. "Israel Says It Will Remove Arafat Whenever It Chooses," *Associated Press* (September 12, 2005), http://203.200.89.67/pti_news.asp?id=166982.

44. Rachel Pomerance, "Jewish Leaders Praise Tough U.S. Stand on Israel at U.N.," *Jewish Telegraphic Agency* (August 2, 2002).
45. Ibid.
46. "Arafat, Israel Trade Blame for Road Map Troubles," *CNN.com* (September 3, 2003), http://edition.cnn.com/2003/WORLD/meast/09/02/mideast.
47. Derrick O'Keefe, "Imperialism's Increasingly Rough Road To Re-Mapping The Middle East," ZNet (September 7, 2003), www.zmag.org/content/showarticle.cfm?SectionID=22&ItemID=4143.
48. Justus Reid Weiner, "'My Beautiful Old House' and Other Fabrications by Edward Said," *Commentary Magazine*, Vol. 108, No. 2 (September 1999), www.commentarymagazine.com/Summaries/V108I2P25–1.htm.
49. Edward Said, "Defamation, Zionist-Style," *Al-Ahram Weekly*, No. 444 (August 26–September 1, 1999), http://weekly.ahram.org.eg/1999/444/op2.htm.
50. "Transcript: David Kay at Senate Hearing," *CNN.com* (January 29, 2004), http://edition.cnn.com/2004/US/01/28/kay.transcript.
51. "The Hon John Howard MP Doorstop Interview" (October 3, 2003), www.pm.gov.au/news/interviews/Interview510.html, accessed September 27, 2005.
52. Susan Jones, "Bush Says He Makes Tough Decisions, Ignores Polls," *CNSNews.com* (October 3, 2003), www.cnsnews.com/ViewNation.asp?Page=%5CNation%5CArchive%5C200310%5CNAT20031003c.html.
53. Tim Radford, "Nelson Mandela: The United States of America is a Threat to World Peace," *BBC News Online* (September 11, 2002), www.commondreams.org/headlines02/0911-01.htm.
54. "Israel's Secret Weapon," *BBC News Online* (March 17, 2003), http://news.bbc.co.uk/nol/shared/spl/hi/programmes/correspondent/transcripts/17_03_2003.txt.
55. "Syria's Weapons of Mass Destruction and Missile Development Programs," U.S. Department of State, www.state.gov/t/us/rm/24135.htm, accessed September 27, 2005.
56. Chris McGreal, "Sharon Shuns BBC," *Guardian* (July 11, 2003), www.guardian.co.uk/israel/Story/0,2763,995987,00.html.
57. "The Universal Declaration of Human Rights."
58. Ibid.
59. "Right to an Adequate Standard of Living," Defense for Children International website, www.dci-pal.org/english/publ/research/2004/report4.pdf, accessed September 1, 2005.
60. See "Concluding observations of the Committee against Torture: Israel," Office of the United Nations High Commissioner for Human Rights, www.unhchr.ch/tbs/doc.nsf/0/daf82ddcda36946e80256609004b7df9?Opendocument, accessed September 1, 2005.
61. "Former Israeli Soldier: We Behaved Like Animals, Criminals, Thieves toward Palestinians," *MIFTAH.org* (December 1, 2003), http://miftah.org/Display.cfm?DocId=2789&CategoryId=12.
62. See "One More Intifada Year," www.palestinehistory.com/time2003.htm, accessed September 1, 2003.
63. Neil Clark, "The Return of Arabophobia," *Guardian* (October 20, 2003), www.guardian.co.uk/comment/story/0,3604,1066569,00.html.

4 PROFOUND CHANGES, INSURMOUNTABLE CHALLENGES (2004)

1. "Israel Challenges Court on Barrier," *Aljazeera.net* (January 31, 2004), http://english.aljazeera.net/NR/exeres/84229909-311F-4FC5-B561-229274258F69.htm.
2. "Israel: Bus Bombing Vindicates West Bank Barrier," *Agency France Press* (January 29, 2004), http://aljazeera.com/cgi-bin/news_service/middle_east_full_story.asp?service_id=71.
3. See "Israel and Palestine Timeline," *Guardian* website, www.guardian.co.uk/israel/page/0,12575,1122113,00.html, accessed September 27, 2005.
4. "Reporters Without Borders calls on Yasser Arafat to act after killing of journalist," *Reporters Without Borders* (March 2, 2004), www.rsf.org/article.php3?id_article=9415&var_recherche=khalil, accessed October 20, 2005.
5. Ben Lynfield, "Hamas Seeks Primacy in Gaza," *Christian Science Monitor* (March 3, 2004), www.csmonitor.com/2004/0303/p01s04-wome.html.
6. Hasan Abu Nimah, "The Gaza–South Lebanon Parallel," *Jordan Times* (March 3, 2004), www.acj.org/Daily%20News/2004/March/March_03.htm.
7. "Hamas Chief Killed in Air Strike," *BBC News Online* (March 22, 2004), http://news.bbc.co.uk/2/hi/middle_east/3556099.stm.
8. Chris McGreal, "Children among 20 Dead as Israeli Army Begins Huge Crackdown on Rafah," *Guardian* (May 19, 2004), www.guardian.co.uk/israel/Story/0,2763,1219823,00.html.
9. Dana Milbank and Glenn Kessler, "Bush Backs Israel's Defense," *Washington Post* (May 19, 2004), p. A19.
10. Chris McGreal, "Ten Die as Israeli Tanks Fire on Peaceful Protest," *Guardian* (May 20, 2004), www.guardian.co.uk/israel/Story/0,2763,1220749,00.html.
11. "Girl, 4, Shot Dead by Israeli Soldiers," *The Age* (May 23, 2004), www.theage.com.au/articles/2004/05/22/1085176039677.html?from=storyrhs.
12. Dan Ephron, "World Court Rules Israeli Barrier Illegal," *Boston Globe* (July 10, 2004), www.boston.com/news/nation/articles/2004/07/10/world_court_rules_israeli_barrier_illegal.
13. Ibid.
14. "U.N. Court Rules West Bank Barrier Illegal," *CNN.com* (July 10, 2004), http://edition.cnn.com/2004/WORLD/meast/07/09/israel.barrier.
15. Khalid Amayreh, "Treason in a Time of Struggle," *Al-Ahram Weekly*, No. 701 (July 29–August 4, 2004), http://weekly.ahram.org.eg/2004/701/re51.htm.
16. Uri Avnery, "The Skin of the Bear," World Crisis website (July 24, 2004), www.world-crisis.com/analysis_comments/499_0_15_0_C39, accessed September 2, 2005.
17. "Arafat Announces Security Shake-up Amid Turmoil," *CNN.com* (July 17, 2004), http://edition.cnn.com/2004/WORLD/meast/07/17/gaza.unrest.
18. "Israel Releases Details of Pull-out Plan," *CNN.com* (April 16, 2004), http://edition.cnn.com/2004/WORLD/meast/04/16/sharon.plan.

19. Ian MacKinnon, "Gaza Withdrawal Aims to Freeze Peace Process," *The Times* (October 7, 2004), www.timesonline.co.uk/article/0,,251-1298668,00.html.

20. Chris McGreal, "50,000 Trapped by Israeli Assault on Gaza," *Guardian* (October 5, 2004), www.guardian.co.uk/israel/Story/0,2763,1319776,00.html.

21. "Arafat's Death: Global Reaction in Quotes," *BBC News Online* (November 11, 2004), http://news.bbc.co.uk/2/hi/middle_east/4001697.stm.

5   END OF THE INTIFADA? (2005)

1. "Abbas Apologizes to Kuwait over Iraq," *BBC News Online* (December 12, 2004), http://news.bbc.co.uk/2/hi/middle_east/4089961.stm.

2. Mike Whitney, "Observations on the Palestinian Election," www.aljazeerah.info/Opinion%20editorials/2004%20opinions/December/14%20o/Obse rvations%20on%20the%20Palestinian%20election%20By%20Mike%20 Whitney.htm, accessed September 2, 2005.

3. See "Democracy: Real World Meaning and Definition," http://encyclopedia.laborlawtalk.com/Democracy, accessed September 2, 2005.

4. See "Defining Democracy," http://usinfo.state.gov/products/pubs/whatsdem/whatdm2.htm, accessed September 2, 2005.

5. Jeffrey Sommers, "Blowback," *ZNet* (September 12, 2001), www.zmag.org/Sustainers/content/2001-09/12sommers.cfm.

6. "West Bank Settlements," Public Broadcasting Network website, www.pbs.org/now/politics/settlements2.html, accessed September 2, 2005.

7. Robert Fisk, "At No Point Yesterday Did Anyone Mention Occupation," *Independent* (February 9, 2005), http://news.independent.co.uk/world/fisk/article10156.ece.

8. "Bush Endorses Sharon's Plan on West Bank," *China Daily* (April 15, 2004), www2.chinadaily.com.cn/english/doc/2004-04/15/content_323464.htm.

9. Richard W. Stevenson, "Bush Supports Plan by Sharon For a Withdrawal From Gaza," *New York Times* (April 12, 2005), http://select.nytimes.com/gst/abstract.html?res=F4071EFD395A0C718DDDAD0894DD404482.

10. Sonia Nettnin, "World Summit, MDGs and Israel," *Alternative Press Review* (September 13, 2005), www.altpr.org/modules.php?op=modload&name=News&file=article&sid=478.

11. "Statement by Senator Rudy Boschwitz, Head of U.S. Delegation," www.unchr.info/61st/docs/L.4-EOV-U.S.A.pdf, accessed September 2, 2005.

12. "Bush Endorses Sharon's Plan on West Bank," *China Daily*.

13. Ian MacKinnon, "Gaza Withdrawal Aims to Freeze Peace Process," *The Times* (October 7, 2004), www.timesonline.co.uk/article/0,,251-1298668,00.html.

14. Edward Said, "What Israel Has Done," *Nation* (May 6, 2002), www.thenation.com/doc/20020506/said.

15. Jennifer Loewenstein, "The Disengaged," *Palestine Monitor* (May 1, 2005), www.palestinemonitor.org/nueva_web/articles/features/the_disengaged.htm.

16. Mark Oliver, "Straw Confirms British Contact with Hamas," *Guardian* (June 7, 2005), www.guardian.co.uk/israel/Story/0,2763,1501156,00. html.

17. "Israel Slams EU Over Contact With Hamas," *Associated Press* (June 16, 2005), www.foxnews.com/story/0,2933,159734,00.html.

18. Conal Urquhart, "Israel Attacks EU over Meetings with Hamas Officials," *Guardian* (June 17, 2005), www.guardian.co.uk/israel/ Story/0,2763,1508566,00.html.

19. Matthew Gutman, "I.D.F., Hamas Council to Cooperate," *Jerusalem Post* (May 17, 2005), www.jpost.com/servlet/Satellite?pagename=JPost/ JP.A.rticle/ShowFull&cid=1116210025340.

20. "UK Helped Israel Get Nuclear Bomb," *BBC News Online* (August 4, 2005), http://news.bbc.co.uk/1/hi/uk/4743987.stm.

21. "BBC: U.K. Sold Nuke Material to Israel," *Associated Press* (August 4, 2005), www.foxnews.com/story/0,2933,164742,00.html.

22. David Leigh, "How the UK Gave Israel the Bomb," *Guardian* (August 4, 2005), www.guardian.co.uk/israel/Story/0,2763,1542077,00.html.

23. Gordon Prather, "Let the Israelis Do It?," *AntiWar.com* (January 31, 2005), www.antiwar.com/prather/?articleid=4644.

24. "UK Helped Israel Get Nukes: Report," *IslamOnline.net* (August 4, 2005), www.islam-online.net/English/News/2005-08/04/article05.shtml.

25. Diana Bahur-Nir, "Extremists Tearing Country Apart," *YNetnews.com*, (July 1, 2005), www.ynetnews.com/articles/0,7340,L-3106541,00.html.

26. Joshua Mitnick, "Israeli vs. Israeli in Gaza," *Christian Science Monitor* (June 29, 2005), www.csmonitor.com/2005/0629/p01s03-wome.html.

27. Uri Avnery, "Arik"s Horror Show," *ZNet* (July 6, 2005), www.zmag.org/ content/showarticle.cfm?SectionID=107&ItemID=8233.

28. Ian MacKinnon, "Gaza Withdrawal Aims to Freeze Peace Process," *The Times* (October 7, 2004), www.timesonline.co.uk/article/0,,251-1298668,00.html.

29. Aluf Benn, "Powell Says Sharon Must Take Hard Look at Policies," *Haaretz* (July 3, 2002), www.haaretzdaily.com/hasen/pages/ShArt.jhtml?itemNo =137662&contrassID=1&subContrassID=0&sbSubContrassID=0.

30. Etgar Lefkovits, "Olmert: Gaza Not Trade-off for West Bank," *Jerusalem Post* (August 10, 2005), www.jpost.com/servlet/Satellite?pagename=JPost/ JP.A.rticle/ShowFull&cid=1123640627311.

31. Joshua Brilliant, "Unilateral Gaza Pull-out Tests Israeli-P.A. Relationship," *United Press International* (August 9, 2005), www.wpherald.com/storyview. php?StoryID=20050809-104045-6348r.

32. See "Text of the Wye River Memorandum," *Arabic News* (October 24, 1998), www.arabicnews.com/ansub/Daily/Day/981024/1998102453. html.

33. Alan Johnston, "Years of Delay at Gaza Airport," *BBC News Online* (April 15, 2005), http://news.bbc.co.uk/1/hi/world/middle_east/4449461. stm.

34. See "Text of The Sharm el-Sheikh Memorandum on Implementation Timeline of Outstanding Commitments of Agreements Signed and the Resumption of Permanent Status Negotiations," www.state.gov/p/nea/ rls/22696.htm, last accessed October 17, 2005.

35. Diana Buttu, "Israel"s Unilateral Disengagement and the Future of Gaza Strip: A Working Paper by the Palestinian Authority Technical Team," *ZNet* (September 5, 2005), www.zmag.org/content/showarticle.cfm?Sec tionID=107&ItemID=8670.
36. "PNA to Celebrate Israeli Withdrawal as Victory for Peace Camp," *Palestine Media Center*, www.palestine-pmc.com/details.asp?cat=1&id=951, accessed October 3, 2005.
37. "Outgoing Ambassador Kurtzer: U.S. will Support Retention of Some Settlements," *Haaretz* (September 19, 2005), www.haaretz.com/hasen/spages/626263.html.
38. "Uzi Dayan Wants 28 Palestinian Towns Annexed to Israel," *Palestine Media Center*, www.palestine-pmc.com/details.asp?cat=1&id=995, accessed October 4, 2005.
39. Abraham Rabinovich, "Clash Humiliates Palestinian Police," *Australian* (October 4, 2005), www.theaustralian.news.com.au/common/story_page/0,5744,16807034%255E2703,00.html.

Recommended Reading

Naseer Aruri, *Dishonest Broker: The U.S. Role in Israel and Palestine* (Cambridge, MA: South End Press, 2003)

Hanan Ashrawi, *This Side of Peace: A Personal Account* (Carmichael, CA: Touchstone Books, 1996)

Ramzy Baroud, *Searching Jenin: Eyewitness Accounts of the Israeli Invasion* (Seattle: Cune Press, 2002)

Francis A. Boyle, *Palestine, Palestinians, and International Law* (Gardena, CA: Clarity Press, 2003)

Noam Chomsky, *Fateful Triangle: The United States, Israel, and the Palestinians* (Cambridge, MA: South End Press; London: Pluto Press, 1999)

Kathleen Christison, *Perceptions of Palestine, Their Influence on U.S. Middle East Policy* (Berkeley: University of California Press, 1999)

Paul Findley, *They Dare to Speak Out: People and Institutions Confront Israel's Lobby* (Chicago: Lawrence Hill Books, 2003)

Norman G. Finkelstein, *Image and Reality of the Israel–Palestine Conflict* (New York: W. W. Norton & Company, 2003)

Sami Hadawi, *Bitter Harvest: A Modern History of Palestine* (Northampton, MA: The Interlink Publishing Group, 1998)

Rashid Khalidi, *Palestinian Identity* (New York: Columbia University Press, 1998)

Ilan Pappe, *A History of Modern Palestine: One Land, Two Peoples* (New York: Cambridge University Press, 2003)

Tanya Reinhart, *Israel/Palestine: How to End the War of 1948* (New York: Seven Stories Press, 2004)

Cheryl A. Rubenberg, *The Palestinians: In Search of a Just Peace* (Boulder, CO: Lynne Rienner Publishers, 2003)

Edward Said, *The Question of Palestine* (New York: Vintage Books, 1992)

Edward Said, *Peace And Its Discontents: Essays on Palestine in the Middle East* (New York: Vintage Books, 1996)

Notes on Contributors

Ramzy Baroud is a veteran Arab-American journalist and former producer at Al-Jazeera Satellite Television. He is also the founder and Editor-in-Chief of PalestineChronicle.com. Baroud started his writing career at a young age and published his first book of Arabic poetry, entitled "Letters of Decision," when he was 18 years old. In 2002, he published *Searching Jenin: Eyewitness Accounts of the Israeli Invasion* with the Cune Press in the United States. The present volume is his third such published work. He has also contributed to numerous essay collections, magazines, and journals. Baroud's articles, commentaries, and short stories have been printed in hundreds of newspapers worldwide, from the *Washington Post* to the *Japan Times*. He has made numerous media appearances, including interviews with the B.B.C., C.N.N. International, Al-Jazeera Television, A.B.C. Radio in Australia, and Democracy Now in New York. He is a renowned public speaker and has spoken at dozens of universities around the world. His articles have been translated into many languages, from French to Japanese to Bulgarian. He holds a Master of Arts Degree in Communication from the University of Washington. He currently teaches Mass Communication at Australia's Curtin University of Technology, Malaysia Campus.

Bill Christison joined the C.I.A. in 1950, and served on the analysis side of the Agency for 28 years. From the early 1970s he served as National Intelligence Officer (principal advisor to the Director of Central Intelligence on certain areas) for, at various times, Southeast Asia, South Asia and Africa. Before he retired in 1979 he was Director of the C.I.A.'s Office of Regional and Political Analysis, a 250-person unit.

Kathleen Christison worked for 16 years as a political analyst with the C.I.A., dealing first with Vietnam and then with the Middle East for her last seven years with the Agency before resigning in 1979. Since leaving the C.I.A., she has been a freelance writer, dealing primarily with the Israeli–Palestinian conflict. Her book, *Perceptions of Palestine: Their Influence on U.S. Middle East Policy*, was published by the University of California Press and reissued in paperback with an update in October 2001. A second book, *The Wound of Dispossession: Telling the Palestinian Story*, was published in March 2002.

Jennifer Loewenstein is a Visiting Research Fellow at Oxford University's Refugee Studies Centre. Her work focuses on the fragmentation of Palestinian nationalism as the result of Israeli occupation policies, and on the failure of a unified national resistance strategy during the Second Intifada. She has lived and worked in the Palestinian refugee camp of Bourj al-Barajneh in Beirut, Lebanon, and in the Gaza Strip where she was the English language editor for the Mezan Center for Human Rights based in the Jabalya Refugee camp. She is a freelance journalist and was among the first internationals into the

Jenin refugee camp after its destruction by Israel in April 2002. An activist and founder of the Madison–Rafah Sister City Project, she was also a senior lecturer in communications at the University of Wisconsin, Madison for 16 years. She has spoken and written extensively about her experiences in Lebanon, Israel, and Palestine. She currently lives in Oxford, England with her husband David and daughter Stella.

Matthew Cassel is a U.S.-based documentary photographer, whose work is aimed at promoting social change around the world. The images seen in this book are part of a larger project Cassel did documenting Palestinian life from 2004–05. His work can be seen at http://justimage.org.

Mahfouz Abu Turk is a Palestinian photojournalist based in the city of Jerusalem. Abu Turk's long experience in the field of photojournalism linked him to leading news agencies and publications around the world including Agency France Press, Associated Press, the Washington Report and others. Currently he works with the Reuters News Agency. Abu Turk's photo exhibits have traveled to many countries around the world, including exhibits in Italy, Greece, Germany, South Africa, the United States, France, and various Arab countries.

Index

Compiled by Sue Carlton

Page numbers in **bold** refer to captions to photographs

Printed and bound by CPI Group (UK) Ltd, Croydon, CR0 4YY

13/04/2025

14656488-0005